# The Psychology of Decision Making

## Second Edition

# FOUNDATIONS FOR ORGANIZATIONAL SCIENCE
A Sage Publications Series
## Series Editor
David Whetten, *Brigham Young University*
### Editors
Anne S. Huff, *University of Colorado* and *Cranfield University* (UK)
Benjamin Schneider, *University of Maryland*
M. Susan Taylor, *University of Maryland*

The FOUNDATIONS FOR ORGANIZATIONAL SCIENCE series supports the development of students, faculty, and prospective organizational science professionals through the publication of texts authored by leading organizational scientists. Each volume provides a highly personal, hands-on introduction to a core topic or theory and challenges the reader to explore promising avenues for future theory development and empirical application.

Lee Roy Beach
Terry Connolly
*University of Arizona*

# The Psychology of Decision Making
## People in Organizations
### Second Edition

Foundations for
Organizational
Science
A Sage Publications Series

**SAGE** Publications
Thousand Oaks ▪ London ▪ New Delhi

*For information:*

Sage Publications, Inc.
2455 Teller Road
Thousand Oaks, California 91320
E-mail: order@sagepub.com

Sage Publications Ltd.
1 Oliver's Yard
55 City Road
London  EC1Y 1SP
United Kingdom

Sage Publications India Pvt. Ltd.
B-42, Panchsheel Enclave
Post Box 4109
New Delhi 110 017  India

Printed in the United States of America

**Library of Congress Cataloging-in-Publication Data**

Beach, Lee Roy.
The psychology of decision making : People in organizations / by Lee Roy Beach and Terry Connolly.— 2nd ed.
    p. cm. — (Foundations for organizational science)
Includes bibliographical references and index.
ISBN 1-4129-0439-0 (cloth) — ISBN 1-4129-0440-4 (pbk.)
    1. Decision making. 2. Organization. I. Connolly, Terry. II. Title. III. Series.
HD30.23.B413 2005
153.8'3—dc22                  2004021807

This book is printed on acid-free paper.

04  05  06  07  08  10  9  8  7  6  5  4  3  2  1

| | |
|---|---|
| *Acquisitions Editor:* | Al Bruckner |
| *Editorial Assistant:* | MaryAnn Vail |
| *Production Editor:* | Laureen A. Shea |
| *Copy Editor:* | Diana Breti |
| *Typesetter:* | C&M Digitals (P) Ltd. |
| *Proofreader:* | Kris Bergstad |
| *Indexer:* | Judy Hunt |
| *Cover Designer:* | Janet Foulger |

*To Ward Edwards, the father of behavioral decision research*

# Contents

# Preface

This book presents an overview of the psychology of decision making. The intent is to be brief so the reader will not get lost in technical details, but to be broad so the reader can understand how the field has developed since its inception as a scholarly discipline in the early 1950s.

To achieve both brevity and breadth requires selectivity. No doubt our selection of topics is biased, as is our interpretation of what they mean and how important they are. The fact is, however, that we have made no effort to be unbiased, because no matter how hard we might try, we would please few of our colleagues, each of whom would happily add or subtract from our selection and gladly quarrel with our interpretations.

On the understanding that he is blameless for what is deficient in the following pages, we would like to thank our colleague Amnon Rapoport for his help and advice.

# 1

# Preliminaries

*R*alph stared at the figures in disbelief; he felt a headache coming on. What happened? After all the planning and work, all the careful analysis and getting his people to buy in, all the sleepless nights and worry, what went wrong? When he took this job he was sure he knew how to deal with the situation—he was the guy who had previously saved three other businesses that had the same problem. Had he been too optimistic? Had his past experience hindered rather than helped? Betty Miller, the company president, clearly believed he was on the wrong track. He hated to prove her right. After all, he was supposed to be the Knight in Shining Armor who would save the firm. Clearly, this Knight was going to have to think things through again.

He flipped back over the figures from previous months, comparing them carefully with the latest report. What were they trying to tell him? Had something changed that he had failed to notice? Was he focusing on the wrong things? Slowly he began to see a pattern. Although not broken out in a way that would make it obvious, the figures suggested that the problem was not with the products themselves but in sales. Some salespeople appeared to be doing a great job, but many more were not. That might be it! He had always read the reports from the viewpoint of fixing the product. Maybe that mind-set blinded him to the possibility that some salespeople simply do not do a good job. He felt like a fool. Most managers made just the opposite mistake, blaming the people first *and the product last. Okay, he was more into product innovation than human resources, everyone knew that. But now that he began to look at the figures this new way, everything began to make sense.*

*Ralph felt a surge of relief and excitement. All was not lost—not yet, anyway. He was going to have to get a lot more information to make the details clear, but he thought he understood the problem. True, it was not something he had ever dealt with before, but he and Betty ought to be able to figure it out. Then it was a matter of coming up with plausible options, deciding on the right one, working hard, and watching closely so he didn't get misled again. It could be done. He almost called Betty to tell her. She probably would be so relieved that she wouldn't gloat. But, on second thought, maybe he would tell her tomorrow so he could enjoy this feeling of relief a little while longer.*

To better understand the problems Ralph faces, we need way of structuring our thinking. The usual way begins with the diagnosis of the decision problem, moves on to selection of an action that will solve the problem, and ends with implementation of the selected action until the problem is solved:

Diagnosis → Action Selection → Implementation

### Diagnosis

The need for a decision arises when anomalous events occur. Often these events stem from internal changes (wants) or external changes (demands), but they also can stem from the realization that an earlier decision was wrong and its implementation is not producing the desired results. In Ralph's case, the anomalous events were the unexpected figures in the monthly report, resulting in the realization that what he was doing was not making things better.

To make sense of the anomalous events, the decision maker must mentally put the events in the proper context in order to give them meaning (*framing*), which allows him or her to draw upon previous experience to decide what to do. If this is a situation that is very similar to a situation that has been encountered before, he or she can use that experience to deal with the events. If the situation is substantially different from previously encountered situations, he or she can set about formulating an action plan that deals with its uniqueness. In Ralph's case, the company's problem had been interpreted as a product problem. But the figures in the reports did not make sense in this interpretation, suggesting that the frame was incorrect. When he began to view the situation as a sales problem, the figures suddenly began to make sense.

Whether the decision maker's framing of the events results in use of previously acquired knowledge about what to do or in formulation of a new action plan, he or she must use the events to guide the fine-tuning of the response. Even past experience usually provides only a general strategy for dealing with the situation. (When one can do exactly what one did before, it is called a conditioned response, which seldom is an effective way to deal with complex situations and almost never is effective for unique situations.) Therefore, the decision maker must *diagnose* the situation by evaluating the states of its most salient features. In Ralph's case, his past experience with product problems provided little help for dealing with the present sales problem, which probably is really a human resource (HR) problem. Therefore, he anticipated having to obtain more information in order to make judgments about precisely what was wrong and how serious it was before he could decide what to do about it.

## Action Selection

We often talk as though the decision maker has some set of potential plans of action (options), and the decision consists of choosing the best from among them. However, consider your own decision making—you frequently have no idea what might be reasonable plans of action. Often you start off in one direction, only to change your mind when things go awry. In fact, decisions seldom are made at a single point. Rather, the process seems to feel its way along, changing in the light of feedback and often leading in directions that never were conceived of when it all began. In Ralph's case, he thinks that with Betty's help he can come up with options from which to choose, but the fact is that once he understands the nature of his sales/HR problem, he will start to do the most obvious things and then adjust his actions in light of how well they work.

The "feeling along" nature of decision making is very difficult to capture in a readable narration, and even more difficult to describe in a tractable theory. It is far easier, for both the theorist and the reader, to talk as though decision options actually exist in full-blown clarity and the choice among them occurs at a single point in time. But this is merely a useful fiction. In Ralph's case, the fiction is useful because we can think of him making choices among different options—even if he makes a sequence of choices in light of feedback about how things are progressing in his search for a solution to his sales/HR problem. The fiction also is useful to Ralph because it allows him to think in terms of rather specific plans of action—even though he knows that anything he decides to do will surely be modified as he goes along.

## Implementation

After a plan of action has been decided upon, it must be implemented. That is, the plan must be used to guide behavior, and the decision maker must monitor its progress toward resolving the anomaly that started everything in the first place. Again, even though Ralph will feel his way along just like anyone else, he may talk as though he has a well-formulated plan—if only because it is easier to communicate with his colleagues and to help his HR people understand what is required of them. He may even believe it himself. But, after the dust settles and he has time to look back over what finally happened, the odds are good that Ralph will see that the route he took does not look much like the original plan. Indeed, if he laid a history of what happened side by side with the original plan, the only things they might share is a common starting point and, if he had successfully solved his sales/HR problem, a common ending point.

## ❖  SOME BACKGROUND

We will return to the "Diagnosis → Action Selection → Implementation" concept because it is the blueprint for the remainder of this book. For the moment, let us leave Ralph, who is busy enjoying his new insight into how to frame his problem, and turn to consideration of some of the larger issues in studying decision making.

## Prescriptive Theory

First of all, decision making is studied by many different disciplines, each of which seems to regard it as uniquely its own. Economists address decision making by constructing axiomatic models that describe the market forces at work in particular circumstances and that prescribe appropriate actions in light of the assumptions underlying the models. Operations researchers follow a similar logic, except that their models tend to be limited to specific problems encountered in specific enterprises. Applied statisticians also model decisions, either prescriptively (e.g., hypothesis testing) or descriptively (e.g., structural modeling).

With the possible exception of structural modeling, the emphasis in most work on decision making has been on prescribing what should be done, not on describing what decision makers actually do, and certainly not on diagnosis or implementation. This is because the models are designed solely to address the tasks involved in choice, which, as we shall see, is but one kind of decision making. Moreover, the models' logic need not mimic or even parallel the cognitive processes of the decision maker, even though their authors often use language that implies that it does. As a result, until quite recently, decision behavior was evaluated in light of how well it conformed to the prescriptive models rather than the other way around. That is, because the models followed logically from what usually were regarded as very attractive axioms, it did not seem reasonable to evaluate them by comparing them to what decision makers actually do. If such a comparison ever was made it was the behavior that was evaluated: Behavior that conformed to the models was judged to be rational and behavior that did not conform to the models was judged to be irrational. Prescriptive theory almost always focuses on choices among options and seldom focuses on either diagnosis or implementation.

Because psychologists, particularly students of organizational behavior, are more interested in describing what people do than in prescribing what they should do, we approach decision making in quite a different way. We are interested in the interplay of group and institutional dynamics and their effects upon the decisions made within and on the behalf of organizations. As a result, we are interested in the ways in which decision makers use information to arrive at decisions, and this is where our story begins.

## Behavioral Theory

Behavioral decision theory began as the study of the degree to which unaided human decision making conforms to the processes and outputs of prescriptive decision theory. Almost from the beginning, however, it has gone beyond this rather narrow mandate by "psychologizing" prescriptive theory in order to make it more descriptive of what decision makers actually do.

*Diagnosis*

Behavioral research on diagnosis is based on the work of Egon Brunswik (1947), who studied perception. In doing so, he developed a model that describes how observers use sensory cues to infer (diagnose) the nature of the world around them. Hammond (1955) generalized this model, called the Lens Model, to more macro-level inferences. The result is that diagnosis has come to be thought of in terms of *policies* that decision makers use to evaluate the characteristics of decision situations prior to making decisions. The Lens Model has provided a powerful way of thinking about policies and has contributed greatly to an understanding of how decision makers use policies in situations as diverse as evaluating the quality of hogs (Phelps & Shanteau, 1978) and evaluating the quality of applicants for jobs as insurance salesmen (Roose & Doherty, 1976). These studies form the foundation of an empirical tradition in the study of policy use that has proved to be of enormous theoretical and applied value.

The rather offbeat Phelps and Shanteau (1978) hog study illustrates how this kind of research is done. In the first of two experiments, seven members of the Kansas State University senior livestock judging team were each given a set of 64 index cards. On each was written a description of a hypothetical female breeding hog. The descriptions consisted of 11 characteristics of hogs, and each hog was said to be high or low on the characteristic (e.g., high body weight, low quality of nipples). The high and low values of the 11 cues across the 64 hypothetical hogs formed a partially replicated factorial design. Each livestock judge was asked to read each description and rate the hog for breeding quality. Thus the 11 cues were the independent variables, each judge's 64 ratings was the dependent variable, and the analysis was done using analysis of variance. The results showed that all of the judges used nine or more of the cues to arrive at their ratings, but it was not clear whether some cues counted for more than others. In the second study, the judges were shown pictures of hogs and rated each hog. This time results showed that most of the cues were used but that they were used in clusters. That is, various cues contributed to an inference about size, others contributed to meat quality, and others to breeding quality. This was interpreted to mean that the judges' policies involved a multi-stage strategy in which cues are integrated into intermediate inferences, which then are combined to arrive at a final decision.

*Choice*

Behavioral research on choice began by comparing decision behavior with the dictates of prescriptive decision theory. The basic concept underlying prescriptive theory is that a decision consists of selecting one course of action, called an *option,* from an array of options. Because most options contain an element of risk, selecting one can be thought of as making a bet, and the goal is to select the option that is the best bet. In short, decision making is seen as analogous to gambling: The decision maker is a gambler who places a bet by selecting one of the options and then waiting to see whether the outcome does or does not materialize. This way of thinking about decision making is called the *gamble analogy.*

The key to choosing the best bet is conceptually very simple. The player should select the option that offers the most attractive payoff package. A simple way to summarize the attractiveness of an option's payoff package is to add up the values of the various payoffs it offers. However, this fails to take into account the possibility that those payoffs may not materialize if the option is chosen. To fully reflect the structure of the situation, the attractiveness of the payoffs must be tempered by the probability of acquiring them. To include the probabilities, the attractiveness of a bet can be summarized by first discounting each payoff by the probability that it will be acquired and then summing the discounted values of the payoffs. Because a probability is a decimal number, discounting is accomplished by multiplying the payoff's value by the probability. The sum of all possible discounted payoffs is called the option's *expected value.* It is assumed that the player should select the option that has the greatest expected value.

❖  BEHAVIORAL THEORY AND RESEARCH

The foregoing is the essence of formal, prescriptive decision theory; it is prescriptive because it is how a "rational" decision maker would make choices if he or she accepted the axioms and assumptions underlying the theory. About 50 years ago (some authorities trace things back 300 years, but 50 will do for us), psychologists became interested in decision behavior. Work by Ward Edwards (1954, 1955) set the paradigm for investigation: How well does the behavior of unaided decision makers compare to what a trained economist or statistician would do using prescriptive theory to make a specified decision?

We will examine a prototypical study in the Edwards tradition in a later chapter. However, a study by Gray (1975) provides a quaint, if atypical, illustration of behavioral research based on the presumption that decision makers' behavior is (or should be) reflected in prescriptive theory. Gray presented third-grade students with an array of six stacks of 10 cards, face down. Each stack contained arithmetic problems of roughly equal difficulty for the children, and the stacks ranged from very difficult at one end of the array to very easy at the other end. The student looked at a problem from each stack and stated how many of the 10 problems he or she would solve correctly if asked to work the problems in that stack. Dividing the estimate by 10 provides the student's assessment of his or her probability of success for each stack. The students' task was to select a stack from which a problem would be randomly selected for them to solve. They were told that if they selected the most difficult stack and got the correct answer, the payoff would be six red poker chips, the next most difficult paid five chips, and so on down to one chip for the easiest problems. If they got the wrong answer, they had to pay the experimenter the corresponding number of poker chips; they were loaned 10 chips to start out, which were deducted from their winnings at the end of the experiment.

The students' choices of problems to solve can be viewed as gambles—they could try a high-payoff difficult problem, but the odds were against getting the right answer. They could try a low-payoff easy problem, but the payoff was so low it hardly was worth the trouble. The students understood the dilemma and, in fact, selected the problems that prescriptive theory would dictate—the appropriate balance between the risk of failure and the magnitude of the payoff. It turned out that these third graders were reasonably efficient gamblers—with one exception. Like real gamblers, many of the students would play conservatively for a while and then, after having built up a supply of poker chips, would take a flyer on the really difficult stack. They almost invariably lost, whereupon they would select easy problems until they had regained their fortune; then they took another flyer.

The agenda that Edwards (1954, 1955) set was to derive a psychology of decision making using prescriptive theory as a starting point, mapping the points at which observed behavior deviated from prescription, and then modifying prescriptive theory to make it descriptive of what decision makers actually do. In short, to transform predictive theory into descriptive theory and then, if necessary, move on to a broader psychology of decision making. In large part, this is exactly what happened, and the story of how this happened is the underlying theme of this book. We begin with prescriptive theory and end having reviewed two generations of descriptive theories with a third generation in the making. The first generation of descriptive theories closely resembles prescriptive theory in that it attempts to retain the general logic and much of the mathematical rigor in its formulation, and it retains the idea that decisions are analogous to gambles. First generation theory has been extensively researched and is broadly accepted as a valid description of human decision making by disciplines outside of psychology, primarily economics. However, from a psychological viewpoint, its resemblance to prescriptive theory is both a strength and a weakness. It gains strength from its legacy of centuries of thinking about decision making that lead up to prescriptive theory, but it is weakened by the constraints this legacy places on its breadth and flexibility. In an attempt to go beyond these constraints, researchers began to explore new ideas about decision making—ideas that bore little or no relation to predictive theory. The result was a second generation of research and theory that is still in the process of coalescing into a unitary body of work.

Second generation research and theory (also called naturalistic research and theory) has its origins in first generation work but grew beyond it in an attempt to more realistically describe how decisions actually are made, notably by professional decision makers such as managers. Second generation work abandons the gamble analogy and views decision making as a form of problem solving. It has been very much influenced by the need for practical knowledge about decision making for systems planning, management, and other real-world applications.

To a large degree, second generation research and theory is based on the work of Herbert Simon. In his classic *Administrative Behavior* (1945), Simon emphasizes that the behavior of a person in an organization is constrained by the position he or she holds in that organization—something so obviously true that it is easy to overlook both its insightfulness and its very broad implications. This means that decision making in organizations is strongly influenced by the structure and norms of the organization, and that decision makers do not entertain the full array of options that an outsider might consider available. Another feature of Simon's analysis is the emphasis on the individual as a decision making agent for the organization, emphasizing that organizations do not themselves make decisions. As pointed out by Davis (1992), after all these years this small but important point is still overlooked by many people who study organizational and group decision making.

Simon is a Nobel Laureate in economics who has produced a stream of useful insights that have inspired large amounts of research by many people. Two of his most famous insights, based on his observations of behavior in organizations, are *bounded rationality* and *satisficing*. Because decision makers' cognitive capacity is rather limited, they must reduce information processing demands by simplifying the problems they encounter. To do so, Simon contends, they construct "small worlds" that are limited representations of the problem at hand. The representation contains only the most salient information, and the decision maker proceeds to make his or her decision based solely upon that "bounded" representation. The decision may in fact be "rational" in that it conforms to the prescriptions of the appropriate prescriptive theory, but the decision maker uses only the information contained in the bounded representation.

Satisficing is another way of reducing the information processing load. This is not a "rational" decision strategy in the sense of following the prescriptions of prescriptive theory, but it allows the decision maker to arrive at a decision without all the computational effort required by prescriptive theory. Here it is assumed that the decision maker has some set of standards that an option must meet for it to be at least minimally satisfactory. The idea is that the first option that comes along that meets all of the standards is the one that is selected. Satisficing is not rational in the prescriptive sense because the decision maker has no assurance that on one or more standards an as-yet-unseen option might not be superior to the option that has been selected, and he or she therefore would fail to select the best possible option. However, the simplicity of this decision strategy presumably makes it worthwhile to risk missing the best option in favor of choosing one that is at least sufficient.

The second generation viewpoint is strongly influenced by decision making in organizations, particularly work-related decisions. Organizational theorists have tended to examine decisions at a higher, more macro, level than do most behavioral decision theorists. The former often treat the organization as the unit and talk as though it makes decisions, presuming something like an organizational mind. The latter focus on individuals, often without specifying the particular context, presuming that an organization's decisions are a function of the collaborative decisions made by its individual members. Things often are confused, however, by a tendency for both organizational and behavioral theorists to switch back and forth between levels of analysis, which muddles things considerably.

Still, observations of individual decision makers in the context of their work provide invaluable information about how decision making takes place. The result has been a number of mini-theories—theories designed to cover some limited kind of decisions but that contribute to an emerging new view about how decision making takes place, particularly in organizational contexts. These mini-theories are beginning to coalesce into more general theories. It is this imminent coalescence that constitutes the second generation of behavioral research and theory.

### Paradigms, Theories, and Models

It is useful to differentiate between paradigms, theories, and models. Although the terms often are used interchangeably, they are not the same thing. In fact they are hierarchically related: paradigms are the most general—rather like a philosophical or ideological framework. Theories are more specific, based on the paradigm and designed to describe what happens in one of the many realms of events encompassed by the paradigm. Models are even more specific, providing the mechanisms by which events occur in a particular part of the theory's realm. Of the three, models are most affected by empirical data—models come and go, theories only give way when evidence is overwhelmingly against them (and sometimes not even then), and paradigms stay put until a radically better idea comes along.

### Prescriptive (Normative) Models

Now to tie all this about paradigms, theories, and models to the study of decision making. As we said above, prescriptive decision theory views the decision maker as a maximizer of expected value. First generation research translated this into the assumption that decision performance will be best if the decision makers' behavior reflects economics' utilitarian paradigm, which means that they strive to acquire desirable payoffs, and if their decision processes correspond to the processes dictated by utility theory and probability theory. That is, decision making, in the sense of acquisition of desired payoffs, will be most successful if the attractiveness of each option is summarized as the sum of the probability-discounted utilities corresponding to its potential payoffs, and if the decision maker chooses the option that offers the greatest sum. If performance falls short of what an economist could achieve by following these prescriptions, the fault must lie in the failure of the decision maker to behave according to the prescriptions. Therefore, by examining the non-correspondence between what the decision maker "should" do and what he or she actually does, first generation researchers and theorists strove to (1) better understand human decision processes and (2) help decision makers perform better. In first generation research, those aspects of utility theory and probability theory that pertain to the decision at hand are referred to as *normative models* because they are seen as defining the norms for correct processing of relevant information—not because it is a social norm to actually behave this way. First generation researchers interpret systematic differences between the prescriptions of the normative models and what decision makers actually do as reflections of people's cognitive limitations and their systematic processing errors. Techniques for helping decision makers overcome these limitations and avoid these errors are called *decision aids.*

In contrast, second generation research is influenced by observations of professional decision makers (managers) and attempts to discover the cognitive processes in which they engage while making various kinds of decisions. This viewpoint lacks the organizing framework provided by prescriptive theory, so it often looks (and is) less systematic than traditional research. At the moment, second generation research and theory consist of a collection of mini-theories, each focusing on some aspect of real-world decision making. There have been a few attempts to construct more encompassing theories, and research on them is presently under way.

Before moving on, it is important to note that by and large, the second generation viewpoint grew out of the first generation, which in turn grew out of the notion of using prescriptive theory as a foundation for behavioral research, so it is not entirely correct to think of the first and second generations as competing with one another. On the other hand, the second generation often has defined itself by how it differs from the first generation, which often makes it look like they all are in competition.

## ❖ THE PLAN

We begin with the basics of prescriptive theory (Chapters 2 through 4). Then we describe the work that led to "psychologizing" some of the central concepts of prescriptive theory and to first generation behavioral theory of decision making (Chapters 5 through 7). This is followed by an examination of work on interpersonal, organizational, and group decisions (Chapter 8) and descriptions of some interesting mini-theories (Chapter 9), with an eye to the implications for second generation behavioral theory. Then we describe a second generation theory that attempts to build on first generation theory and on subsequent research results to produce a descriptive psychological theory of decision making (Chapter 10). The book ends with a short recap, specification of needed research, and some predictions about the future (Chapter 11).

## ❖ SUMMARY

We have characterized decision making as a sequence of events: diagnosis, action selection, and implementation. We have introduced the idea of prescriptive theory and its gambling analogy. And we have discussed two generations in the construction of a psychology of decision making: the first generation, which adheres to the structure and spirit of prescriptive theory, and the second generation, which grows out of a broader appreciation of cognitive and organizational psychology. In the course of this we have described how parts of prescriptive theory were used as normative models by researchers, how differences between normative prescriptions and observed decision behavior were used to construct the first generation behavioral theories, and how dissatisfaction with the breadth of these theories prompted research leading to a second generation of behavioral theories of decision making.

# 2

# Framing

*R*alph and Betty were walking back to their offices from the cafeteria. It
had been a working lunch and Betty had no recollection of what she had
eaten—she thought it might have been sort of yellow. She agreed with Ralph
that their problem wasn't with the product, as he had insisted earlier, and that
their top priority was to focus on sales. Then they had discussed the possibility that their hiring procedures were the root of the difficulty. It looked like they
were hiring people who were ill suited for selling the company's unique line
of products. Earlier she had talked with their Human Resources (HR) people
about hiring procedures, but at the time she hadn't known exactly what to ask.
Anyway, it was clear that the HR folks thought they were doing the best that
could be done and that hiring was pretty much a crapshoot at best. She wasn't
happy with their attitude, but she didn't know enough to confront them.

At lunch she and Ralph had agreed that a good salesperson had a mix of
talents, but it was a mystery what the mix might be. In an offhand remark,
Betty had joked that it would be nice to clone the salespeople who already did
a good job. There had been a moment of silence when they both recognized that
the joke was right on target.

Betty turned the cloning notion over in her mind as they walked along. It
made sense—not literally, of course, but certainly what they wanted was a whole
sales force of people like the best people they already had. This immediately raised

15

*two questions: (1) How can you figure out what makes the best people the best? (2) How can you train current employees to be like them or select new employees who are already like them? And what on earth guided HR's present selection process? Whatever it was, it surely didn't work. She and Ralph both wanted to swing into action, to solve their problem before things got any worse. But what exactly were they going to do? As they parted to go to their separate afternoon meetings, Ralph suggested they talk with his sister-in-law, who worked at the local college. Maybe she had come across something that might help.*

Actually, Betty and Ralph have come farther than they might realize. Common sense tells us that identifying the problem is a large part of solving it, and common sense has much to commend it. In our terms, identifying the problem means framing it properly. Improper framing causes one to invest, as Ralph had earlier, in trying to solve the wrong problem. Betty and Ralph have now reframed the problem from one involving products to one involving their sales force. Then within this new frame they have begun to explore their options. The key concept is to clone the good performers by getting rid of (or retraining) poor performers and hiring people who have the characteristics of the good performers. After their discussion, they both were ready to get to work.

Getting to work is dangerous when you do not know what to do. It is one thing to know what your goal is; it is another thing to know how to reach it. But Betty and Ralph are asking good questions, and when you have no answers it always is a good idea to go to someone who might have them—in this case, Ralph's sister-in-law at the college. But before we see what happened when they talked with her, let us examine framing more closely.

### ❖ FRAMING AND REFRAMING

Framing involves embedding observed events in a context that gives them meaning. Events seldom occur in isolation; the decision maker usually has some idea about what led up to them—what is going on and why. This knowledge supplies the context, the ongoing story that gives coherence to one's experience, without which everything would appear to be random and unrelated. Incoherent experience sometimes occurs under extreme stress (and can be induced by drugs, or may accompany some kinds of illness), but under normal circumstances most of us are aware of a meaningful flow from the past to the present and into the future.

Sometimes, however, events do not fit into this ongoing flow. Often these anomalous events can quickly be reconciled with experience. For example, you realize that a letter you are awaiting did not arrive, prompting you to recall that yesterday was a holiday and there was no mail delivery. But when anomalous events cannot be easily reconciled, they may signal the need to reframe the situation. For example, if you are sitting in your office peacefully answering your e-mail and the fire alarm sounds, your first reaction is to be startled by the loud, intrusive noise. This may be followed by a moment of confusion about what is going on, then you quickly make sense of things by assuming that the building is on fire. Once you recognize the fire alarm for what it is, the flow of your experience is changed—you no longer are in a peaceful e-mail-answering situation, you are in a fire situation, and your behavior must change accordingly. Now seemingly trivial events that previously had escaped your notice, or that might not have made much sense had you focused on them, become meaningful—the smoky smell of which you had been only faintly conscious, the clamor of voices down the hall, the sound of sirens in the distance.

Of course, as was the case with Ralph and the monthly reports, the anomalous events may not be as dramatic as a fire alarm. In fact, events often are so subtle that we miss their importance, or it is so easy to erroneously reconcile them with our current frame that we fail to notice that they in fact signal the frame's inadequacy. Ralph looked at the figures every month and failed to see their message—he thought they were telling him that he still had not solved the product problem. Only when it became clear that his efforts were getting him nowhere and things were getting progressively worse did he realize he had misinterpreted (misframed) the situation. Because the figures did not send an unequivocal message, he had to think hard about what they meant. When the reframing insight came, his entire approach to the problem changed.

Wagenaar and Keren (1986) provide an example of what follows from framing situations in either one way or another. They instructed half of a group of individuals to frame a decision from the viewpoint of a public official and the other half to frame it from the viewpoint of a parent. The decision was about whether to impose a law requiring children to wear seatbelts when traveling in an automobile. Information was presented about accidents in which children were hurt. Half of each framing group (parent or public official) received statistical information (each year 100 out of 150 juvenile victims of traffic accidents could have been saved if they were wearing seatbelts) and half received anecdotal information (a story about a little girl who died because she was not wearing a seatbelt). The participants were asked to make a decision about the law and to explain how the information influenced their decision. It was found that participants operating under the parental frame were more likely to favor the law when presented anecdotal information about the little girl than when presented statistical information, and participants under the public official frame were more likely to favor the law when presented with the statistical information. In short, framing provides the context within which new information is used, and different frames put the focus on different kinds of information.

The most prominent line of decision research on framing has focused on how people differentially frame problems that are stated in terms of possible gains or possible losses. Tversky and Kahneman (1981) presented 150 participants with the following problems and asked them to choose which option in each pair of options they would prefer to play.

*Problem 1*
A1: A sure gain of $240
A2: A 25% chance to gain $1,000, and a 75% chance to gain nothing

*or*

*Problem 2*
B1: A sure loss of $750
B2: A 75% chance to lose $1,000, and a 25% chance to lose nothing

As we saw in Chapter 1, the generally accepted way to evaluate these options is to multiply the potential gains or losses (dollars) by the chance of winning or losing that outcome. This is called the *expected value* of the option, and if one option has a larger expected value than the other, it is regarded as the better of the two options.

The research found that when choosing between A1 and A2, 84% of the participants chose A1, even though the certain gain of $240 is less than the expected value of $250 for A2. When choosing between B1 and B2, 87% of the participants chose B2, even though the expected value for B2 is a loss of $750, which is equal to the certain loss of $750 for B1.

The results illustrate the often-repeated finding that people tend to avoid taking risks (they choose the sure thing) when outcomes are framed as gains and that they tend to take risks (they choose the gamble) when outcomes are framed as losses, even when the only difference is in how the outcomes are stated. That is, the wording of the problem can influence how people frame it and, as a result, how they decide to deal with it.

This research finding ought not to come as a surprise. Advertisers, politicians, and everyone else who tries to influence people's behavior know that the way in which things are described influences how people frame situations. Most of us have learned to discount the hyperbole of such descriptions, but we clearly are not immune to their effects—we still buy heavily advertised products and we still vote for the politicians who use the right words.

Framing goes beyond mere wording. Indeed, the fact that wording has an influence at all merely indicates how pervasive framing is and how sensitive it is to relevant information. The Nobel Laureate Herbert Simon (1945) has suggested that decision makers reduce information processing demands by constructing limited representations of situations because they cannot cognitively deal with a great deal of information. The representation is called a "small world." The problem with relying on a small world representation is that it might not include the right things, be too simplistic, or just be wrong. Hence it behooves us to be rather flexible, to be sensitive to signs that the representation needs correction (reframing). Of course, some people appear amazingly inflexible, retaining their frame in the teeth of disconfirming information that other people would regard as overwhelming. Consistent to a fault, their overconfidence in their frame's correctness makes them vulnerable to serious error. At the other extreme are those who seem unable to stick with one frame for any length of time. Flighty and inconstant, they see every side of every issue; seeing it first this way and then that, they never resolve much of anything. It is best to be somewhere between the two extremes, flexible but not flighty.

❖  EXPERTISE AND FRAMING

Experts often exhibit the desirable flexibility without flightiness. As a result of research in both cognitive science (Anderson, 1981) and in behavioral decision making (Wright & Bolger, 1992), a great deal has been learned about what makes people experts at one or another task and how they approach problem solving and decision making.

At first the research results appear to be conflicting: experts sometimes are awful and sometimes they do a very good job. Shanteau (1992) analyzed the results of many studies and found that experts perform better in domains involving physical processes and less well in domains involving human behavior. In short, they do better in inherently predictable domains and worse in inherently unpredictable domains. Even at that, experts generally do better than novices, and they clearly approach tasks differently than novices. Part of this difference is that experts can use their experience to frame situations rapidly and accurately. Then they use the underlying meaning of the situation provided by the frame to guide their task performance—and use of the underlying meaning provides flexibility because it allows the expert to vary his or her approach to the particular problem at hand without losing track of the larger picture. That is, having framed the situation, experts use the frame to draw upon their knowledge about what to expect in the situation and what variations are reasonable (and what they mean), as well as knowledge about what has worked in the past and how that might be adapted to the present situation. Lacking the depth of experience, novices must rely on the surface characteristics of the situation to guide their performance of the task, with the result that they are more likely to do things "by the book," thereby failing to utilize the nuances of the situation profitably. In short, framing allows an expert's performance to be informed by a significantly richer store of information than a novice's and, at the same time, injects a degree of flexibility and adaptability that is unavailable to the novice.

The superiority of expertise is not merely due to having access to memories of past experience, although that plays an important role. Studies of chess experts, for example, show that when they are shown chess pieces randomly arranged on a board, they are no better at remembering the pieces' locations than are novices. In contrast, when the pieces are placed in locations that might reasonably occur in an ongoing game of chess, experts are far superior to novices in recalling the locations (Chase & Simon, 1973; de Groot, 1965). What is more, the experts can start with the given arrangement and anticipate what moves might occur two or three steps ahead. The conclusion is that chess experts, and presumably other kinds of experts, can recognize meaningful patterns of events, and having recognized (framed) them can use them to perform the tasks that the situation demands.

## ❖ THE NATURE OF FRAMES

It is reasonable to ask how frames are cognitively represented, and how they come to be shared by different people. That is, what is the essence of a frame—how does it give meaning and how does it relate to ongoing experience? And how do different people come to have what they at least think are the same frames for a situation?

We think of the frame of a situation as the decision maker's cognitive image of the situation because to us the word *image* implies both visual and narrative representation. To get the idea, recall what you were doing yesterday at noon. Do you have a picture in your mind's eye of where you were and who you were with? Do you remember the conversation? Could you tell us in a phrase or two what was going on?

Now consider the following about your recollection:

- Do you see your companions and the locale in your mental picture? (Can you see yourself? If you can, you know this is not an exact memory because you never see yourself unless you look in a mirror.)
- Can you recall the conversation verbatim—maybe even hear your companions' voices in your head? In fact, you are unlikely to recall the conversation word for word, just the gist of it.
- Is your brief description of what was going on simply a list, or does it focus on your understanding of the why and wherefore of what took place? It is probably much more meaning-laden than would be the description by an outside observer who merely recounted the events.

In short, your version of what happened yesterday at noon is a rather complex representation comprising both visual and auditory components that are held together by the story-like meaning of what was going on.

When we ask you about yesterday, we are in effect asking you to recall the frame you placed on events and then to color in the details; by and large, memory is a store of frames and referents from which we reconstruct the past, rather than a store of exact recordings of what occurred (Neisser, 1982). The frame you currently are using for yesterday noon might change dramatically if we were to tell you something you did not know about one of the people you were talking with (presuming that you were talking with others). Suppose we told you that this morning one of those companions had checked into a hospital for treatment of an acute psychiatric problem? As in the fire alarm example, your first response might be to be startled. Your second response might be to review yesterday's conversation to see if something suggested that this might happen. Finally, you might completely reinterpret what was going on yesterday in light of this new information and reframe the situation or parts of the situation.

Researchers have studied the nature of framing, and the results are instructive, if a bit overwhelming. Instead of using the term *frame*, much of the research uses the term *schema* (singular) or *schemata* (plural). Subspecies of schemata are given labels to denote the particular roles they play. Thus, *scenarios* (Jungermann, 1985; Jungermann & Thüring, 1987; Thüring & Jungermann, 1986) and *mental models* (Johnson-Laird, 1983) are researchers' labels for schemata that play a role in forecasting and problem solving. *Knowledge partitions* (Dinsmore, 1987) is the label for schemata that play a role in inference. *Episode schemata* (Rummelhart, 1977) and *causal models* (Einhorn & Hogarth, 1986) are labels for schemata that play a role in reasoning about complex chains of events that lead up to some specified event. *Script* (Schank & Abelson, 1977) is the label for schemata that play a role in dealing with social situations. *Prototype* (Rosch, 1976) and *stereotype* (McCauley, Stitt, & Segal, 1980) are labels for schemata that play a role in classifying people, objects, and events. *Self-concept* (Markus & Nurius, 1986; Markus & Wurf, 1987) is the label for schemata that play a role in organizing one's knowledge about oneself. In short, many areas of research, under various labels, have studied schemata and their use in different situations, but the underlying concept is pretty much the same. And this concept is what we mean when we talk about frames in decision making.

As you can see, a considerable amount is known about framing— each of the areas cited above has an enormous literature associated with it. While it is beyond the scope of this book to review all of this, we can derive from it a formal definition of a frame: a frame is a mental construct consisting of elements, and the relationships among them, that are associated with a situation that is of interest to a decision maker. The elements are salient current events and associated past events. Relationships define the expected interactions among the elements—violations of these expectations indicate that the frame is not a valid representation of the situation of interest. If these violations are regarded by the decision maker as important enough, they prompt revision of the frame, either through its complete replacement or through reinterpretation of various of its elements or relationships.

It perhaps is impractical to try to think of frames in this formal, rather esoteric way. A more down-to-earth definition is that the frame guides the decision maker's interpretation of what is going on. It derives from the decision maker's knowledge about events that led up to the situation in question and his or her private theories about how people behave and what makes things happen. It therefore tells the decision maker what to expect. The frame may be in error, but until feedback or some other form of information makes the error evident, the frame is the foundation for understanding the situation and for deciding what to do about it. In fact, knowing the frame the decision maker is using goes a long way in predicting and understanding the decisions he or she makes—which is useful for other people who must interact with the decision maker.

### ❖  SHARED FRAMES

Unless one is a hermit, few decisions are made in isolation and few fail to have an impact on someone else. Indeed, decision making is essentially a social behavior, even when there is nobody else present, because one anticipates how others will react and factors this into the decision. And, of course, a large proportion of our decisions are made in concert with other people—we ask for advice, we use others as sounding boards as we deliberate, we ask them what they would do. Organizations per se do not make decisions, but individuals in organizations do. And when they do, they must take others into account.

In order to take others into account when making decisions, the decision maker has to assume that he or she knows how they frame the situation of interest. Clearly, if we think your frame is different from ours, in order to avoid conflict or censure we must try to make decisions that will not be anomalous from the viewpoint of your frame, or we must try to bring our frames and yours into alignment so our decision will not look outlandish or stupid to you. If you are our boss or a colleague with whom we must coordinate our work, this becomes especially important.

People align their frames in two ways. First, they talk about them—discussion permits them to iron out the differences and come to some mutually shared idea about the nature of the situation and its demands and about what their options might be. (Or, if they cannot align them, they can at least understand where they differ.)

The second way frames become aligned is more subtle. People who share a similar view of the world, a similar set of beliefs and values, tend to frame situations similarly. This shared set of beliefs and values is called a *culture* (Trice & Beyer, 1993). Thus we can speak of a country's culture—the inhabitants' shared worldview. And we can speak of an organization's culture—the members' shared worldview. We even can speak of a marriage's culture, or a family's culture, or a friendship's culture—whenever two or more people have in common a set of beliefs and values that induce similar interpretations of events. In short, people who share cultures often arrive at similar frames for situations, frames that might be very different from those arrived at by outsiders.

If you have traveled in foreign lands, you no doubt have encountered situations that you framed in one way due to your cultural background and that the local people framed in quite another way. One of us lived in the Netherlands for a while and frequently heard observations about how shallow Americans tend to be (present company always excepted, of course). The nub of the argument was that Americans become too familiar too quickly, because we frequently use first names from the moment we meet someone and we are rather open about personal information such as marital status, our families, and our attitudes about things in general. Dutchmen, and many other Europeans for that matter, tend to be much more guarded; friendships are built over years and one often knows very little about the personal lives of people with whom one has worked for a long time. This is more than just a difference in style. American values favor openness and straightforwardness, and we distrust people who behave otherwise. Dutch values favor discretion and privacy, and they distrust people who behave otherwise. In both cases, our respective values influence how we differentially frame social situations and our subsequent expectations about how we and others should behave. We each interpret observed behavior in light of our respective frames and draw the logical conclusions: they often see us as shallow and we often see them as stuffy.

Organizational cultures induce perhaps even more commonality in framing than do national cultures. The population of any nation will have a variety of subcultures. While they all may share a few core beliefs and values that define them as part of that nation's larger culture, they also will have substantial differences, and the resulting differences in how they frame things are the stuff of which local politics is made. Variety also exists in organizations, but it tends to be less. If people substantially dislike the dominant culture it usually is easier to leave than to bring about change. Therefore, most of the people who are attracted to and remain in an organization are fairly comfortable with the beliefs and values that make up its culture and with the way in which the organization's members tend to frame situations. Indeed, it has been shown that there is a substantially greater tendency for people to leave an organization—law firms, in this case—when there is a conflict between their values and the organization's values than when the two sets of values are similar (Sheridan, 1992).

If this sounds too abstract, consider the members of a religious congregation. Presumably, it is the common core of beliefs and values that makes membership attractive. People who do not hold those beliefs and values are not attracted to the congregation. As a result, there is a greater similarity of worldview among the members than there would be within some randomly selected group of people. This does not mean that there are no disagreements within the congregation, but it means that the things they disagree about are peripheral to their central core of beliefs and values (often, how those beliefs and values ought to be translated into action).

Any organization is like this congregation—there is culture consisting of a central core of shared beliefs and values, sometimes larger, sometimes smaller, but shared nonetheless. The larger the shared core, the more similar will be the frames that the organization's members derive for situations. This means that individuals usually can make decisions for the organization that will neither surprise nor outrage other members (Beach, 1993a; Weatherly & Beach, 1996). On the other hand, if the core is small, conflict will tend to arise because everyone with be playing from a different sheet of music, so to speak. That is, if the core is small, different people will tend to have different frames for the same situation, and a decision made by any one member will look wrong, foolish, or malevolent to other members.

Of course, even if two people frame a problem in the same way it does not mean that they will automatically choose the same way of dealing with it. In fact, they may not even come up with similar options from which to choose. However, if the frames are similar, they can at least understand where the other person is coming from and can at least think about the choice using the same assumptions the other person is using. So, conflict may arise, but it is conflict about how to deal with the problem, not about what the problem is. Presence of a shared culture does not ensure that things always go smoothly, but absence of one almost certainly ensures that they will not.

There is a downside to a widely shared culture in an organization. Because it predisposes the members to frame things in particular ways, it often makes them overlook alternative frames. This "groupthink" (Janis, 1982) phenomenon is often observed, and its dangers are broadly recognized—in utter unanimity everyone marches off in the wrong direction. Equally bad, however, is the fact that frames that do not fit well with the culture get very short shrift. This means that novel viewpoints and fresh ideas are quickly squelched.

Perhaps more important, a shared culture makes necessary organizational reforms very difficult to bring about. Consider an organization that has been around for a long time and has functioned in a rather stable, predictable environment. People who disliked its culture have left, and people who found the culture attractive have come and stayed. In short, everyone is pretty happy and they all see the world pretty similarly.

Then that stable environment begins to change—not radically perhaps, but change nonetheless. The members, who often do not have a very clear view of what is going on outside the organization, fail to see the danger, but the leader does. If the only way to deal with the danger is for the organization to radically change, to try new innovative approaches to problems it does not yet comprehend, the leader may be in for trouble. Revolutionary changes often clash with the core beliefs and values of the organization's culture, and it is the attractiveness of this core that makes the organization attractive to its members. Anything that threatens this core, that violates these beliefs and values, is framed as a threat and is regarded as patently wrongheaded and dangerous. This frame leads to decisions that protect the core values and results in resistance to the proposed changes, often rationalized by a disbelief that the threat is great enough to justify revolutionary change. Every executive can tell stories of sincere efforts to convince employees that change was necessary, of efforts that were actively or passively subverted, not because of the effort they would require, but because the proposed changes flew in the face of the organization's culture.

Organizational change is an interesting topic, but we must not let it lead us astray. The point is that people who share beliefs and values, and who have a common experience as a result of long association with one another, tend to frame problems in much the same way. This is valuable in that it is efficient—decisions end up being coordinated because they are predicated on the same set of assumptions. However, the range of admissible frames is limited by the culture. Frames that fall outside the range tend to be regarded with suspicion or rejected out of hand. When problems arise that cannot be addressed by the frames within that range, the culture becomes a liability—it does not permit the organization to address the problems because it does not allow its members to understand (frame) problems adequately, and they therefore cannot make the appropriate decisions.

### ❖  INFORMATION AND FRAMING

In much of what has been discussed thus far it may appear that framing is some magical process that through a flash of insight leads to a clear understanding of the situation and the problems it presents. In fact, framing often is the result of hard work and thoughtful examination of events. True, the mind abhors a vacuum and usually frames events almost automatically—but when the stakes are high and we are making a conscious, conscientious effort to be careful, this first frame usually is regarded as provisional. In business, for example, going with the first hunch is dangerous, and even when it appears to be the overwhelmingly correct frame, people usually make sure by checking it against the facts.

Betty and Ralph arrived at their understanding of their sales problem both by Ralph's analysis of the monthly reports and by Betty's insightful remark about cloning. His use of information showed him that his first framing of the company's problem was wrong and suggested that the real frame had something to do with sales. Her remark further defined the sales frame by focusing their attention more closely on building a good sales force. But the frame is not yet fully developed; they both want to get to work to solve the problem, but action is premature until they more clearly delineate the frame—it is still to loose to provide any clear guidance for action. The only way to tighten it is to gather information. Perhaps they ought to talk to their customers about what they value in salespeople and who they think does the best job. In light of what they find out, they perhaps should devise ways of predicting success for job applicants (or design appropriate training programs for old employees). They also might want to find out what HR currently is doing when it evaluates job applicants to see why current practices are producing such bad results.

In short, initial framing may be fairly swift, but when the stakes are high common sense argues against settling for that first impression. Instead, we must seek information against which to test the validity of the initial frame and to guide us in tailoring a frame that best fits the facts. After that initial, almost instantaneous, framing a lot of time and work is invested in fleshing out our understanding of the situation and in making judgments (inferences) about those parts of it that are not wholly clear.

❖  SUMMARY

Framing serves to tie events to the decision maker's ongoing experience, thereby endowing those events with meaning. However, a frame is a fragile thing: When challenged by events that conflict with it, the decision maker is quick to amend it or to replace it altogether—although people differ in the degree to which they are flexible in this regard. Experts may well be experts because their training and past experience allow them to recognize situations and apply familiar frames to them. Once the situation is framed, the expert's knowledge about what to expect and what has worked or not worked in the past can be brought to bear on the current problem.

Because almost every decision ultimately is a social decision, people make efforts to understand others' frames. When they perceive differences between those frames and their own, they make efforts to align the frames through discussion and persuasion. Fortunately, when people have a history of shared experience, they tend to frame situations similarly in the first place, thus reducing the amount of work needed to align their frames. An organization's culture—the beliefs and values shared by members of the organization—promotes similar frames and therefore can contribute to coordinated decision making.

# 3

# Policy

*P* *rofessor Karma Howell not only had a unique first name, she had a smile
warm enough to melt steel. Her students loved her, and so did Ralph, in
a proper brother-in-lawish sort of way.*

*Ralph and Betty sat in Karma's cramped office listening to her describe the
research on decision making. They had told her that they wanted to clone their
best salespeople. She thought that this was a novel way of putting it, but that
the technology existed to do it—well, not genetic cloning, of course, but identifying the salient attributes of good salespeople and formulating a policy for
using those attributes to guide decisions about hiring or training salespeople.
She explained that the technology had its weaknesses, but that it could at least
introduce order and reason to the selection process. Whatever its faults, the
technology probably would lead to better overall results than the company's
present methods. By the time they left, Ralph and Betty knew the next step in
solving their sales problem.*

The purpose of this chapter is to examine the use of policy in decision
making. This follows directly from our previous discussion of framing.

When a situation is framed, the decision maker can make decisions about it in one of three ways:

1. Recognition. The situation is so similar to one that he or she has encountered before that behavior that worked before can be used again—or, at least, a variation of what worked before can be used.

2. Inference. The situation is familiar enough that the decision maker can make an educated guess about what to do.

3. Choice. The situation is sufficiently unique that neither recognition nor inference provides adequate guidance, and the decision maker must explore his or her options and choose the most promising option.

Recognition and inference both involve policy, the subject of both this chapter and the one that follows.

## ❖ RECOGNITION

When a decision situation is encountered, the decision maker uses its salient features to probe his or her memory. If the probe locates a contextual memory that has features that are virtually the same as those of the current situation, the latter is said to be recognized. The advantage of recognition is that the decision maker can draw upon his or her knowledge about the previously encountered situation to guide behavior in this situation. In decision making, old behaviors that are used in new but similar situations are called *policies*. In the psychology of learning, they are called *habits*. In social psychology they are called *scripts*. In all cases the point is to add efficiency to the process by using precedent rather than engaging in choice for every situation.

One of the most thorough explorations of policy for decision making was done by Gary Klein (1993) and his associates. Their studies focused on crucial, real-life decision tasks such as firefighting, Army tank platoon command, and design engineering. The key is that the decision makers are highly familiar with the situations in question and that they have extensive training and experience in dealing with those situations. Upon encountering a situation of the same type, they draw upon their training and experience to act appropriately. Klein calls this "recognition-primed decision making," and his description of it is called the RPD model.

There are three levels to the RPD model. The most basic level is the simple match, in which the situation is recognized and what has been done in the past is done again. The second level involves more evaluation; the decision maker performs mental simulations of variations on past behaviors and what might happen if one or another variation were used here. The third level applies when there are apparent flaws in the variations, requiring major modifications and more complex mental simulations. That is, recognition primes the decision about what to do, but it does not wholly determine what to do.

The mental simulations are an important key to recognition-primed decision making. Klein has gathered descriptions of what decision makers think about when making decisions and shows that they imagine "what might happen if they did this," and "what might be the result of doing that," where both "this" and "that" are drawn from past experience. Past behaviors have not all been successful, and past failures inform current decision making as much as, or more than, past successes. Thus when they think about whether some act might successfully deal with a situation, decision makers can use past failures to help them see flaws in the action under consideration, and to guide modifications (or rejection) of the action. The point is recognition of situations does not necessarily result in blind application of a policy based on past experience; it often prompts consideration of modifications and revisions while providing the general strategy for approaching the decision.

❖ INFERENCE

The RPD model strikes a responsive chord in most people who hear about it. The lowest of the three levels is closely related to learning and memory research in psychology. The middle level allows for minor modification of learned behavior, introducing a cognitive flavor and accounting for the fact that behavior seldom is exactly the same from one time to another, just as situations are never identical. However, the RPD model's account of the highest of the three levels is too vague to be of much use either in studying decision behavior or in helping decision makers do their jobs. For the necessary specificity, we must turn to an older model, the Lens Model (Brunswik, 1947). While the Lens Model does not directly address all of the issues raised by the RPD model's third level, it provides a more systematic treatment of the processes involved when it is not wholly clear what to do in a familiar situation.

It all began with Egon Brunswik, an Austrian psychologist who came to the United States just before the outbreak of World War II and who specialized in the study of perception. Specifically, he studied how people use perceptual cues to make decisions (inferences) about the state of their surrounding environment. Let us take a moment to explore the underlying logic of Brunswik's position because that logic is the basis of all that follows in this chapter.

It is widely accepted by perceptual psychologists that one's mind does not directly experience the objects and events in the world around one. Instead, sensory information permits the mind to construct mental representations of those objects and events (e.g., Prinzmetal, 1995; Yantis, 1995). There are many ways to demonstrate that what seems to be direct experience of the external world actually is a mental representation built from sensory information, but let us concentrate on just one:

Consider a table that has a rectangular top. When you look at the top what do you see—a square, a rectangle, a trapezoid? In fact, the image of the table's rectangular top forms a trapezoid on the retina of your eye, but you perceive that table top to be rectangular. That is, in order to make the table top look realistic, an artist would have to draw it as a trapezoid; the nearer edge of the table would be longer than the farther edge and the two sides would form acute angles with the nearer edge and obtuse angles with the farther edge. When you looked at the artist's drawing you would see a table with a rectangular top.

Look around you for a table. Then look at it analytically, as an artist would, and you will see that its rectangular top is in fact presented to your eye as a trapezoid. Moreover, if you walk around the table you will note that the trapezoid changes shape as you move. But your perceptual system is never tricked into thinking that the top changes shape as you walk around it. This is called "perceptual constancy," and it has been studied for a hundred years (James, 1983). For our purposes, it serves as evidence that what you experience (a solid rectangular table top that does not change as you move around) and what is presented to your senses (a trapezoid that changes shape as you move) are not identical. In fact, your perceptual system must use the dynamic sensory information about the table in order to make inferences that tell you there is a

**Figure 3.1**    Brunswik's Lens Model

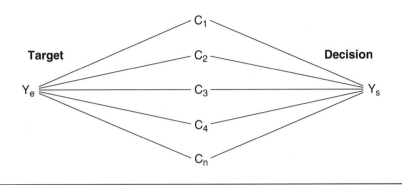

stable object out there—otherwise the contents of your experience would be in constant flux.

Brunswik (1947) summarized his idea about perceptual inference in the form of the Lens Model, diagrammed in Figure 3.1. To make it simple, imagine that your perceptual system is called upon to identify some target object ($Y_e$). Light and air surround the target and convey information to you through your vision, hearing, and other senses. These are cues ($C1, C2, C3$) that convey information about the target. On the basis of these cues you must make a decision ($Y_s$) about the nature of the target.

Suppose the target's outline on your retina indicates that it is small. Your color receptors sense that it is white. And because of the way in which its surface reflects light you infer that it is covered with something soft, perhaps fur. You smell alfalfa on its breath, you can feel the radiance of its body heat, and your hearing tells you that it is nearly silent when moves. You see that the pointy part of the target (its nose?) is constantly twitching, and even more telling, there are two long white appendages that project upward from just above and slightly behind the pointy part (ears?). And the round things between the pointy part and the (assumed) ears are pink (eyes?). This must be a rabbit!

Actually, all of this happens virtually instantaneously and with little effort on your part—your perceptual system is designed to make inferences and it does so without much help from your conscious mind. This is especially true if the situation is framed so that there are a limited number of possibilities to begin with. If we had told you that we were at a country fair it would have limited the possibilities so much that the system would not have had to work very hard. However, if we told you that we were in a pet store, you might have expected the target to be a dog or cat, which would have required your perceptual system to work a little harder to avoid error.

Identifying targets is but one function of the perceptual system. It also serves to make comparisons among targets. Suppose we framed the situation as a county fair and told you that your job was to judge the rabbits. Now there are lots of rabbits and your perceptual system is called upon to make comparisons among them. This requires some additional effort, and your conscious mind now will be called upon to augment your automatic perceptual processes. Now you must be more discriminating; the cues will again be size, coloring, texture of the fur, and so on, together with whatever else livestock judges use when judging rabbits. This time, instead of merely inferring that the target is a rabbit (which you now take as given), you must use the cues consistently (a *policy*) when deciding about each of the rabbits so you can tell which are winners and which are not. In short, you must evaluate each rabbit's location on an underlying scale, where the best rabbits are on the high end and the worst are on the low end. Then you must select the winner based upon the rabbits' locations on this scale—presumably you would select the one that was highest on the scale.

### ❖  APPLYING THE LENS MODEL

Enough about rabbits. The idea is that Brunswik's (1947) apparently simple description of how the perceptual system identifies targets has hidden within it a great deal of sophistication. It applies both to basic perceptual decisions and to higher-order decisions that permit ordering of the targets on an underlying scale, usually related to preference. And it is here that we return to Ralph and Betty and their cloning problem.

When Betty and Ralph talk about cloning their good salespeople, they mean that they would like to know how to look at a job applicant (target) and make a good guess (decision) about whether he or she will turn out to be a successful salesperson. The first step is to turn the inference process around and find out what makes successful salespeople successful. The second step is to use this knowledge to devise a policy for using information about potential job applicants in order to decide how well they are going to do (which is not unlike judging which rabbits are at the winning end of the scale). The third step is getting the HR folks to use this policy to select new salespeople or to design a program for retraining failing salespeople. Let us look at each of these steps in turn.

### The Left Side of the Lens

To simplify things, let us assume that you have been hired to do the work for Betty's company. Let us assume further that the company has a pretty good performance evaluation scheme in place. The first step in discovering what makes a good salesperson ($Y_e$) would be to sit down and read the performance evaluations of both the good performers and the poor performers, concentrating on what differentiates them. What you learn should be augmented by discussions with supervisors and with the salespeople themselves. Eventually you should get a fair idea of some of the differences between the two groups.

Unfortunately, much of what you learn will not be very valuable. That is, much of what you learn will be about how good salespeople behave in the selling situation, but you seldom have direct information about selling behavior when you are judging the applicant's suitability for hiring. This is the crux of the problem: You usually have to make your evaluation on the basis of only tangential information—and this could have been one reason the HR people told Betty that hiring was hardly better than a crap shoot.

On the other hand, things may be better than they appear. For one thing, you know who the good and bad salespeople are, and you have their original job applications somewhere in their personnel folders. We can think of the information on job applications as potential cues for predicting whether an applicant will turn out to be successful or unsuccessful. Except that now you can turn things around—by knowing who the good salespeople are, who the so-so salespeople are, and who the poor salespeople are, you can look back at the cues on their applications and see which cues would have been the best predictors of later performance.

The procedure is fairly straightforward. First you have supervisors rate each salesperson for performance, perhaps on a scale from 1 (poor) to 7 (excellent). Then you go to each person's original job application and code the answer to each question on the application so that it can be entered into a computer (i.e., you must convert qualitative information to quantitative information, coding yes/no answers as 1 or 0, and assigning numbers to different levels of more complicated answers.)

For each salesperson, you now have a set of data consisting of his or her performance rating and one coded answer for each of the $n$ questions on the application. Then across all salespeople you do a multiple regression analysis using the performance ratings as the dependent variable and the coded answers to each of the $n$ questions on the application as the $n$ independent variables. This analysis will yield an equation that describes the structure of the relationship between the cues (the independent variables) and performance (the dependent variable) for the sales force as a whole:

$$Y_e = a + B_1C_1 + B_2C_2 + B_3C_3 + \cdots + B_nC_n. \qquad \text{(eq. 1)}$$

This regression equation is a statement of the optimal policy for using the cues to predict performance. $Y_e$ stands for the supervisors' ratings of performance, $C$ stands for a coded answer to a question on the application (questions 1, 2, 3 and so on up to $n$ questions), and $B$ stands for the standardized regression weight for each question, called the *beta weight*. The $a$ is merely a scaling constant that has no particular importance for us at the moment. A cue (question) that has a large beta weight can be regarded as contributing more information to predicting performance than a cue with a small weight.

In addition, the analysis yields an indication of how well this equation fits the data, expressed as the square of the multiple correlation coefficient, $R^2$. This coefficient can be interpreted as the degree to which the equation is capable of predicting the performance ratings. Of course, because the equation is derived from data across all of the salespeople, because the ratings are done by different supervisors, and because there is bound to be noise (error) in the data, the equation can never perfectly predict the performance ratings for every one of the salespeople. But if $R^2$ is large, it means that the cues from the application permit reasonably accurate prediction across the group as a whole. If it is small, you must assume that the cues are not very diagnostic—you have the wrong cues, they are not measured accurately, or it simply is not possible to predict performance in this situation.

## The Right Side of the Lens

The use of multiple regression in the way just described is a pretty standard use. Moreover, it does not have a lot to do with human decision making. So, turning to the right side of the lens in Figure 3.1, let us consider the role of the HR people in the hiring process.

As noted above, the purpose of an application is to provide information for an HR employment officer (let us call him Hank) to make a decision about how well an applicant will perform. Use of equation 1 might appear to eliminate Hank from the process; a clerk could merely obtain the required information and put it into the equation. However attractive (and cheap) this substitution might appear to Ralph and Betty, it is unlikely to work. The equation is mechanical and inflexible. It treats every applicant the same, acknowledging no mitigating circumstances and making no exceptions. As such, its blind application probably is an invitation to a lawsuit.

Human intellect clearly has its limitations, but it excels in its ability to detect exceptions to rules (anomalies). Indeed, it tends to go to sleep when things are constant, but when something unique comes along it is quick to seize on it. Therefore, the intellect of the people in HR (Hank in particular) should be used, not subjugated to the inflexible application of equation 1. You need the HR people to make sure the equation does not blindly commit injustices or do stupid things. For example, if you have no cue in the equation for some kind of very diagnostic information, perhaps because it has never arisen before, you could overlook the best applicant you have ever had. Let us say that the applicant has owned his own highly successful company in the same field as Betty's company, but his physician told him that the stress of running it was going to kill him. He decides therefore to sell his company and to go to work as a salesperson for a similar company—he knows the business inside and out, he was his own best salesperson, and he wants to work for Betty. Because this has never happened before, there is no way to put this information in equation 1, so somebody has to override the system and hire him before he goes to a competitor.

Even for more mundane cases, Hank has to be active in the hiring process—laws must be observed and information has to be interpreted. Equation 1 is merely a policy guide. So, the question becomes one of helping Hank align his hiring policies with the policy described by equation 1, while retaining his discretion in unique cases.

The first step is to find out what Hank is doing now—what policy characterizes his use of information about the applicant to evaluate acceptability. This involves returning to the Lens Model. Your evaluation of how the cues could be used to predict good sales performance involved the left side of the lens in Figure 3.1. Your evaluation of how the cues are used by Hank involves the right side. In the past, Hank read the applications, talked with the applicants, and made a decision about how acceptable the person was, that is, placed him or her on a scale of preference for hiring.

The question of interest is about Hank's policy for using the cues on the application to make his decisions. You can find this out by performing an analysis very like the one you did before, except that this time the resulting equation will describe Hank's policy (equation 2) rather than the optimal policy (equation 1). First, you present Hank with the applications for each of the people on the sales force (with identifying information blanked out). Do not tell him that these are people who have already been hired so he will treat them as new applicants and rate their acceptability (on a scale from 1 to 7). For each salesperson, you now have the coded answers on their original application (which you already coded for the earlier analysis) and Hank's acceptability rating. Once again you do a multiple regression analysis, this time using Hank's rating as the dependent variable $(Y_s)$ and the same coded cues $(C)$ you used before. The analyses will yield an equation of the following form:

$$Y_s = a + B_1 C_1 + B_2 C_2 + B_3 C_3 + \cdots + B_n C_n. \qquad \text{(eq. 2)}$$

Note that the form is the same as equation 1, but some of the components will be different. The things that are different are $Y_s$, which is Hank's acceptability rating; $a$, which again is an uninteresting constant; and the beta weight, $B$, for each cue, which indicates the relative influence (importance) of the cue to Hank's ratings. Notice that the coded cues, $C$, in equation 2 are the same as in equation 1. That is, you used the same information from the applications in the analysis for equation 2 as you used for equation 1. This means that if Hank's policy for using the cues (equation 2) is different from the optimal policy (equation 1), it will show up as differences between the beta weights in the two equations.

In addition, having Hank's acceptability ratings allows you to see how good a decision maker he is; you merely correlate his ratings with the ratings the supervisors made for the salespeople. This correlation is called the *achievement coefficient,* and it indicates how well Hank's judgments of acceptability (which presumably reflects his prediction of the applicant's performance) correspond to the supervisors' performance ratings. However, a low achievement coefficient is not necessarily an indictment of Hank. Let us look more closely at this, and then let us look at how we might help Hank do a better job if he is not doing too well.

Consider Hank's dilemma. He has the answers to the questions on the application, which may not be very good predictors of performance in the first place. So, if he does poorly, it could be for either of two reasons: (1) nobody could do a good job with the information on the application, or (2) another person might do a good job but Hank cannot.

The difficulty of Hank's task is revealed by the $R^2$ for equation 1. If it is low, the cues are not good predictors of rated performance, and we should not expect Hank to do very well either. The low $R^2$ puts an upper limit on Hank's achievement coefficient (actually on the square of his achievement coefficient), so he will be unable to do better than that no matter how hard he tries.

On the other hand, if the $R^2$ for equation 1 is high but Hank's achievement coefficient is low, there is only one place the problem can lie—he must be weighting the cues in a way that lowers his ability to predict accurately. As we observed above, this will be revealed by differences between the beta weights in his equation and the beta weights in equation 1. The remedy is to train Hank to weight the information in the appropriate manner.

If Hank is poor at predicting performance, it does not necessarily mean that the $R^2$ will be low for equation 2. This is because the $R^2$ for equation 2 indicates how well equation 2 is able to account for *his* ratings on the seven-point scale, not how accurate these ratings are (which would be achievement). He may be using the cues all wrong, but as long as he uses them in a consistent manner the equation will be able to account for his ratings and the $R^2$ will be high. To the degree that he is inconsistent in his use of the cues, it becomes more difficult to account for his ratings and, therefore, the $R^2$ is reduced.

## Making a Recommendation

Now you have equations for both the left and right sides of the Lens Model, and you know that you are not simply going to replace

Hank with a clerk who knows how to use equation 1 because you need Hank's intellect and experience to deal with unique cases.

What, then, might you recommend to Betty and Ralph about how to clone their best salespeople? One recommendation might be to go ahead and have a clerk code the data from each job seeker's application and enter it into a computer that is programmed to apply equation 1 and yield a score (the predicted $Y_e$). Except instead of replacing him with the equation, Hank could be given this score together with other information that is unique to the applicant and asked to make an overall decision about the qualifications of the applicant. This would mean that Hank would not have to learn to use the cues the way equation 1 uses them; he simply would use the output of equation 1 as information upon which his decision could be based. This would leave him in control, but it also would make sure that the information on the application was presented to him in a form that was both concise and valid. Of course, you would have to do a follow-up study to see if this new arrangement improved the sales force, which, after all, is the point.

## ❖  PROBLEMS WITH THE LENS MODEL

While the logic of the Lens Model has its attractions, it is rather simplistic, and the appropriateness of the multiple regression analyses can be questioned on at least two grounds.

First, equations 1 and 2 presume that the cues are additive—that the information provided by each cue simply piles on top of the other information, and as the pile increases, the applicant moves higher on the preference scale. However, it does not take much imagination to understand that information conveyed by some cues sometimes amplifies what is conveyed by other cues, rather than just adding to it, so the applicant would move up the scale in ever-increasing steps. Amplification is described mathematically as a multiplicative combination of information instead of the additive combination assumed by the model. That is, the cues may be non-independent (multiplicative), but the mathematics of multiple regression requires them to be independent (additive) if the equation is to make sense. The problem is important because even if the cues are not independent, the analysis will blindly impose additivity on them, with the result that the optimal policy (equation 1) or the decision maker's policy (equation 2) will appear to be much simpler than it really is.

Second, the equation assumes that each cue is linearly related to the dependent variable. For example, the larger the cue value the higher the applicant will be on the preference scale. However, some cues have a curvilinear relationship to preference, for example, low and high values of the cue are associated with low preference and medium cue values are associated with high preference. Unless special steps are taken, the analysis will blindly impose linearity on the cues, and the resulting equations will suggest a greater simplicity than actually exists.

Those who defend the Lens Model point out that multiple regression is very robust. For example, it is possible to include non-independence in the equation by combining coded cue values before they are included in the analysis. However, they argue that from a practical standpoint there often is little gained by doing so. This was demonstrated very early on by Kort (1968), who showed that unless cues are very highly dependent (in which case one or the other might best be eliminated as redundant), the $R^2$ for the equation that uses combined coding usually is not much different from the $R^2$ for the equation that treats the cues as independent.

The argument continues that the equations do not have to be absolutely accurate representations of the environment or of the decision maker's policy to be valuable. That is, they can get you in the ball park even though they might not be right on the mark. As such, it usually is cheaper and less work to assume independence (or drop one of the dependent cues, or combine the dependent cues into a single measure), go with the simple equation, and then temper its use with a little common sense.

These same defenders of multiple regression use a similar argument in regard to curvilinear cues. Unless the curvilinear relationship is especially crucial, the analysis's imposition of linearity may not do much damage. By recoding the cue (so now both low and high values of the cue are recoded as low numbers to use in the equation, and medium values are recoded as high numbers), it is possible to derive a more accurate equation, but it often does not buy much for the effort; the $R^2$ may stay pretty much the same. Of course, there are other forms of non-linearity than curvilinearity, but much the same argument is made for them.

## ❖  THE LENS MODEL IN RESEARCH

The Lens Model has been used in many studies of decision making. In one of the earliest, Frederick Todd (reported in Hammond, 1955) examined 10 clinical psychologists' ability to use patients' responses to Rorschach cards (ink blots) to predict the IQ of each of 78 patients. IQ tests had previously been given to the patients, and their Rorschach responses had previously been coded using a standard coding system. The results of each patient's IQ test was $Y_e$ and his or her coded Rorschach responses were the cues. Each clinician was given the coded Rorschach responses for each patient and asked to make a decision ($Y_s$) about each patient's IQ. Using multiple regression to obtain the optimal policy (across patients) yielded an $R^2$ of only .23, which means that it objectively is very difficult to predict IQ from Rorschach responses. The 10 clinicians' median achievement coefficient (squared) was .22, which means that their achievement was about as good as could be expected given that IQ cannot be reliably predicted from Rorschach responses. The median $R^2$ for their policy equations was .72, which means that even in the face of this unpredictability they tended to use the cues consistently—which is the best strategy in a low-predictability situation and which probably accounts for their achievement being as high as it was.

Among the more interesting results of early policy research is, for example, Rorer, Hoffman, Dickman, and Slovic's (1967) finding of no consistency among the policies of the attendants in a mental hospital in judging whether patients should have weekend passes; imagine how confusing that must have been for the patients. Similarly, Slovic, Rorer, and Hoffman (1971) found four different policies being used by various radiologists for judging malignancy of ulcers. Dawes (1971) modeled the decision policies of the admission committee for a doctoral program and found that replacing the committee with its own policy equation (called "bootstrapping") resulted in better predictions of applicant success than using the committee itself, presumably because the committee's membership changed over time and it therefore was not wholly consistent. Roose and Doherty (1976) studied how agency managers for an insurance company used application information to hire new agents and found that they relied too highly on a non-diagnostic cue; training them to use the optimal policy promised a substantial increase in successful hires.

Somewhat later, Dougherty, Ebert, and Callender (1986) studied how applicant information is used by employment interviewers in a large corporation; they had very consistent policies, but it was not clear that they were the best policies. Over the years there have been many studies done in the context of businesses or other organizations, but for proprietary reasons or because there is no payoff for the investigators to do so, little of this has been published in the scientific literature.

### Social Judgment Theory

Since the 1970s, the point of view represented by the Lens Model and its applications has come to be known as Social Judgment Theory (Hammond, Rohrbaugh, Mumpower, & Adelman, 1977; Hammond, Stewart, Brehmer, & Steinman, 1975). In addition to examining interesting practical problems, such as the selection of bullets by the Denver Police Department (Hammond & Adelman, 1976, and see chapters in Brehmer & Joyce, 1988, for other applications), fundamental psychological issues also have been addressed. Among these is how people learn to use cues appropriately (Klayman, 1988). It is found that people learn most quickly when the cues have a simple, linear relationship to events $(Y_e)$ and when the task content gives rise to reasonable hypotheses about weighting, but learning often is surprisingly slow. It turns out that having to learn by trial and error is very inefficient, but efficiency can be increased through provision of "cognitive feedback" (Hammond, 1971) consisting of information about the optimal policy. There also has been Social Judgment Theory research on decision processes in small groups, focusing largely on conflicts resulting from differences among the group members' various decision policies and how these differences can be reconciled (Rohrbaugh, 1988). An article by Hammond, Harvey, and Hastie (1992) provides a Social Judgment Theory analysis of social policy formation.

### ❖  SUMMARY

In this chapter we have examined how the Lens Model can be used to study both the decision maker's policy and the optimal policy. Moreover, the degree to which these policies account for $Y_e$ and $Y_s$, as well as the degree to which the latter are correlated (achievement), permits us to prescribe different courses of action—replacement of the decision maker with mechanical application of the optimal policy or training the decision maker to use the optimal policy. As it has been developed in Social Judgment Theory, the logic of the Lens Model is applicable to a broad range of non-laboratory, socially interesting areas of decision.

# 4

# Choice

*R*alph, Betty, and Hank sat at the large conference table in Betty's office, a stack of application folders looming over them. Although the stack contained only a small proportion of all the applications they had received, it still looked daunting. Their task this morning was to select three new salespeople, which had seemed simple enough until they sat down to do it. They waited for the coffeepot to brew its magic, hoping that caffeine would show the way.

Ralph was thinking about how far they had come. Under the guidance of his sister-in-law, Professor Karma Howell, they had used the Lens Model to evaluate their good salespeople and, in turn, to evaluate applicants. It was a lot of work, and Hank hadn't been very comfortable at first.

Now they had before them the application information for 23 applicants identified by the Lens Model analysis as more or less clones of their best salespeople. None was a perfect clone, of course. Each had a different constellation of characteristics that made him or her unique. The Lens Model identified all 23 of them as about equal in sales potential, which wasn't much help when you only had three jobs to offer.

So there they sat. Ready to make decisions. Having no idea how to go about it. Ralph thought it was comical that they had invested in all that analytic stuff up front only to be faced with having to use their intuition to do the hardest part. He cleared his throat, to indicate that official business was about *to begin, and stated the obvious: they had all read the 23 applications, and it now was time to choose three. There was a long pause. Finally, Betty proposed that they start at the top of the stack and work their way down, discussing the pros and cons of each applicant. Then each of them should rate the acceptability of the applicant on a scale from 1 to 5, with 5 meaning outstanding. They could average their ratings of each applicant and select the three who had the highest averages. Nobody else had a better idea, so they agreed.*

*Twelve hours later, after endless discussions and too much coffee, after displays of temper and attempts at conciliation, after wandering in a shared haze of confusion and uncertainty, they finally began to average their ratings. There was good news and bad news. In the course of their discussions it was clear that they agreed on the best applicant, and indeed she got an average rank of 5. Unfortunately, seven other applicants also got an average of 5, and six more candidates got an average of more than 4.*

*It was awful. They had long ago stopped focusing on the applicants and now were wholly engrossed in resolving their differences. Betty swore that she was going to put all the names on a list, pin it to the wall, and throw darts to select the new people. Hank was pouting because neither Ralph nor Betty was inclined to let his opinions prevail—after all, he had been doing this sort of thing for years. Ralph was simply tired and had long ago lost confidence in his own ability to make reasonable decisions. He tried to console himself with the thought that all over the world there were managers faced with this same problem, but it didn't help much. All three felt that they had shirked their duty, that because they were managers they ought to be able to be more decisive, but they were so sick of the whole thing they simply wanted resolution.*

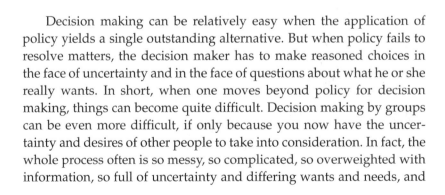

Decision making can be relatively easy when the application of policy yields a single outstanding alternative. But when policy fails to resolve matters, the decision maker has to make reasoned choices in the face of uncertainty and in the face of questions about what he or she really wants. In short, when one moves beyond policy for decision making, things can become quite difficult. Decision making by groups can be even more difficult, if only because you now have the uncertainty and desires of other people to take into consideration. In fact, the whole process often is so messy, so complicated, so overweighted with information, so full of uncertainty and differing wants and needs, and so hemmed in by social expectations that it is a wonder anything ever gets decided.

Researchers have approached choice in two ways. One way is to ignore the confusion and complexity and assume that the process has an underlying orderliness to it. The resulting description trades realism for simplicity. However, within the limits imposed by this trade-off, it provides concrete methods for determining what decision to make. The other way is to focus on the confusion and complexity and to assume that they are integral to the process. The resulting description trades simplicity for realism. It captures more of what actually goes on in decision making, but it does not provide much concrete help to the decision maker faced with a problem (March & Shapira, 1982). In this chapter we will examine the first of these two ways of describing decision making, the one that trades realism for simplicity. Then, in the following chapter (Chapter 5), we will examine the research on the two central concepts that comprise this description in an attempt to evaluate its validity. Following that (Chapters 6 and 7), we will examine the second of the two ways of describing decision making, the one that trades simplicity for realism.

❖  PRESCRIPTIVE DECISION THEORY

The primary approach to imposing order on decision making is through the use of prescriptive decision theory's normative models.[1] Prescriptive theory has its roots in the very reasonable assumption that decision makers strive to do what is best for themselves or for the organizations for which they are making decisions. "Doing best" usually is interpreted as deciding on the option that offers the most desirable payoff, be that maximum benefit or minimal loss. Note that this requires two guesses: a guess about what the payoffs (i.e., the consequences or results) will be if the option in question is chosen and a guess about how valuable those payoffs will be when they actually accrue to the decision maker (March & Shapira, 1982). In a perfect world the decision maker would always know the payoffs and their future values. Good sense would then dictate that the decision maker choose the options that offer the payoffs that will be most valuable when he or she receives them.

But the world is not perfect, and decision makers seldom can be sure of the consequences of their decisions. Even if they could be sure about what will or will not happen, they cannot know that those consequences will turn out to be as good or as bad as they thought they would be when the decision was made. Indeed, as Ralph and Betty and Hank found out, decisions are steeped in doubt and uncertainty and mired in riskiness. In fact, one can think of most decisions as gambles. Each option is a potential bet, and the decision maker has to choose which bet to make. Each bet can be characterized by its potential gains if things turn out one way and its potential losses if they turn out another way—where the way things will turn out frequently is beyond the decision maker's control.

This gamble analogy has a long history. The philosopher and mathematician Blaise Pascal (1623–1662) is credited with having put the issue most clearly when addressing the question of whether or not one should believe in the Christian God. Let us assume that the decision maker will not know for sure about the existence of God until Judgment Day. The decision is to believe (option 1) or not to believe (option 2). If the decision maker chooses option 1, belief, and it turns out that God exists, then the outcome will be a blissful eternity in heaven. However, if the decision maker chooses option 1 and it turns out that God does not exist, the decision maker is out whatever time and effort he or she had invested in worship and other religious observances. Weighing the enormous benefits of eternity in heaven against the relatively small costs of religious behavior makes option 1 very attractive.

Option 2, disbelief, is a very different story. If it turns out that God exists, failure to believe will result in eternity in hell. If God does not exist, the disbelieving decision maker really has lost nothing because he or she invested nothing in religious observances. Weighing the enormous costs of being in hell against the trivial benefits of not having invested in religious behavior makes option 2 very unattractive. Pascal argued that the choice between option 1 and option 2 is very easy; the decision maker should choose to believe in God.

About 100 years later, Daniel Bernoulli (1738) was asked by a group of young noblemen to prescribe a rational method of gambling. His prescription was much the same as Pascal's, if a bit more formal. He noted that in most gambles the objective (money) payoffs for winning and losing are fairly clear and that in many cases the probabilities of winning and losing are known (and if not known, can be guessed at). He prescribed that for each bet the payoff for winning should be multiplied by the probability of winning and the payoff for losing should be multiplied by the probability of losing. Then these two products should be added together (note that the payoff for losing often is a negative number because you lose money, so its product with the probability is a negative number and adding it actually turns out to be subtracting it). If the sum is negative, that is, if the expected value is negative, one should refuse the bet. If there are two or more bets, the gambler should select the one with the largest sum, the largest expected value.

Now, why would you only play positive expected value bets and bets with the larger expected value? After all, on any bet you will not receive the expected value, you will receive the payoff for winning or lose the payoff for losing. So, what does the expected value have to do with anything? The answer is that if you play a bet repeatedly, the expected value represents the amount that you will most likely end up with in the long run. But what about a one time, unique bet? Well, that is controversial. Some people claim that the expected value characterization of bets is irrelevant for unique bets, others claim that it still serves as a handy guide for evaluating unique bets and that maximization always is the best strategy.

Bernoulli did two other important things. He noted that the value of winning or losing a dollar is less for a rich person than for a poor person. Therefore, the dollar amount of the payoffs really does not accurately describe the attractiveness of those payoffs to the two people. Hence the dollar amounts should be replaced by their subjective worth, which is called *utility*. This accounts, for example, for why a rich man might be willing to accept a bet that a poor man might spurn—the loss would be of minimal importance to the former and devastating to the latter.

Bernoulli also outlined the logic for insurance. Suppose a merchant were shipping products to the New World. How much should he pay to have someone else assume the financial loss if the ship were to sink or be captured by pirates? (The flip side of this question is how much should the other person demand for assuming the loss?) Bernoulli suggested that when the merchant sends the ship out, he is taking a gamble: Winning means the ship gets to the New World and back, and the payoff is the profit. Losing means the ship is lost either coming or going, and the merchandise and the profit are lost with it. If, say, 6 ships out of 10 generally make it, Bernoulli assumed that the probability of this particular ship returning safely is .60 and the probability of this ship failing to return is .40. If the utility of the profit is $X$, the utility of the ship itself is $Y$, and the utility of the cargo's wholesale value is $Z$, the utility of winning is $X$ and the disutility of losing is the sum of losing the profit $(-X)$, losing the ship $(-Y)$, and losing the cargo $(-Z)$.

That is to say, the worth of the bet (sending the ship and its cargo to the New World)—its expected utility—is the product of the probability of the ship returning (.6) multiplied by utility of winning $(X)$ added to the probability of the ship being lost (.4) multiplied by the disutility of losing (the sum of $-X$, $-Y$, and $-Z$). If, after the computations are done, the expected cost of losing is greater than the expected benefit of winning, the merchant should be willing to pay someone to insure his possible loss. Of course, if the insurance costs more than the potential profit, then the merchant ought to keep the ship at home.

Insurance is interesting in light of the question about the applicability of expected value to unique gambles. An insurance company makes bets against each of its many policy holders—the company bets the policy holders will not have losses and the policy holders bet they will. The company ensures that it makes a profit by setting premiums so that the expected value of its bet against each policy holder is positive.

Treating insurance policies as bets makes sense for the company because it issues so many policies that they are more like repeated plays of the same bet than like unique bets. But does it make sense for the individual policy holder? After all, insuring your life, or house, or ship actually is a unique bet for you. Clearly there is risk, and clearly you want someone else to assume it, and clearly a loss would be a financial blow, but is expected utility the best way of reasoning about whether to insure and how much to pay? Do people actually make such calculations, or do they merely buy the most coverage for the lowest price, if they even bother to shop around? That is, maybe insurance companies are betting, but policy holders are merely buying a product that will reduce their anxiety.

After a couple of hundred years of muddling along, the expected value approach to gamble evaluation received a thorough analysis by von Neumann and Morgenstern (1947). They called gambles *games*, and two kinds were identified, games against nature and games against persons. The two examples given above are games against nature—God either exists or not and the ship will either make it or not; there is no opponent actively playing against the decision maker. Games against persons, on the other hand, pit the wiliness of the decision maker against the wiliness of an opponent or coalition of opponents.

Von Neumann and Morgenstern's work gave rise to modern microeconomics as well as to the psychological study of decision making. It is, of course, the latter that is of interest here, and that interest will focus on how gambles (decision options) can be analyzed so that their worth to the decision maker can be evaluated. This brings us to the art of decision analysis, using decision matrices, expectation calculations, and decision trees, all three of which are related methods for characterizing gambles and evaluating their worth.

### Decision Analysis: Games Against Nature

*Decision Matrices*

Consider the matrix at the top of Figure 4.1. This is called a decision matrix, and it is for a game against nature. For simplicity, only two decision options occupy the left axis and only two states of nature occupy the top axis; outcomes occupy the cells. To add life to this, put yourself in the place of an executive for a timber company in 1980 when Mount Saint Helens, in Washington State, began to belch steam and ashes. You have logging crews and expensive equipment on the mountain when you hear from the geologists that the mountain might erupt. Because volcanology is a relatively new science, the geologists cannot say for sure that an eruption will take place, nor can they tell you when it might happen. All they can say is that it is likely, is getting more likely, and that it could happen at any time—then again, it might not happen at all.

The manager has two options, to evacuate the crews and equipment (option 1), or to leave them on the mountain (option 2). Nature has two states, eruption or failure to erupt; the manager assesses the probabilities as .80 for eruption and .20 for failure to erupt.

If the manager chooses option 1 and the volcano in fact erupts, the crews and equipment will have been saved and the manager will be a hero, but if it does not erupt the company will sustain the costs of evacuation and the loss of productivity while the crews and equipment are elsewhere, and the manager will be judged a fool. If he or she chooses option 2 and the volcano erupts, the crews are likely to be killed and the equipment is likely to be lost and the manager will be blamed, but if it does not erupt, productivity will continue and the manager will be judged to be competent. What to do?

**Figure 4.1**    A Decision Matrix

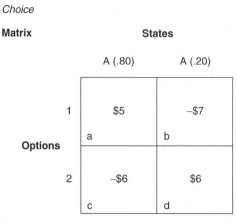

*Choice*

**Matrix**                                    **States**

**Equations**

$$EV_1 = PU_{1A} + (1 - P) U_{1B} = .80 (\$5) + .20(-\$7) = \$2.60$$
$$EV_2 = PU_{2A} + (1 - P) U_{2B} = .80 (-\$6) + .20(\$6) = -\$3.60$$

Which option is most attractive depends upon how the manager values the safety of the crews, the replacement costs for the equipment, continued productivity, and being judged a hero or a fool. Not all of these are readily assessed in dollars—crew safety or being a hero, for example. But the manager has to balance them out somehow, even if he or she does not explicitly assign numbers to them or do calculations for each of the two options. In fact, what the lumber company actually did was evacuate its crews (which cost very little) and take the loss in productivity (which cost a lot), but left its equipment there so productivity could be easily resumed if the volcano calmed down. Of course, it did not calm down, its massive eruption flattened most of the forest and destroyed all of the equipment. So the final result was a mix of good and bad; the crews were safe, productivity would have been lost whether the crews stayed or not, and the equipment had to be replaced.

*Expectation Computations*

In order to evaluate the relative attractiveness of the two options in the top matrix in Figure 4.1, we must calculate the expectation for each.

The process is the same as for Bernoulli's ship gamble. Suppose we have the matrix in Figure 4.1, and that the amounts in the cells are the payoffs. Again let us assume that the probabilities for the two states of nature are $P(A) = .80$ and $P(B) = .20$.

Now we can construct the two equations in Figure 4.1, one for each option. Comparing the calculated expected utility ($2.60) for option 1 with the calculated expected utility (–$3.60) for option 2 shows that option 1 is more attractive and thus should be the choice. Choosing the option with the larger expected value is called *maximizing expected value.*

*Decision Trees*

Note that the matrix in Figure 4.1 is two dimensional, options and states of nature, and that each dimension is divided into two, options 1 and 2 and states A and B. Of course, decisions can be much more complicated than this, more dimensions divided into more parts. But it is difficult to comprehend more complex matrices. Equations are better able to handle increased complexity, and are useful for calculations, but they lack intuitive clarity for many of us. As a way of drawing a helpful picture of a decision, decision trees are far superior to either matrices or equations.

The tree in Figure 4.2 describes the decision in the matrix in Figure 4.1. A tree usually starts with a box that indicates a choice point for the decision maker. Events that are outside his or her control are indicated with a little circle. So, beginning on the left, we see a box indicating that the decision maker has to choose between two options, 1 and 2. The circles indicate that whichever option the decision maker chooses an event will occur—which means that nature takes on state A or state B. The numbers on the branches from the circle indicate the probabilities of the states, and the numbers at the ends of the branches indicate the payoffs. Each path through the tree from left to right tells a story about what might happen if the decision maker chooses one or the other option. The top path says that if option 1 is chosen and state A occurs, the decision maker will gain $5. The next path says that if option 1 is chosen and state B occurs, the decision maker will lose $7. And so on for the other paths.

The rub, of course, is that the decision maker does not know which state will occur, so the paths through the tree actually are stories about gambles. The gamble aspect, the uncertainty, is injected by including the probabilities in the scenarios. To do this we begin on the right and "fold back" (Raiffa, 1968) the utilities, which means that we discount

**Figure 4.2**    A Decision Tree

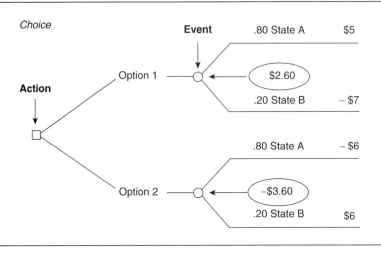

them by multiplying them by the probabilities.[2] Then we sum the discounted utilities across all of the branches to the right of the circle, thus deriving the overall utility for that option. This sum is written in the oval near the event circle. Note that all of these numbers are the same numbers we used in the equations in Figure 4.1, and the calculated expected utilities (in the ovals) also are the same. Again, because the expected utility ($2.60) for option 1 is greater than the expected utility (-$3.60) for option 2, maximization prescribes the choice of option 1.

### Decision Analysis: Games Against Persons

The general logic of games against persons is the same as for games against nature, so all that has been said above still applies. The complication is that while nature may not be wholly predictable, it is not actively trying to compete with the decision maker. Von Neumann and Morgenstern (1947) viewed games against persons as analogous in structure to the interactions of firms. In some cases (called zero-sum games) the payoffs are symmetrical in that anything that is a gain for the opponent is a loss for the decision maker, and vice versa. Thus if one firm gains market share as a result of a decision, the other firm loses that market share. In other cases (called non-zero-sum games) the payoffs to the two players are contingent on their respective decisions

**Figure 4.3**    The Prisoner's Dilemma

*Choice*

**Other Person Confesses**

| | | Yes | No |
|---|---|---|---|
| | **Yes** | him: 5 yrs<br>you: 5 yrs | him: 10 yrs<br>you: 0 yrs |
| **You Confess** | | | |
| | **No** | him: 0 yrs<br>you: 10 yrs | him: 1 yr<br>you: 1 yr |

but are not symmetrical. The most famous, if somewhat depressing, example of a non-zero-sum game is called the Prisoner's Dilemma.

### The Prisoner's Dilemma

Suppose that you and a friend have been arrested for a major theft. You are taken to separate rooms in the police station and subjected to questioning. The officer explains your dilemma to you, and you, being a good decision analyst, draw the matrix in Figure 4.3. Your options are to confess (option 1) or not to confess (option 2). Similarly, your friend's options are to confess or not to confess.

If you both confess, you both will get five years in jail. If you confess and your friend refuses to confess, the prosecutor will throw the book at him, giving him 10 years in jail, while you go free. Similarly, if he confesses and you do not, they will throw the book at you, giving you 10 years, while he goes free. If neither of you confesses, the prosecutor will get you both on lesser charges with the assurance of a year in jail for each of you. Your dilemma is to decide whether to confess given that you and your friend are in separate rooms and you do not know if he will confess.

In one sense the Prisoner's Dilemma is not actually a dilemma because the optimal choice for you clearly is to betray your friend, to confess no matter what he does. This way you get off completely if he does not confess and you get only five years if he does. His best choice is precisely the same—not knowing what you are going to do, he should confess. Thus, instead of getting off free or only getting one year, you both assure yourselves five years in jail. Moreover, confession is the optimal choice if you think there is any chance at all that your friend will confess, and the same is true for him. That is, the expected values for your two options will be better for option 1 no matter what probabilities (other than zero) are used to describe your uncertainty about whether your friend will confess.

The Prisoner's Dilemma is a dilemma in yet another sense, in that most people are very uncomfortable with the prescription to confess no matter what. They think that if the other person is a friend, they ought to behave honorably, trust him, and refuse to confess. However, honor is not part of the normative analysis of the dilemma, which presumes you always look out for your own best interests.

The Prisoner's Dilemma has real-life counterparts in such things as OPEC (Organization of Petroleum Exporting Countries) members' decisions about whether to undersell their fellow oil-producers and liquor distributors' decisions about whether to break the agreement not to advertise on television. OPEC was founded so that oil-producing nations could present a united front to the oil-consuming nations. OPEC members agree on a price that all will charge for their oil, but it is in the interest of any single member to charge less than the agreed-upon price because its sales volume would be immense. However, doing so would encourage other members to lower their prices, thereby reducing the profit for all OPEC members. The only way for OPEC to operate successfully is for all of its members to abide by the agreement, which has not always happened.

Similarly, liquor distributors agreed not to advertise their products on television in an attempt to avoid government oversight of their advertising practices. If they each behave honorably, all is well. However, it is in the interest of any single distributor to break the agreement, thereby increasing its sales. If one succumbs to the temptation and the others follow suit, the entire agreement falls apart.

### Change Versus the Status Quo

Speaking of dilemmas, the same word is used to describe another kind of situation, but this time the prescribed decision can be more satisfying. The situation is one in which an opportunity arises that, if it works out, can make your life better than it is now, but if it does not work out, can make your life worse than it is now. That is, the opportunity is a gamble, and the status quo is more or less a sure thing; you have a pretty good idea what the future will look like if you stick with the status quo, but you do not know for sure what will happen if you abandon the status quo for the opportunity.

Behn and Vaupel (1982) call this problem the Basic Decision Dilemma, an example of which is a heart bypass decision. Assume that you are a 59-year-old executive who has had angina pain for a year. Your physician says that an artery is 90% blocked. Medical therapy has proved to be inadequate. You can have surgery or endure the pain. The physician tells you that given your age and your rotten physical condition (too many hot dogs and not enough exercise), there is a 10% chance you will die on the operating table, but there is a 90% chance you will survive the surgery and be free of angina pain for a good long time. Your dilemma is whether to stick with the status quo and endure the pain or to have the surgery, which can either result in death or leave you free of pain. Figure 4.4 shows the decision tree for this kind of decision.

As before, the box on the left indicates the act of making a decision (have surgery, forgo surgery). The lower branch represents the opportunity (surgery), which is called the risky alternative because it is a gamble. An event, the little circle, will occur that will determine whether the gamble leads to success, with probability $p$, or failure, with probability $q$, where $p + q = 1.00$. Success will bring the best payoff (absence of pain); things will be better than they will be if you stick with the status quo. Failure will bring the worst payoff (death); things will be worse than they will be if you stick with the status quo. The upper branch

**Figure 4.4**    Basic Decision Dilemma

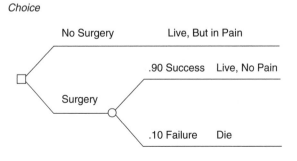

represents the status quo (forgo surgery), which is called the riskless alternative, and its payoff is somewhere between the best and worst payoffs offered by the risky alternative (you will continue to have angina pain, but you will not be dead).

Decisions of this general form are very common for both individuals and organizations, and from a normative viewpoint their resolution is rather simple. The decision maker should calculate the expected utility of the risky alternative and compare this to his or her utility for the payoff for the riskless alternative. If the expected utility for the risky alternative is greater, he or she should abandon the status quo and pursue the opportunity. If it is less, he or she should stick with the status quo.

Decisions of this kind may look simple from the normative viewpoint, but they are wretched in real life. Doubtless, candidates for bypass surgery consider the possible consequences and the chances that things will go wrong, but how does one assign utilities to things like death? In addition to this problem, there also is the old question of applying expected value to a unique decision. If you have the surgery, you either will get well or be dead, and you will not play the gamble repeatedly. So, while the tree certainly lays out the dilemma, it is not wholly clear that maximization of expectation is the best way to make the decision.

### Individuals and Organizations

In all of the above, we have talked as though the decision maker is a single individual. Part of the beauty of the normative analysis, made clear by von Neumann and Morgenstern's (1947) discussions of coalitions, is that the decision maker can be either an individual or a group. The analysis is not about the decision maker per se, but about the structure of the decision. True, the decision maker's utilities and probabilities may be used in the analysis, but whether these are for an individual or a group is of no relevance to the analysis.

### ❖ VARIATIONS ON EXPECTED VALUE

Only two variables contribute to the computation of an option's expected value: payoffs and probabilities. In most normative analyses, the payoffs are assumed to be known to the player, and they often are. Sometimes the probabilities also are assumed to be known, but frequently they are not. However, even when everything is known, things are not very straightforward. It has been clear for over 200 years (Bernoulli, 1738) that a payoff of a given magnitude will be valued to different degrees by different people. Moreover, different levels of a payoff have correspondingly different amounts of psychological worth to each person, which is called the *utility* of the payoff to the person. When probabilities are known to the player, it is assumed that he or she uses them in determining the option's expected value. When the probabilities are not known, the player must rely on hunches about the likelihood of winning or losing—that is, probability belongs to the player, which is called the player's *subjective probability* of winning or losing.

Edwards (1955) identified the four variations of the expected value model contained in Figure 4.5. Cell 1: When the player knows the objective probabilities and his or her utility is isomorphic with the objective value of the payoffs, the computations described above constitute the *expected value (EV) model*. Cell 2: When the player knows the objective probabilities but has non-isomorphic utility, the computations constitute the *expected utility (EU) model*. Cell 3: When the player has only his or her subjective probabilities but has isomorphic utility, the computations constitute the *subjective expected value (SEV) model*. Cell 4: When the player has only his or her subjective probabilities and his or her utility is not isomorphic with the objective value of the payoffs, the computations constitute the *subjective expected utility (SEU) model*. The SEU model is a wholly psychological model, which makes it very interesting to behavioral researchers.

**Figure 4.5**    Edwards's Four Variations on the Expected Value Model

|  | **Probability** | |
|  | **Objective** | **Subjective** |
| **Isomorphic** <br><br> **Utility** | Cell I: EV | Cell 3: SEV |
| **Non-Isomorphic** | Cell 2: EU | Cell 4: SEU |

❖  SUMMARY

We began our discussion by examining the normative model of decision making. The underlying assumption is that people strive to do what is best for themselves, choosing the option that offers the most desirable consequences. This is, of course, complicated by the fact that consequences will occur in the future, so the decision maker cannot be completely certain that he or she actually will receive them or that they will be all that is anticipated if they are received. This uncertainty makes decision making analogous to gambling; the decision maker bets on the most promising alternative and waits to see how things turn out.

Over the years a technology for analyzing decisions has developed, based on the gamble analogy. Thus decisions can be cast in decision matrices, subjected to expected value computations, or analyzed with decision trees. In all cases the goal is to make the structure of the decision as clear as possible in order to clarify the decision maker's thinking.

The gamble analogy also prompts characterization of decisions as games. Games can be against nature or against an opponent, the most famous of which is the Prisoner's Dilemma.

Both probability and value have subjective counterparts, subjective probability, and utility, and it is possible to retain the mathematical rules of the expected value formulation but substitute subjective components. The result is four variations on expected value: EV, SEV, EU, and SEU. The last, SEU, has been of great interest to behavioral researchers because it is a wholly psychological model whose components are subjective probability and utility.

❖  NOTES

1. In choice research, expected value theory, probability theory, and utility theory are referred to as normative components of prescriptive theory because they are seen as defining norms for correct processing of relevant information.

2. Discounting means, for example, that a payoff of $10 is less attractive if the probability of receiving it is only .30 than if the probability is .90.

# 5

# Subjective Probability and Utility

*H*ank was feeling a little introspective. He, Betty, and Ralph had spent more time than any of them could afford trying to choose the best applicants from the pile. He had tried to behave as rationally as possible, but the information on the applications always left him in doubt—he never had a feeling that he was as well informed as he should be.

A while back he had told Betty that selecting new employees was a crap shoot. Apparently she thought he meant it was sheer chance. What he really meant was that there was a lot of uncertainty involved—he was convinced that uncertainty was a big part of the whole process for him.

On the other hand, uncertainty was not the only part of the process. It also was true that he tried to anticipate the outcomes that might result from hiring a particular applicant. It wasn't all that difficult. He merely tried to imagine the applicant in various situations that might arise and how he or she would handle them. Of course, he had very strong views about what was the right thing to do in those hypothetical problem situations. If it seemed like applicants would do what he preferred them to do, he liked them. If not, he didn't.

In decision research, riskiness, doubt, and uncertainty are captured by probability and value is captured by utility. Recall from Chapter 4 that two (EV and EU) of the four variations on the normative theory of choice use objective probability to represent the decision maker's uncertainty about whether the various outcomes actually will be attained if the option is chosen, and two (SEV and SEU) use subjective probability to represent this uncertainty. Similarly, two (EV and SEV) use value to represent outcomes' worth and two (EU and SEU) use utility.

❖  THE NATURE OF PROBABILITY

All four variations on the normative theory of choice assume that the probabilities have the mathematical properties required by probability theory—that is, that they are "real" probabilities and not just any old decimal numbers. This is equivalent to saying that uncertainty is appropriately represented as a probability.

While this assumption is not difficult to accept for objective probabilities, it seems rather shaky for subjective probabilities: Who knows where they come from? On the other hand, if subjective probabilities are not "real" probabilities, the SEV and SEU models lose their claims to normative (prescriptive) status. Because of this, a good deal of research in the 1960s through the early 1980s centered on whether those claims were valid by examining how well subjective probability conforms to probability theory. To understand this research we must briefly review the rudiments of probability theory.

### A Brief Review of Probability

Probability theory is an abstract, axiomatic mathematical system of rules for assigning numbers to sets of hypothetical elements (Kolmogorov, 1950). As such, it has nothing to say about events in the real world—that comes later when the user of the theory ties its concepts to specific events of interest.

Mathematical probability theory begins with a set of hypothetical elements, consisting of individual elements ($A$, $B$, etc.), unions of elements ($A \cup B$), intersects of elements ($A \cap B$), and complements of elements ($A - B$).[1] A number can be assigned to each of these elements. The number assigned to an empty set of elements is .00 (which defines the lower limit of the range of acceptable numbers). The number assigned to a subset of elements is equal to the sum of the numbers assigned to each of its constituent elements (which defines additivity). The number assigned to the set of all elements is 1.00 (which defines the upper limit of the range of acceptable numbers). Thus the numbers assigned to the elements in question must lie between .00 and 1.00, and the system is additive.

Assignment of numbers to individual elements occurs when we attempt to use probability theory for real world applications. To do this we use one of three definitions.

The first definition is *necessary probability*, exemplified by the probability of a three being observed on a roll of a single die being equal to $1/6 = .17$. That is, because a die (one of a pair of dice) has six sides, only one of which has three spots on it, and because we assume the die is unbiased and the roll is fair, the probability of .17 is necessary given the physical structure of the die. If we were speaking of a deck of cards, the probability of drawing a three would be $4/52 = .08$, because there are four cards with threes on them in the deck of 52 cards.

A second definition is *frequentistic probability*, exemplified by actuarial tables used in the insurance industry. For example, by knowing the past relative frequency of thefts of the kind of car you want to insure, your insurance company can judge the probability that your car will be stolen—"The probability (past relative frequency) of theft of this kind of car is X." Then they can set the premium high enough to make it worth taking the risk of insuring you. Similarly, when a particular weather pattern is observed, the weather service can use the past relative frequency of rain under these conditions as the probability that it will rain this time—"The probability (past relative frequency) of rain under these conditions is X." Note the conceptual leap in going from the relative frequencies of past events to the probabilities of future events. It depends heavily on the assumption that however the process operated in the past, it will continue to operate in the same way in the future—thieves will continue to have the same taste in cars and climatic systems will continue to operate as they have before. Moreover, it assumes that the relative frequency for a collective of past events is applicable to a single future event (theft of your particular car or occurrence of rain today).

The third definition is *subjective (personal) probability*, exemplified by my statement that "I think the probability is about .75 that Senator Smog will run for President." This is a statement about my certainty (uncertainty) about future events. It is not at all clear where these probabilities come from, but they are quite distinct from necessary and frequentistic probability. There is no necessity for Senator Smog to run for President (except perhaps in his own mind), and it is not at all clear how relative frequency would apply. If he had never run before, the relative frequency would be undefined (because you would have to divide by zero), so does that mean that there is no way of assessing a probability that he will run in the future? If he ran in the last election, would it mean the probability of his running this time is 1.00? But even then, he only ran one time out of the something like 50 U.S. presidential elections, so does that make the probability that he will run again 1/50 = .02? Neither necessary nor frequentistic probability make any sense in this kind of situation.

Probability theory is deceptive in its simplicity. Exploring the logical implications of those few rules for assigning numbers to elements has permitted mathematicians to derive the useful tools of modern statistics. One aspect of these logical implications, *conditional probability*, has been of particular interest in behavioral research on probability judgment. To understand conditional probability, let us begin with an intuitive description, then move to a formal statement, and then explore its importance to research on subjective probability.

### Conditionality and Bayes' Theorem

When the probability of one event is modified by the fact that some other event already has occurred, the modified probability is called a conditional probability. Thus Hank may think that the probability that a new job seeker will be successful is .50, if only because he does not know anything to sway his opinion one way or another. Then he reads the answer to the first question on the person's application. The information in that answer modifies Hanks uncertainty—making him less uncertain about success or more uncertain. The new probability of success is correspondingly higher or lower than the beginning probability—let us say that it goes up to .65. Then Hank reads the second answer and modifies the .65 either upward or downward, and so on until he has read the answers to all the questions on the application or until he becomes sufficiently certain about success to hire the person or sufficiently uncertain about success to turn the person down. That is, Hank's subjective probability (uncertainty) is conditional upon the answers in the application.

Formally, conditional probability is an algebraic consequence of the axioms we described above. Let us consider two events that, for reasons that will be clear in a moment, we will call $H$ and $D$ rather than $A$ and $B$. The numbers (probabilities) assigned to elements $H$ and $D$ will be written as $P(H)$ and $P(D)$. Conditional probability, written $P(H \mid D)$, is defined in terms of the intersect of $H$ and $D$, written $P(H \cap D)$ as well as $P(H)$ and $P(D)$. Thus the conditional probability of $H$ given that $D$ has occurred is defined as $P(H \mid D) = P(H \cap D) \div P(D)$, which is read as "the conditional probability of $H$ given $D$ is equal to the probability of the intersection of $H$ and $D$ divided by the probability of $D$." Conversely, the conditional probability of $D$ given that $H$ has occurred is defined as $P(D \mid H) = P(H \cap D) \div P(H)$, which is read as "the conditional probability of $D$ given $H$ is equal to the probability of the intersection of $H$ and $D$ divided by the probability of $H$." Multiplying both sides of the two equations by $P(D)$ or $P(H)$, respectively, and rearranging terms, yields:

$$P(H \cap D) = P(H \mid D)\, P(D), \text{ and}$$

$$P(H \cap D) = P(D \mid H)\, P(H)$$

Because the left sides of both of these equations are the same, the right sides must be equal to one another:

$$P(H \mid D)\, P(D) = P(D \mid H)\, P(H)$$

and, dividing both sides by $P(D)$,

$$P(H \mid D) = \frac{P(D \mid H)\, P(H)}{P(D)} \qquad \text{(eq. 3)}$$

Equation 3 is called Bayes' Theorem, after the Reverend Thomas Bayes (1958) who first recognized its primary implication. To make that implication clear, let us say that $H$ stands for *hypothesis* and $D$ stands for *data*. Starting on the right, we begin with the probability that a hypothesis is true before we procure data about it, $P(H)$, called the *prior probability*. Then we gather some data, $D$, and compute the probability that these data would have been obtained if the hypothesis were indeed true, $P(D \mid H)$, and divide it by the probability that these data would have been obtained whether or not this hypothesis were true. This fraction is called the *likelihood*. Then we multiply the prior probability by the likelihood to arrive at $P(H \mid D)$, the *posterior probability* that hypothesis $H$ is true in light of the observed data, $D$.

Recalling Hank and the new job seeker, Hank's prior probability of .50 for the success was revised to .65 in light of the job seeker's answer to the first question on the application, indicating that the answer had a large impact on Hank's opinion—called the *diagnosticity* of the data, which is reflected in the likelihood. In effect, Hank had to ask himself, "How probable is it that this applicant would have given this particular answer if he were going to succeed, relative to the probability he would have given it whether or not he were going to succeed?"

❖  SUBJECTIVE PROBABILITY, BAYES'
     THEOREM, AND DECISION RESEARCH

Because the normative legitimacy of the SEV and SEU models rest on the legitimacy of subjective probability, for 20 years or more the agenda for many behavioral decision researchers was set by the question of how closely subjective probability conformed to probability theory. This work addressed three issues: measurement of subjective probability, subjective probabilities for simple events, and the revision of subjective probabilities in light of data.

### Measurement Issues

Before you can do reasonable research on how closely subjective probability conforms to probability theory, you have to decide how to measure subjective probability. Clearly, if different measurement methods yield different results, it is going to be difficult to evaluate conformity. This is not the place for a tutorial on methodology; suffice it to say that many methods have been tried (direct assessment, psychophysical measurement, inferences from bets, confidence ratings, and verbal statements such as "sure thing" or "toss up"). Early on, comparisons were made among these (e.g., Beach, 1974; Beach & Phillips, 1967; Beach & Wise, 1969; Galanter, 1962; Wise, 1970). Of course, the measurement technique one uses is going to be dictated in part by the demands of the research setting and task, but based on the research, and judging from the frequency with which researchers use it, direct assessment appears about as good as any other method (von Winterfeldt & Edwards, 1986). That is, simply asking people to give a number to represent their opinion about the probability of an event appears to produce data that are not markedly different from data produced by the other methods, and the procedure is simpler than for most other methods. The least attractive method involves verbal statements—individuals may be consistent in what they mean when they use statements like "sure thing," "very likely," "unlikely," but there is very little agreement across individuals about the level of probability represented by the statements (Lichtenstein & Newman, 1967). The irony of this is that many experiments, both in behavioral decision research and in other areas, rely on rating scales anchored with verbal statements of this kind.

Direct assessment can be done in two ways. One way is to ask people to state the probability. The other way is to ask them to state the relative frequency (or proportion) with which an event might be expected to occur ("The probability of a given person having characteristic X is .10" versus "Ten people out of 100 can be expected to have characteristic X" or "Ten percent of these people have characteristic X"). For a long time it was assumed that all direct assessments were equivalent, but as we will see later, this may not be true, and what one concludes about the nature of subjective probability depends upon which kind of assessment, stated probability, or relative frequency (proportion) one asks decision makers for.

### Accuracy and Coherence for Simple Events

One way of evaluating the conformity of subjective probability to probability theory is to study areas in which it is possible to calculate objective probabilities (necessary or frequentistic) and then compare decision makers' assessments with them. This is called *accuracy*. It frequently is found that people tend to give assessments that are a bit too high for objectively low probability events and a bit too low for objectively high probabilities (e.g., Preston & Baratta, 1948). This generalization ignores many exceptions, but as a summary it is roughly correct.

Sometimes participants' assessments bear almost no discernible relationship to objective probabilities, but that does not mean that they do not conform to probability theory. It is quite possible for a person's probabilities to be *coherent* (i.e., interrelated in the ways demanded by probability theory) even if they are inaccurate—it merely means that the person is not well informed about the necessary probabilities or the relative frequencies for the domain in question. Ignorance is not the same as incoherence.

Coherence among subjective probabilities that are inaccurate, or for which there are no objective counterparts, can be measured by having participants assess the probabilities for each of the events and each of the compounds (unions, intercepts, or conditionals) in a set. Then the experimenter analyzes the degree to which the assessments "fit together" in ways dictated by probability theory.

For example, Peterson, Ulehla, Miller, Bourne, and Stilson (1965) presented participants with a list of personality traits and for each asked a question of the form, "How many people in a hundred are witty, brave, and so on," for $P(A)$, $P(B)$, and so on. Then they asked for conditional probabilities with questions of the form, "One hundred persons are known to be brave, how many would you expect to be witty?" for $P(A \mid B)$ and, "One hundred persons are known to be witty, how many would you expect to be brave?" for $P(B \mid A)$. Recall from our previous definition of conditionality that $P(A \mid B) P(B) = P(B \mid A) P(A)$. Therefore the product of the participants' assessments of $P(A \mid B)$ and their assessments of $P(B)$ ought to be equal to the product of their assessments of $P(B \mid A)$ and their assessments of $P(A)$. To test this, Peterson and his colleagues merely correlated the two products across participants; the mean correlation was .67. This may not seem very high, but the experimenters recognized that asking people to do a strange task like this is unlikely to produce very stable assessments, so they measured the reliability of the assessments; the mean reliability correlation was .72. Because response unreliability (.72) places an upper limit on coherence, the correlation of .67 for the latter is quite encouraging. Even higher coherence for assessments of familiar, concrete events was obtained in other studies. For example, Barclay and Beach (1972) obtained correlations in the high .70s, .80s, and .90s both for group data and for individual participants.

## Accuracy and Coherence in Probability Revision

Recall that Bayes' Theorem follows directly from the definition of conditional probability, and it can be interpreted as a mechanism for revising probabilities in light of data. As a result, it affords a way of examining the accuracy and coherence of subjective probabilities in a more dynamic situation than for single events. Edwards and his colleagues were the first to do "Bayesian" studies of accuracy and coherence. They used variations on what was called "the bookbag-and-poker chips task." This consisted of showing participants two or more cloth bags (bookbags were the forerunners of backpacks as the conveyance of choice for students' textbooks). Each bag contained a mixture of blue and red poker chips. The proportion of blue chips differed from one bag to another, and participants were told the proportions for each bag.

Out of the participants' view, the experimenter randomly selected one of the bags, drew a sample of chips from it and told participants the proportion of blue chips in the sample. Then, for each of the bags of chips, the participants assessed the probability that that bag was the one that had been selected.

Because the bag to be sampled was randomly selected, the number of bags determined the prior probability for each being the selected bag: If there were two bags the prior probability for each was .50, if there were three the prior probability for each was .33, and so on. The proportion of blue chips in the bag determined the likelihood; if a bag's proportion was high and the sample had lots of blue chips in it, the likelihood was high that the bag was the one that had been selected—if the proportion was low but the sample had lots of blue chips in it, the likelihood was low that the bag had been selected. Thus the posterior probability (each bag's probability of having been selected in light of the composition of the sample of chips) was jointly determined by the prior probability and the likelihood, and this should have been reflected in the probability assessments given by the participants for each of the bags.

There were two major findings (Phillips & Edwards, 1966). First, participants tended to treat the prior probabilities of the bags as if they were more equal than they actually were. Second, participants tended to be less influenced by the data (the blue chips in the sample) than they should have been. As a result, their posterior probability assessments were *conservative* relative to the posterior probabilities that a statistician would arrive at using Bayes' Theorem. Close examination of the data showed that participants' posterior probabilities after the first data were moderately accurate, but that successive draws from the same bag (remember that the posterior after one observation of data becomes the prior for the next observation of data) led to increasingly severe conservatism (Peterson, Schneider, & Miller, 1965).

Conservatism was robust in that it was obtained in many replications of and variations upon the bookbag-and-poker chips experiments, and in even more realistic tasks of comparable logical structure. Although training sometimes reduced conservatism in a specific task (e.g., Christensen-Szalanski & Beach, 1982; Peterson, DuCharme, & Edwards, 1968; Wheeler & Beach, 1968), the general conclusion remains that, compared to Bayes' Theorem, decision makers' revised subjective probabilities are neither accurate nor coherent.

## ❖ REEXAMINATION OF SUBJECTIVE PROBABILITY

By the late 1980s, it was generally agreed that probability theory does not adequately describe subjective probability—or, put another way, subjective probability does not conform to probability theory. However, most investigators persisted in their belief that the four variants of the expected value model were descriptive of choice, and subjective probability is a component of two of those variants. One might think, therefore, that these researchers would move from testing the fit with probability theory to investigating the nature of subjective probability itself, in the hope of salvaging the SEV and SEU models. This is not what happened. For the most part, interest in subjective probability simply evaporated. It disappeared from the agendas of conferences, both in the United States and abroad. It was as though everyone simply was bored with the topic and anxious to move on to something else. And then a new voice, with new data, was heard calling for a reexamination of our conclusions about subjective probability judgments.

The new voice belonged to Gerd Gigerenzer. In the late 1980s he and his colleagues undertook a reexamination of the literature on subjective probability. Their conclusion was that it is necessary to differentiate between decision makers' assessments of relative frequency, which implies long-run probabilities of events, and assessments of the probabilities of unique events (Gigerenzer, 1991).

It has long been known that people are very good at assessing proportions (Peterson & Beach, 1967), and Gigerenzer's studies show that when decision makers make assessments in the form of relative frequencies or proportions, many of the problems with subjective probability are greatly reduced or disappear. However, when asked for probabilities for unique events, the problems are strongly in evidence. Gigerenzer's conclusion is that frequentistic judgments made by people who are reasonably familiar with the domain of interest are apt to conform reasonably well to the demands of probability theory. Probability assessments for unique events are not very apt to conform to probability theory. This conclusion makes sense in light of many statisticians' strong opinions that applied probability theory only addresses long-run relative frequencies, and has no meaning for single events (e.g., von Mises, 1957).

In fact, it has been clear for quite a long time that it is necessary to differentiate between judgments for long-range and for unique events (Lopes, 1981). Beach, Barnes, and Christensen-Szalanski (1986) proposed that decision makers use different *judgment strategies* for different *judgment tasks* encountered in different *judgment environments*, and that the final judgment is *contingent* upon all three. The strategies fall into two categories, aleatory and epistemic. (An aleator is a dice player, hence aleatory refers to necessary and frequentistic probability. Epistemology means knowledge, hence epistemic refers to the use of knowledge to derive subjective probabilities.) The general idea is that the decision maker selects one or the other strategy depending upon how he or she frames the judgment task (whether chance appears to be an important component, whether repeated versus unique events are involved, whether statistical or causal logic is the norm for the domain in question). He or she then applies the selected strategy with more or less rigor depending upon the demands of the judgment environment (the payoff for accuracy, whether the judgment can be revised later, the degree to which the decision maker's credibility is on the line, the quality of the information with which he or she must work).

More recently, Gigerenzer, Hoffrage, and Kleinbolting (1991) proposed a process model for both aleatory and epistemic judgment based on work by Egon Brunswik. Thus things have come full circle; we began with Brunswik in Chapter 3 and we seem to have come back to Brunswik.

## ❖  THE NATURE OF UTILITY

We now turn to the fit between subjective worth and utility theory. Unfortunately, the research on subjective worth does not provide as clear a test of its fit with theory as the research on subjective probability provides; the evidence is more indirect.

As we have seen, the methods for comparing decisions with normative prescriptions are inherent in the nature of the normative theory itself. Because prescriptive theory views choices as gambles, and the usual prescription is to maximize expectation, it is widely accepted that studying choice means studying how people deal with gambles. As in Bernoulli's example in Chapter 4, the decision about sending a ship to the New World, this can consist of deciding to take or not to take a gamble (send the ship or not), or deciding on a fair price for a gamble (insurance). Or, as in the example of the lumber executive and Mount Saint Helens, it can consist of choosing the best from among two (or more) bets. In the laboratory, participants might be presented with a pair of gambles for which the expected value of gamble M is greater than that of gamble N, in which case they are predicted to choose M. In successive presentations, the payoffs can be systematically changed so that at some point the expected value for gamble M becomes less than that of gamble N. Of interest is the point at which decision makers switch from preferring gamble M to preferring gamble N, from which, with a little algebra, one can infer the utilities underlying their choice of one bet over the other.

## ❖ UTILITY THEORY

Just as formal probability theory is a way of assigning numbers to events, and not a theory about decision makers' uncertainty, utility theory is another way of assigning numbers to events and not a theory about what is valuable to decision makers. In application, however, utility theory is used to represent preferences among potential (or obtained) outcomes of a decision, and the question is how usefully it does its job.

As Yates (1990) has pointed out, there are two ways of relating preference to the "objective" value of outcomes. The first is called a *value function,* which represents the increase in the strength of the decision maker's preferences as a function of the outcomes' objective value. It is as if there were a scale in the decision maker's head on which the various outcomes are placed, such that the ordering of their locations are consistent (higher scale values mean higher preference), and the distances between the ordered outcomes on the scale represent meaningful differences in preference for the outcomes (the scale is ordinal). This first kind of scale is the most common view of utility—the relative preference of various outcomes.

The second way of relating preference to the objective value of outcomes is called a *utility function*. Here the assumption is that preference reflects both the value of the outcome to the decision maker *and* his or her feelings about risk (i.e., uncertainty about whether the outcome will or will not occur). Using conventional expected value logic, this means that preference is for gambles rather than merely for the outcomes. Hence it is as if there were a scale in the decision maker's head on which the various gambles are placed such that the ordering of their locations is consistent and the distances between them are meaningful. This second kind of scale is the one used in most discussions of utility in decision theory and research.

There are numerous versions of utility theory (von Winterfeldt & Edwards, 1986), but they all make three fundamental assumptions:

*Connectivity.* They assume that the decision maker can judge his or her preferences (or indifference) when faced with two gambles.

*Transitivity.* They assume that preferences among gambles are consistent such that if gamble M is preferred to gamble N, and gamble N is preferred to gamble O, gamble M is preferred to gamble O.

*Summation.* They assume that the preference for a gamble is greater than the preferences for any of its component parts. For example, the preference for a gamble that offers a payoff of $50 and a movie ticket must be greater than the preference for the $50 alone or for the movie ticket alone. That is, the preference for a compound outcome of a gamble is a combination (usually the sum) of the preferences for the component outcomes.

If these and some ancillary enabling assumptions are met, it can be formally shown that gambles can be arrayed according to preference on an underlying scale of utility.

Because utility theory is an abstract method of attaching numbers to events, it is not altogether meaningful to talk of testing it. However, it is meaningful to talk of testing the degree to which decision makers' preferences conform to its assumptions and implications, and it is here that the behavioral decision research has focused, but—to repeat—the tests, which are far fewer than one might expect, have been less direct than in similar research on probability theory.

## Research Results

- If the connectivity assumption holds, decision makers' preferences ought to be robust because connectivity means that they know what they prefer. Instead, it is found that preferences change depending upon task characteristics, measurement methods, context, and the probabilities with which they are associated (e.g., Fischhoff, Slovic, & Lichtenstein, 1980; Fryback, Goodman, & Edwards, 1973; Schoemaker, 1980; Slovic & Lichtenstein, 1983).

- If the transitivity assumption holds, the order of decision makers' preferences should be reliable. Research shows that this frequently is not the case and that intransitivity is easily induced (e.g., Tversky, 1969).

- If the summation assumption holds, preferences for compound gambles ought to be a function of the sum of their component gambles. Again, research finds that this is not always the case (e.g., Shanteau & Anderson, 1969).

To convey the flavor of the research that leads to these conclusions, consider a study by Tversky (1967). Using inmates in a federal prison as participants, Tversky asked each inmate to state the price he would ask to sell his right to play a particular gamble. Everyone in the room was given the same gamble, and the idea was that each inmate should ask a price lower than anyone else's so they, and not someone else, could sell the gamble to the experimenter. (Because the experiment was set up so that the inmates might not get the opportunity to play their gamble, in which case it became worthless, it was better to sell it and make at least the sale price.) On the other hand, they should not sell the gamble for less than the worth of the gamble (i.e., for less than its expected value). The gamble's probabilities were presented as a pie diagram with a spinner attached to the center. If the spinner landed on one section of the pie, the inmate who got to play would win some stated amount, and if it landed on the other section he would win nothing. Thus the expected value of the bet was the product of the probability of winning, from the pie diagram, and the inmate's value for the payoff. The payoffs were in cigarettes and candy, which were used by inmates as currency within the prison. There were simple gambles and compound gambles—the latter had compounds of the payoffs that had been offered for some of the simple gambles and were designed to test the summation assumption described above.

The presumption was that the competition to sell the bet would drive down the inmates' selling prices until the lowest price asked would be equal to the subjective expected utility of the gamble. That is, $\$_s = (P \times V)$, where $\$_s$ is the lowest price any inmate in the group asked for the bet (in cigarettes or candy), $P$ is the probability of winning (from the pie diagram), and $V$ is the inmate's private value for winning whatever has been offered as the payoff. Because Tversky knew the probability of winning and the price asked by the inmate who under-priced everyone else, he could figure out what that inmate's value must have been for the payoff:

$$\$_s = P \times V,$$
$$V = \$_s/P,$$

which is to say, the price divided by the probability reveals the inmate's value for the payoff.

To state the complex results rather simply, Tversky found that inmates' asking prices suggested that they in fact evaluated the gambles in terms of the product of the probability and the value of the payoff, and that value appeared to be additive, both of which are congruent with utility theory. However, the inmates consistently set selling prices higher than the expected value of the gambles. In any strict sense, utility theory does not allow for what appears to be the inmates' desire for a profit margin or, interpreted another way, their value for retaining the gamble (a value for gambling). On the other hand, common sense finds both of these explanations reasonable.

Utility theory generally assumes that the value for a payoff must be the same whether it is a "sure thing" or whether it is part of a gamble. To test this, in one condition of the experiment Tversky's inmates simply set a price on each of the payoffs. Later, when these same payoffs were then included in gambles, the inferred value for them (using the equation) was not the same as the simple prices. This result contradicts the utility theory assumption and implies that value is not independent of risk, which means that the simple expected value equation is not an adequate description of the determinants of participants' utility for the gamble.

This is but one of a number of studies that obtain data suggesting that utility theory is not a very good description of human preferences, even in well-controlled experimental conditions.

## ❖ SUMMARY

We have been examining the two components of the expected utility model: subjective probability and utility. We began with the mathematical formulation of probability and then moved on to examine Bayes' Theorem, which is a consequence of the definition of conditionality. Behavioral studies comparing subjective probability with the demands of formal probability theory show that some similarity often is found for simple events but that there is consistent error for more complex events and for the revision of subjective probability.

After a hiatus, research on subjective probability returned in a new line of work by Gigerenzer (1991) that claims to refute many of the negative conclusions previously reached. It appears that both accuracy and consistency may be linked to decision makers' use of different strategies for assessing subjective probabilities, depending on the demands of the problem and the environment in which the problem is encountered.

Finally, we examined some of the basic assumptions of utility theory and described the general results of attempts to evaluate its adequacy as a description of human preferences. In fact, it does not come off too well. All in all, what with the unsettled question about whether probability theory adequately describes human uncertainty, the failure of utility theory makes acceptance of the expected value approach to choice highly tenuous.

## ❖ NOTE

1. Recall that the union of elements is both $A$ and $B$, that the intersect is either $A$ or $B$, and the complement is what remains when $B$ is subtracted from $A$ (or vice versa).

# 6

# Heuristics and Biases and Prospect Theory

*T*he three newly hired salespeople were settling into their jobs and already things were looking better. Ralph sat back in his chair and pondered what had happened, determined to learn something useful. He recalled his misdiagnosis of the original problem as a product problem and how his view of things changed when he reframed it as a sales problem. He went over the conversations with Professor Karma Howell and how he, Betty, and Hank had used multiple regression (he hadn't even known the term three months ago) to design criteria for hiring new people. He thought about the process of going through the files of all the applicants for sales jobs and the utter hopelessness they had felt as they bogged down in the details. It had been long and hard, but somehow they had muddled through.

He was surprised about how much he wanted to understand what had gone on—to identify the various things they had done that produced progress as well as the things that had led them down blind alleys. Perhaps it was time to talk with his sister-in-law the professor again to put all this in perspective.

*Perhaps someone already had thought this stuff through; no use reinventing the wheel. He called her for an appointment.*

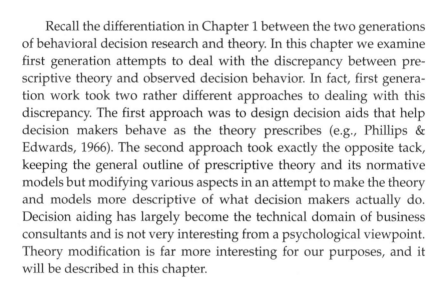

Recall the differentiation in Chapter 1 between the two generations of behavioral decision research and theory. In this chapter we examine first generation attempts to deal with the discrepancy between prescriptive theory and observed decision behavior. In fact, first generation work took two rather different approaches to dealing with this discrepancy. The first approach was to design decision aids that help decision makers behave as the theory prescribes (e.g., Phillips & Edwards, 1966). The second approach took exactly the opposite tack, keeping the general outline of prescriptive theory and its normative models but modifying various aspects in an attempt to make the theory and models more descriptive of what decision makers actually do. Decision aiding has largely become the technical domain of business consultants and is not very interesting from a psychological viewpoint. Theory modification is far more interesting for our purposes, and it will be described in this chapter.

❖   PROBABILITY ESTIMATES

As we saw in Chapter 5, people's intuitions about probabilities often are poor. The interesting thing, though, is not that people make mistakes—it is that people tend to make similar mistakes. That is, people in general tend to be systematically *biased* in comparison to the answer prescribed by probability theory. This suggests that something psychologically interesting is going on.

It is relatively easy to generate research findings by looking for systematic biases between typical responses to probability problems and the normatively correct answers. For example, a very commonly found error is known as "gambler's fallacy," the belief that chance processes are self-correcting, so that in coin tossing, several heads in a row means some tails are "due" to balance things out. After all, the probability on a coin toss presumably is .50 –.50, which means about an equal number of heads and tails should be obtained in the long run. Of course, the key is the phrase, "in the long run." In the short run there can be a distinct imbalance between heads and tails, and the pattern leading up to the next toss does not tell you anything about how it will turn out.

Researchers have discovered dozens of biases comparable to the gambler's fallacy. People have poor intuitions about the effects of sample size, so that, for example, they expect similar distributions of daily percentages of boy and girl babies at large and small hospitals—when in fact the small hospital with its fewer births is likely to have greater variance in the percentages of boys and girls from day to day (Tversky & Kahneman, 1974).

Another example: People seem to believe that probabilities combine by averaging rather than by multiplying, so that if you combine a very unlikely event with a very likely one you end up with a moderately likely combined event—when, clearly, the combined event cannot be more likely, and will generally be less likely, than its least likely component (Tversky & Kahneman, 1983). Even more, people make predictions without adjusting for the fact that their predictive information is imperfectly correlated with the outcome they are predicting, as when they use standardized test scores to predict later school performance (Kahneman & Tversky, 1973). (The normatively correct rule is to make less extreme predictions than the predictors suggest, discounting more and more as the predictors get less and less accurate, until with useless information you should simply predict that performance will be the average.)

There is even evidence (Kahneman & Tversky, 1973) showing the reverse of the conservatism phenomenon discussed in Chapter 5. For example, if people are given a description of a man on a college campus that fits their image of a tennis pro—muscular, sun-tanned, white shorts and T-shirt—they tend to think he really is more likely to be a tennis pro than a professor, despite the fact that there are vastly more professors than tennis pros on a college campus, and the description is not very diagnostic. A statistician using Bayes' Theorem from probability would adjust her initial, base-rate estimate (much more likely to be a professor) only a little in the direction indicated by the evidence. Most of us adjust too much, more than the quality of the evidence would justify.

As more and more of these biases were identified, Tversky and Kahneman (1974) suggested that they were not just random mistakes, but rather that they reflected the operation of a few simple rules of thumb or *heuristics*. People use these heuristics, generally without being aware of doing so, because they are quick and easy and they often yield answers that approximate the correct answers to the probability questions they face every day. The three main heuristics Tversky and Kahneman proposed are as follows:

## Representativeness

People expect samples from processes or events to reflect the characteristics of the underlying processes and events. This is a perfectly reasonable expectation, except that they expect the reflection to be better than it really is. If the coin is fair, they expect even short runs of tosses to turn up equal numbers of heads and tails, setting themselves up for the gambler's fallacy. In fact, runs of several heads or several tails in a row aren't all that uncommon. Similarly, after you have discussed the upcoming election with your friends you may end up pretty sure your candidate is going to win, despite the fact that your friends are probably much like you and constitute a very unrepresentative sample of the U.S. voting public. Representativeness errors come, then, when people expect small, non-random samples to reflect the underlying process as well as large, random samples really do.

## Availability

If something is frequent or probable, it is usually easy to bring examples to mind, which is to say, the examples are highly "available" to us. It's easy to think of friends who have dogs as pets, but hard to think of friends who keep tigers. Good bet: Dogs are more common pets than are tigers, and the "ease of recalling examples" rule gives us good guidance. However, some things come to mind for reasons other than their frequency. Especially dreadful or dramatic causes of death, like homicide or plane crashes, are widely reported and easy to recall, so people tend to overestimate their probability compared to less dramatic events like suicide or car wrecks (Fischhoff, Lichtenstein, Slovic, Derby, & Keeney, 1981). Rock climbing seems much more dangerous than swimming, though vastly more people drown each year than die rock climbing. Things people have seen recently come to mind more readily, and thus seem more probable, than things they saw weeks ago.

## Anchoring and Adjusting

When people try to estimate something, like a probability or an amount of money, they may start with an initial guess (the anchor) and then make adjustments as they think of reasons why the anchor might be too high or too low. For example, a manager may start with last year's budget and adjust it to reflect business growth since last year. Once again, this is a sensible process. The problem is that his or her adjustments tend to be insufficient—people adjust in the right direction, but not enough. Interestingly, the effect shows up even when the anchor is obviously irrelevant. In one demonstration, students were asked to estimate how many countries are represented in the United Nations and given a starting number obtained randomly by spinning a wheel. Those who got a high number adjusted downward, those who started low adjusted upward, but neither adjusted enough, and they ended up wide apart (Tversky & Kahneman, 1974). Northcraft and Neale (1987) observed the same thing when real estate experts estimated the value of houses; the anchor was the owner's asking price, a number the professionals all disparaged and claimed to ignore but that biased their estimates anyway.

### Critique of Heuristics and Biases

Researchers have argued at length about what precisely has been learned from the "heuristics and biases" program of research (see, for example, Cohen, 1993; Jungermann, 1983). On the one hand, searching for errors or "biases" has inspired dozens of studies of the sorts of mistakes people (sometimes) make when they try to deal with probability problems; having a short list of "heuristics" that seem to underlie these very different sorts of mistakes at least helps us organize the results in a helpful way. On the other hand, the heuristics have never been connected adequately to other major concepts in psychology: They lack much theoretical substance. There also has been a tendency to expand the list as time goes on, without being very clear about exactly what the "new" heuristic means in terms of decision making in general or when we might expect it to be applied. The net result is a list of imperfectly defined, rather atheoretical, hypothetical processes that can be used for post hoc accounts of almost any decision maker's behavior, however bizarre. As always, concepts that explain everything explain nothing.

There are two different questions here. First, does the heuristics and biases research suggest that people are liable to make mistakes when they make probability judgments? For all the passionate debate among researchers, the answer is almost certainly "Yes," but it is hard to determine when and how often these mistakes occur. At least some of the studies have compared human performance to normative models that other researchers deem to be inappropriate; others may have misled the participants into solving the wrong problem; others may simply show what college students do when they are bored or unmotivated to think hard about the right answer. But even setting these studies aside, and with an optimistic view of human abilities, there is a core of worrying evidence. It points pretty convincingly to the fact that even apparently simple probability problems can be tricky, that people are likely to reach poor conclusions if they rely on their unaided intuition about these problems, and that getting help from textbooks or computers or experts may be a smart move.

The second question about the heuristics and biases research is, "What does it tell us about the way people think about these problems?" Even if we agree that the results of their thinking are sometimes poor, does the research tell us about what they are actually doing? Are they trying to be intuitive statisticians and failing? The evidence suggests that, in fact, they are often doing something else altogether—most often, trying to understand the causal influences in the situation (Barnes, 1984). For example, Tversky and Kahneman (1982) showed that causal influences creep into judgments of simple correlations. It is easier to think about sons' heights being correlated with fathers' heights than vice versa, though from a statistical point of view the correlation is identical. People can think of *why* a father's tallness causes a son to be tall, but not why the son's height should influence the father's height. People understand situations by building causal models rather than statistical models, and they judge probabilities from the logical consequences of these causal models—as in stringing together a narrative of events, motivations, sequences, and results in trying to understand the evidence in a criminal trial (Hastie & Pennington, 2000; Pennington & Hastie, 1986). If asked, people can state their judgments in the form of a probability, but that doesn't mean they are thinking in probability terms (Beach, Christensen-Szalanski, & Barnes, 1987). They seem to be more like intuitive causal modelers than intuitive statisticians, but if they are asked the question in a different way they sometimes look like they can think statistically.

To illustrate the effect of the question on causal versus statistical thinking about probabilities, consider the following (Beach, 1990). Suppose that an experimenter were to *randomly* select a church in the United States and visit it one Sunday afternoon in June, the traditional month for weddings. He stands outside and waits for the wedding party to emerge. Then he approaches the best man and asks, "If I were to randomly select a couple that is getting married this afternoon somewhere in America, what is the probability that they will still be married to each other ten years from now?" Assuming that he knows the divorce rate, the best man would probably give it, in probability form, because that was what he was asked for.

Now what if the experimenter instead asked, "What is the probability that the couple for whom you were just best man will still be married to each other ten years from now?" For the experimenter, the change in question does not change the problem—he randomly selected this couple and he knows absolutely nothing about them as individuals; for him, they are interchangeable with any other American couple getting married on that or any other day. But for the best man, the change of question reflects a substantial change in the framing of the task. The divorce rate for the population at large may influence his answer, but only if he is particularly cynical. (Indeed, if he really thought the probability of his friends' marriage working was only about .50, he might well have declined to be their best man on the grounds that it would be a poor investment of his time.) Rather, his answer to the second question, the one that is specific to his friends as individuals, is properly based upon his knowledge about them and his theories about what causes successful and unsuccessful marriages.

❖  UTILITY

It is assumed by utility theory that payoffs can be described by their "objective" market value, which is stated in terms of money. In this view money is money, its source is unimportant, and one's present asset value is the sum of all of one's different forms of wealth as well as one's expectations for future income. Even presuming decreasing marginal utility for additional money, it is convenient to assume that a dollar is a dollar. This is called the *fungibility* of money.

A little reflection reveals that for most of us money is not fungible. Consider the person with $20,000 in the bank earning 4% interest who takes out a 7% loan to buy a $18,000 car. Or the person who refuses to purchase a pair of pants for $30 because they are too expensive but who then pays $40 for a pair of comparable quality because they are marked down from $70. Clearly, the $20,000 in the bank and the money borrowed for the car are different kinds of money to the car buyer, and the $30 "saved" by buying on sale is not the same as the $30 "squandered" by buying at full price. The point is, people value different categories of money differently, and this means that utility is a far more complicated concept that it may at first appear.

Von Winterfeldt and Edwards (1986) introspected about the different kinds of money that made up their own personal finances and came up with four categories:

*Quick Cash.* The money in one's wallet, credit card, checking account

*Capital Assets.* Money in one's house, car, investments, retirement fund

*Income and Fixed Expenditures.* Salary, taxes, house payments, utility payments, insurance

*Play Money.* Money reserved for extravagances such as vacations, household extras, risky investments, sports cars

Thaler (1985, 1990) refers to categories such as these as "mental accounts." He suggests that we exercise self-control over spending by treating different parts of our assets in different ways. Thus we might force ourselves to save by putting money in a Christmas Club (which usually pays no interest) even though the money could more profitably be used to pay off a credit card account (on which the interest often approaches 20%). We allow ourselves to spend pocket money for fun, but would never touch the grocery money for anything but food. Windfalls, such as winning $50 at a charity raffle, may not be regarded as "real money" and can therefore be spent frivolously.

## ❖ PROSPECT THEORY

Despite all the evidence that probability theory does not describe decision makers' uncertainties very well, and that utility theory does not describe their thoughts about value either, it remains clear to many decision researchers that uncertainties and value do affect choices. Indeed, it is hard to think of any sensible choice that doesn't consider how attractive, and how likely, one judges the consequences of choosing each option to be. It is also clear that, while variants of the expected value model (EV, EU, SEV, SEU; see Chapter 4) are not entirely successful in describing actual choices, they often come close. Researchers have continued to tinker with variants of the expected value model in an effort to improve their ability to account for observed decision behavior.

Kahneman and Tversky's (1979) prospect theory is by far the most important effort in this direction and is the landmark achievement of first generation behavioral research and theory.[1] It is clearly in the expected value tradition: The value of an uncertain "prospect" is determined by a weighted average of the decision maker's valuations of the various consequences of the prospect, where the weights reflect his or her assessment of the likelihood of each consequence. However, the elements of the model are rather different from those in the standard expected value model.

### Wealth

In the standard expected value model, the carrier of value is the individual's total wealth. That is, if one outcome of a gamble is winning $1,000, the outcome is treated as (Total wealth + $1,000). Since most of us have only the haziest idea of what our total wealth might be, this is obviously not psychologically realistic. In prospect theory, value is carried by departures above or below some reference point, typically the status quo. Winning $1,000 is, plausibly enough, treated as (+$1,000), losing the same as (−$1,000). It is gains and losses that count, not total wealth. (The theory is a little vague about what reference point is operating in some situations. The status quo is often plausible, but plenty of us would evaluate a pay raise by comparison with what our deadly rival got, or feel we had gained if a speeding ticket we expected to pay $100 for was reduced to $50.)

### Value

In prescriptive theory, value (utility) is related to outcome quantity (e.g., money) by a "utility function," often assumed to be of the "diminishing marginal utility" form. This means that more money always adds more utility, but at a declining rate; for every dollar you gain, the less the next dollar means to you. Similarly, a $1 gain for a rich person adds less to his or her utility that a $1 gain for a poor person. For gains, prospect theory's value function reflects this by rising steeply at first for small gains and then proceeding upward more and more slowly for larger and larger gains. For losses (outcomes below the reference point), the value function plunges swiftly downward for small losses, dropping more and more slowly for larger and larger losses. The result is that the two parts of the value function form a slanted letter "S" going through the origin (no gain, no loss = 0 value) at the middle of the "S." Again, this adds psychological realism: Losing $20 feels much worse than winning $20 feels good. This is reflected in people's unwillingness to play a coin-toss game where heads wins $20 and tails costs $20. The $20 win would move them up the gains curve, but the $20 loss would move them much farther down the losses curve, so a .50 possibility of getting a small-value gain compares poorly with a .50 possibility of getting a large-value loss. This bit of realism, referred to as "loss aversion," is built into the value function via the steeper slope for losses.

### Probabilities

The third modification prospect theory makes in the standard expected value model is its treatment of probability. Instead of using "real" probabilities or subjective probabilities as the weights given to the value elements, it uses *decision weights, $\pi$*. That is, prospect theory discounts value by multiplying by $\pi$, which is a weight that corresponds to that probability. The theory is designed so that when probabilities are small, the decision weights are somewhat larger than the probabilities up to a probability of about .30, then they become increasingly smaller than the probabilities as the probabilities increase toward 1.0. This is intended to reflect a variety of oddities in the way people treat small and large probabilities, such as their strong reactions to the difference between "a very small probability" of some dreadful disease and "no chance at all."

These three elements—wealth as an anchor point, an S-shaped value function defined as gains and losses relative to the reference point and steeper for losses than for gains, and decision weights instead of probability—have enabled prospect theory to be more descriptive of decision behavior than prescriptive theory, while retaining prescriptive theory's general logic. The result is that prospect theory is remarkably robust in accounting for a wide range of choices in laboratory studies. Its authors later published a significant modification called cumulative prospect theory (Tversky & Kahneman, 1992) to deal with some difficulties and to expand its applicability, and the theory now enjoys widespread acceptance. Economists, in particular, have been delighted to have a behavioral theory that is more realistic than prescriptive theory but that still retains the formal features that are familiar to them. As a result, prospect theory is commonly used in economic analysis.

To the extent that it accurately describes behavior, prospect theory suggests a number of ways in which one might make one's life happier. For example, how should you deal with a series of gains (gifts, unexpected payments, found money) and losses (traffic tickets, lost wallets, dental bills)? Prospect theory suggests a rule, and it seems like a good one: segregate gains, consolidate losses (Thaler, 1990). Pay off all your losses in a single payment, if possible, so you only feel the pain of the steep downward part of the loss portion of the value function once. Conversely, segregate your gains: Keep them separate from one another, deposit them separately one at a time, so you are repeatedly going up the steep part of the gains portion of the value function. Most of us would get more pleasure from receiving a $50 rebate check today and a $100 birthday gift tomorrow than we would from a single check for $150. Notice, also, how unpleasant it is to pay off a large debt in installments, especially when the thing we bought has already worn out.

An interesting shift occurs if we combine our earlier framing discussion (Chapter 2) with prospect theory's value function, with its "risk seeking for losses, risk aversiveness for gains" property. Simply changing the way people describe a choice can alter what they want to do! In an example suggested by Kahneman and Tversky (1984), research participants were told about a dangerous disease that was expected to kill 600 people in the U.S. Two alternative public health policies were proposed. Option A would save 200 lives. The outcomes for option B were riskier: there was a 1/3 chance that it would save all 600 lives, but a 2/3 chance that it would not save any lives. A majority of the participants indicated that they would play it safe and take option A. They were then asked to choose between two other options. If option C were adopted, 400 people would die, while option D offered a 1/3 chance that no one would die, and a 2/3 chance that 600 people would die. Offered this choice, a majority of the participants chose D: the 600 dead did not seem that much worse than the 400 dead, and there was a real chance that no one would die. Notice, however, that option A is exactly equivalent to option C, and option B to option D. If you chose A in the first pair, why would you choose D in the second? Simply shifting the description from "lives saved" to "lives lost" seems to have shifted many of the participants from risk aversion to risk seeking, and from the certain option to the risky one.

It is easy to dismiss findings like this as parlor games, wording tricks that confuse people, and as unrepresentative laboratory tasks that have no bearing on real-world choices. However, the evidence suggests that this would be premature. Barbara McNeil, a researcher at Harvard Medical School working with a distinguished group of colleagues (McNeil, Pauker, Sox, & Tversky, 1982), presented a difficult medical choice (surgery or radiation for operable lung cancer) to three groups of participants: graduate students, patients, and physicians. Half the participants were given the mortality rates for the two treatments, the others were told the survival rates. (Note: Survival rate plus mortality rate = 100%—everyone who isn't alive is dead, and vice versa.) These two alternative ways of describing the options had a significant effect on the choices of the students, replicating the earlier findings. But what is really striking, and really worrying, is that the wording difference also had a substantial effect on the choices made by patients, and by their physicians as well. Even people with a substantial stake, and real expertise, in thinking hard about these choice can be swayed by simple changes in the way options are described: survival (gains) versus mortality (loss). Apparently the gain/loss framing effect is not just a clever laboratory trick; it could have real life and death consequences. (The obvious cure, if you worry that you might have fallen into this trap, is to try rephrasing your problem into the other frame, from gains language into losses language, or vice versa, and see if your choice is still the same. If it isn't, you need to think more deeply about what you really want to do. "Option A has a 95% survival rate [i.e., a 5% mortality rate] while option B . . .")

## ❖ CRITIQUE OF PROSPECT THEORY

Prospect theory, for all its empirical richness, remains rooted in the gambling metaphor for choice. It treat "prospects" as gambles, with possible gains, possible losses, and some equivalent of a roll of the dice or a spin of the wheel to determine what happens. Gambling requires you to make your decision, to place your bet, and then await the verdict of the wheel, the dice, or the cards. Outside the laboratory, however, in government and business, for example, as well as in their personal lives, decision makers are seldom so passive. Instead, they actively work to influence events so as to make their choice the right choice (Isenberg, 1984). Working managers scorn passivity, and keep out of situations that require it. Like most of us, they strive to control events rather than let events control them. Of course, people—managers included—sometimes make decisions in the gambling way, but allow for the effects of effort: "There's a 20% chance of this new product succeeding if you launch it now, but I can turn that into a 60% chance if you hold off for a month and let me make improvements to it." But it does seem that real-world decision makers—us, once people get out of their laboratories—generally do not deal with decisions in ways that much resemble gambling.

Gambling ideas go back to the very beginnings of serious thinking about decisions. One can trace decision theory to efforts, notably by Daniel Bernoulli (1738), to advise real gamblers on how much various gambles were worth. Very early on, the bet's expected value became the accepted way of assessing its worth. On the other hand, Bernoulli presented a troubling example of people's unwillingness to accept his advice, known as the St. Petersburg Paradox.

Pretend that you are offered the opportunity to play a game in which you toss a coin until it comes up heads, then the game stops and you get paid. If the first toss is heads, the game stops and you win $2. If the first toss is tails and the second is heads, the game stops and you win $4. If it is tails on the first two tosses and heads on the third toss, you win $6, and so on. How much would you pay to play the game? The expected value rule gives advice: there is a .50 chance the game will end on the first toss, and pay $2, a .25 chance it will end on the second toss and pay $4, and so on. Because of the way the game and its payoffs are structured, it turns out that the expected value for every toss is $1, that is, if you multiply the payoff for each toss by the chance of receiving it, the answer for every toss is $1. So, if you were to add the expected values of the tosses together for a string of tosses, it turns out that the expected value of this gamble is infinite. This means, theoretically anyway, that the game offers the chance to win an infinite amount of money and, therefore, you ought to be willing to trade your entire wealth for the opportunity to play. Most people, however, do not find the game very attractive; they might pay a few dollars to play, but certainly not their entire wealth. Expected value is not even a rough guide to what people decide to do in this situation.

It sometimes is easy to see how expected utility works for a string of identical decisions (like bets on coin flips) because it closely approximates the average payoff over the long haul. But what about single, unique decisions that are made just once? These are, after all, the most interesting decisions because they are the ones we encounter every day.

Lola Lopes (1981) has been one of the most visible and persuasive critics of using the expectation rule in evaluating unique gambles, suggesting instead that people do (and should) use some combination of (a) worst-case outcome and (b) upside potential in evaluating risky options. Some people emphasize one factor, some the other, but most people give at least some weights to both, and the resulting preferences are different from those predicted by the rule to maximize expected utility.

The celebrated economist Paul Samuelson (1963) reports offering a colleague a coin-toss bet where he would win $200 if he won and lose $100 if he lost. The colleague declined the bet even though its expectation is ($200 × .50) + (–$100 × .50) = $100 – $50 = $50.

The colleague explained his decision: "I won't bet because I would feel the $100 loss more than the $200 gain [just like prospect theory, which was formulated 20 years later]. But I'll take you on if you promise to let me make 100 such bets. . . . One toss is not enough to make it reasonably sure that the law of averages will turn out in my favor. But . . . a hundred tosses of the coin . . . will make it a darn good bet. I am, so to speak, virtually sure to come out ahead in such a sequence, and that is why I accept the sequence while rejecting the single toss" (p. 109).

Samuelson declared his colleague to be irrational because he was not willing to use expectation to guide his decision about the single bet. According to Samuelson's logic, because the expectation of $50 is the same for every bet, if you are willing to play a series of bets, you ought to be willing to play a single bet—the probabilities are the same no matter if the bet stands alone or if it is one of a series.

Lopes, on the other hand, argued that the colleague's behavior was quite sensible. Of course, there's a chance that you might lose 100 tosses in a row and end up paying out $10,000, but the chance is very tiny, about $1/10^{30}$, and most of us ignore it. In contrast, on a single toss there is a substantial chance (.50), relatively speaking, that you will come out behind. On the series of tosses, the chance is small enough to ignore, and the potential of winning money is good.

Like Samuelson's colleague, most people think quite differently about the single bet and the series. Keren and Wagenaar (1985) found that when they were offered a choice among gambles to play just once, 68% of their experimental participants chose the bet with the best chance of paying at least something instead of an alternative bet that had a higher expectation. When the same gambles were offered with an option to play 10 times, however, 67% chose the one with the higher expectation. Lopes's two-factor model does a good job of explaining these preference shifts between single and repeated play.

Perhaps the ultimate test of the adequacy of prospect theory's reliance on the gamble metaphor is the behavior of real-life gamblers. Laboratory studies that give students hypothetical gambles or gambles for small amounts (usually provided by the researcher) are one thing, but if real gamblers do not even behave as prescriptive theory requires, then something is seriously wrong with the gambling metaphor.

First of all, the very fact that gamblers even go to casinos indicates that they are not trying to maximize expected value; the games are designed to have negative expected value for the players, even if they play skillfully. In the long run, the casino always comes out ahead, even if a few players make a killing now and then.

Second, even when they get there, gamblers do not strive to maximize expectation. Gideon Keren and Willem Wagenaar (Keren & Wagenaar, 1985; Wagenaar, 1988) studied the customers in casinos in the Netherlands. Interviews showed that gamblers not only do not think about expected value, they in fact attend to a variable that is not even part of predictive theory, normative models, or prospect theory: luck. In their view, someone who is lucky on a given evening will win irrespective of the objective probabilities involved. Players do not believe they can influence the turn of the roulette wheel or the fall of the dice, but they do control the choice of what they bet on and, if "their luck is running," their choices will work out well. Chance favors no one, but luck favors some. This, of course, is what keeps casinos in business.

If you must gamble, research on gamblers might help you play more skillfully (or, perhaps, less foolishly). One group of decision researchers (Payne, Laughhunn, & Crum, 1980) identified what they called the "house money effect," the common observation that people tend to treat money they have won differently, and more carelessly, than they do their own money—the money they brought with them to the casino (recall Thaler's idea of mental accounts). A gambler who wins money early in his visit tends to play wilder bets (and lose more quickly) with this "house" money than he does with his own money, as though the winnings weren't real money. (Notice also how playing with chips rather than with cash increases this feeling that it isn't real money changing hands). Few gamblers who win early manage to quit while they are ahead (perhaps coupled to the belief that the win suggests that their luck is running), and the house soon gets its money back. Once a gambler is behind, the temptation is to keep on playing to try to break even for the evening (likely emphasized by the gambler's fallacy noted above—the belief that one's luck has to change after a long run of losses). Not surprisingly, most casino gamblers mostly lose.

One study (McGlothlin, 1956) suggests that this "getting even" effect may open an opportunity for horse race bettors to make a little money. In racetrack "tote" betting, money bet on any one horse changes the odds on the others. Bettors who are behind for the afternoon may try to break even by wagering on a long shot in the last race, which means that the odds on the favorite become more attractive—sometimes attractive enough to offer a bet with positive expected value. Neither of us, the authors, is an authority on practical gambling, so we cannot tell you whether or not this practice works. If it does not, we bear no responsibility. If it does, remember where you got the advice.

This brings us to the end of our examination of the first generation of attempts to deal with the fact that people do not behave according to prescriptive theory and its normative models for probability, utility, and maximization of expectation. Our attention has focused on the first generation's two main accomplishments, heuristics and biases and prospect theory. For years, these two bodies of work, both of which were pioneered by Tversky and Kahneman, have occupied center stage in behavioral decision research and theory. Both had an enormous influence on researchers, to some degree by legitimizing ventures beyond the strict limits of prescriptive theory and its logic. In addition, both have had enormous impacts outside of psychology, inspiring studies in business, education, economics, and elsewhere. This is a rich legacy for any two experimenters, and Tversky and Kahneman certainly are the two names most often cited in the decision literature.

With all the success of heuristics and biases and of prospect theory, both lines of research seem to some observers to overlook an important component of decision making. Personal experience with difficult decisions convinces most of us that we are not logic machines; our decisions seem more based upon feeling and emotion than on clear-headed thinking. This insight has motivated a large number of researchers to move beyond characterizations of decision making based on prescriptive theory and normative models and to focus on the role of feelings and emotions in decision making. This was the beginning of the second generation of behavioral research and theory. The next chapter describes what this research has found.

### ❖ SUMMARY

We have examined attempts to deal with mounting evidence that unaided human decision making does not conform to prescriptive theory and its component normative models for probability, utility, and maximization of expectation. The goal of the first generation attempts was to build a behavioral theory that would account for this lack of fit but retain the general flavor of prescriptive theory and its normative models. The major result of this effort was heuristics and biases and prospect theory.

Critics of heuristics and biases focus on the lengthening list of biases, most of which have no discernable relation to one another other than being attributable to one of the three heuristics. Critics also point out the lack of theoretical links between heuristics and any other area of psychological theory. In short, the research stands alone, which somewhat limits its value in the search for an encompassing behavioral theory.

Critics of prospect theory are considerably kinder. Prospect theory generally does a good job of accounting for data in typical laboratory studies involving gambles, which is what it was designed to do. Problems arise, however, with attempts to apply it outside the laboratory, where results are very mixed. Moreover, prospect theory retains the gamble metaphor from prescriptive theory, and this metaphor is increasingly seen as inappropriate for many, if not most, real-world decisions, particularly for unique decisions.

Whatever their strengths and weaknesses, both heuristics and biases and prospect theory have legitimized research that strays from prescriptive theory and normative models. Indeed, they have freed researchers to search for behavioral aspects of decision making that have no counterparts in prescriptive theory, thus encouraging them to construct a second generation of behavioral theories that bear increasingly less resemblance to prescriptive theory. This is a major contribution to decision research, and the following chapters will describe the results of the resulting search and attempts at theory construction.

❖  NOTE

1.  Prospect theory was cited as a major contribution in earning Kahneman the Nobel Prize in economics in 2003. Tversky, who died in 1995, would clearly have shared the award but for the rule that Nobel Prizes are never given posthumously.

# 7

# Emotions

*R* *alph left Professor Karma Howell's office and walked across the campus. He liked being here; the trees were beautiful, the newly mown grass smelled wonderful, and everything seemed so peaceful. He sat down on a bench to savor the pleasure he felt in the moment, slipping back to thoughts about what he had just learned from his sister-in-law. He certainly could see his own experience in her descriptions of heuristics and biases, and he thought much of prospect theory made good sense. But he still lacked the sense that the picture was complete. He thought about all the uncertainty, misery, and strife involved in the decisions he, Betty, and Hank had made, and he wondered where they fit into the theories and models. It was intuitively very clear to him that all that emotion had not been merely ancillary to the decisions; it was an integral part of them.*

*He got up and walked toward the parking lot; it was time to get back to work. He had another appointment with Karma next week, and he was going to bring up his thoughts about emotions. Perhaps there was research that could help him better understand this part of decision making.*

If you glance back over the chapters so far, you will see that almost everything we have discussed looks at the thinking side of making decisions. Decision makers think about the available options: they think about the outcomes each option might lead to, and they think about how likely each outcome is. They think about how desirable or undesirable the outcomes might be. And they think about how to put all this information together to select the best option. In this emphasis on cognitive activity—thinking—we have faithfully reflected most of the research on decision making for the last 50 years: nearly all of it has looked at decision making as the product of logical thought.

Anyone who has actually made an important decision, however, knows that thinking is only part of what goes on, and not always the most important part. Try to recall the last important decision you made—buying a car, choosing a college or a job, asking someone out on a date, deciding on whether to have surgery. You probably remember how much emotion was involved. You were worried about spending so much money on the car, you felt hopeful about the new college or job, you were delighted when the person you asked for the date said "yes," and you were terrified when you thought about the surgery. Making a decision is not just a matter of deliberative thinking; it involves strong emotions as well.

Decision researchers knew about emotionality all along, of course, but they generally treated it as a distraction from the main event. Emotions were seen as a source of irrationality, and therefore as something that had to be kept under control so we could think straight. As a result, decision-related emotions were pushed to the edge of research attention, or ignored altogether.

Recent research reflects a change of view; emotions are no longer seen as merely disruptive, they now are seen as playing a central role, sometimes complementing deliberative thought and at other times overwhelming it. In part this view stems from researchers' personal experience, in part from the freedom from prescriptive models afforded by the heuristics and biases research and prospect theory, and in part from research in areas other than decision making that have begun to investigate emotion. To some degree, the latter began with findings by Damasio (1994), who found that patients who have injuries to one specific part of their brains are incapable of feeling certain emotions and, as a result, make terrible decisions in simple gambling games. They can think perfectly well, but their emotional impairment makes them poor decision makers.

In this chapter, we will survey some of the decision-related work on emotion, beginning with work on how decisions are influenced by mood—the simple matter of feeling happy or sad while decisions are being made. We then look in more detail at how specific emotions, such as disappointment and regret, influence decision makers' choices and their satisfaction with those choices. We will then examine how emotional influences spread to feelings of confidence in judgment and decisions, and how emotions link past decisions to future decisions, often with unfortunate results. Finally, we will see how emotions influence how decision makers deal with risk. Not all of these areas of research are fully mature, but the findings in each are interesting, suggesting ways in which people can understand and incorporate their emotions into their decision making.

## Mood

Most of us know that being in a bad mood—feeling angry and upset after a row with the boss, or feeling depressed after getting a low grade on an important exam—can have a marked effect on a wide range of behaviors, including our decision making. But would you expect that being in a mildly positive mood would have much effect? Suppose, for example, that you showed up for a psychology experiment and the researcher welcomed you to the lab with a warm smile, said, "Thank you for coming," and gave you a small bag of candy. Would you expect this small positive experience to have an effect on your creativity, your intelligence, your risk aversion, or your decision efficiency?

### Isen's Research

The smile, thanks, and candy treatment is the trademark experimental device of Alice Isen, a psychologist at Cornell University, who has for more than 30 years studied the effects of mild positive emotion on all sorts of mental performance. The effects she has discovered are remarkably varied. For example:

*Creativity.* The Remote Associates Test (RAT) (Mednick, Mednick, & Mednick, 1964) is commonly used to test for individual creativity. A typical RAT item gives you three words (e.g. "book," "up," and "mate") and asks you find a fourth word that relates the other three to each another ("check" might work in this example). Isen, Daubman, and Nowicki (1987) found that participants who had received the mild positive emotion treatment scored better on this test, indicating heightened creativity, than did untreated control participants.

*Risk and Loss Aversion.* Being in a mildly positive mood makes people less eager to spoil things by taking a loss. For example, Isen and Patrick (1983) found that positive mood participants were reluctant to gamble with the experimental credits they had earned for participating in an experiment, and demanded better odds before they would do so. Similarly, Isen, Nygren, and Ashby (1988) found that positive mood participants were more sensitive to losses, and Carnevale and Isen (1986) found participants who were in a positive mood were more likely to persist in trying to find good win-win agreements in bargaining tasks. The combination of better creative performance (to invent possible solutions) and desire not to incur a loss (to motivate persistence) seems to have made participants who were in a positive mood superior bargainers.

*Complex Problems.* Isen and Means (1983) studied participants choosing (hypothetically) between different cars—a complex set of tradeoffs for most of them. The control participants took nearly twice as long as the positive mood participants—they were just less efficient. In a similar study, however, medical students doing medical diagnostic tasks were no faster overall than the controls, but reached the correct answer earlier in the session, spending the rest of the time checking their answers and continuing to work the problem beyond the goal given by the experimenters (Isen, Rosenzweig, & Young, 1991). Positive mood seems once again to have improved both cognitive ability and motivation, but it showed up in different ways in the medical task study than it did in the car choice study.

These are remarkable effects to obtain from a simple smile and some candy (or, in some of the studies, a report that one did well on an earlier task). As Isen (1993) summarizes her findings:

> positive [mood] tends to promote exploration and enjoyment of new ideas and possibilities, as well as new ways of looking at things. Therefore people who are feeling good may be alert to possibilities and may solve problems both more efficiently and more thoroughly than controls. However, people who are feeling good respond cautiously in dangerous situations or when caution is otherwise appropriate. (p. 273)

The mood state of mild positive emotion—feeling good—clearly has a surprisingly broad and substantial effect on the way we make decisions.

## Regret and Disappointment

Regret is, by far, the most studied emotion in connection with decision making, even more than its near neighbor, disappointment. (Interestingly, related positive emotions, such as elation and rejoicing, have been relatively neglected. Perhaps decision researchers find the dark side more interesting.) The term *regret* has been used for a wide range of negative emotions associated with decisions, from the merely conventional "regret" one claims when politely declining an invitation to the persistent anguish one might feel for years after a car accident that one caused. To decision researchers, part of the interest is not just that people feel regret when decisions turn out badly, but that they know ahead of time this might happen, and often shape their decisions to avoid it. Regret can be both a result and a cause of a decision.

As with so much of recent decision research, an important stimulus to work on regret came from a small study by Kahneman and Tversky (1982). Participants read a short scenario in which two investors each lose $1,200, one by buying a particular stock, the other by holding onto the same stock as its price dropped. Which investor feels more regret? By a huge margin (92%), participants thought the first investor would feel worse: A bad outcome resulting from action, it seems, generates more regret than the same bad outcome resulting from inaction. It does not take much imagination to see that this finding, if general, could have important implications: Would a patient be biased against a beneficial but risky surgery in favor of the riskier option of sitting and waiting (Spranca, Minsk, & Baron, 1991)? Does this connect to the widespread moral intuition that there is a difference between active and passive euthanasia—between actually taking steps to kill someone rather than simply standing back and allowing them to die (Spranca et al., 1991)?

On the other hand, exactly the opposite results were obtained by Gilovich and Medvec (1995) when they asked people to look back on their lives and to describe the things they regretted. By a margin of better than 2:1, the participants reported more regrets for inactions than for actions, for the things they had *not* done (not marrying the girl, not finishing their education, not quitting smoking) rather than the things they *had* done (taking the job, learning to play the guitar, moving away from home).

In retrospect, the focus on action and inaction may have been a red herring. The issue seems not to be whether or not one took action, but whether or not what one did (or did not do) was justified. For example, Marcel Zeelenberg (Zeelenberg, van den Bos, van Dijk, & Pieters, 2002) asked participants to consider the emotions of two soccer coaches whose teams had just lost a game, the first after making changes to his team (taking action), the other after making no changes (inaction). Which coach feels more regret? It turns out that the answer is, "It depends." Losing after a change is seen as regrettable if the team had been winning, but not if it had been losing—changing a losing team is justifiable. Conversely, if the team had been losing, taking action was justified, and thus not regrettable, even if it led to another loss. The regrettable thing was leaving the losing team unchanged and then losing. Losing after making changes was less regrettable—at least the coach did the right thing. Notice how thought and emotion get woven together here. The question is not just the outcome of the decision (losing the next game) or the decision the coach made (changing the team or not). It's whether or not the coach's decision was reasonable or defensible—in a word, justifiable (Connolly & Zeelenberg, 2002).

This need to justify one's decisions shows up very clearly in studies of an important medical decision: whether or not to vaccinate one's children. Initial studies (Asch et al., 1994) suggested that mothers were reluctant to vaccinate when there was any substantial risk of side effects from the vaccine. Some researchers suggested that the action-regret link might be behind this reluctance—causing the child's sickness yourself seemed worse than leaving it to fate—and that there might be a general tendency called "omission bias" that affected such decisions. More recent research has shown this not to be the case. Indeed, the reverse may actually be true. When the risks from the disease and the vaccine are carefully balanced, most people are inclined to vaccinate (Connolly & Reb, 2003). Interestingly, both pro-vaccine and anti-vaccine participants appear to be taking the course of action that will minimize their expected regret; they just expect to regret different things. The pro-vaccinators think that the child's sickness from the disease is more regrettable; the anti-vaccinators think sickness from the vaccine side effects is worse. Once again, regret is not driven by what you decide to do, it is driven by what you think is justified.

We must not leave the topic of regret without noting the contribution made by economists to the topic. It seems clear that regret is driven by comparisons: the outcome I received versus what I might have received, or expected to receive, or had beforehand; the choice I made versus the other alternatives that were available; the way I decided (e.g., carelessly) versus the way I could have decided (e.g., carefully). Economic choice theorists (e.g., Bell, 1982; Loomes & Sugden, 1982) turned this into an elegant formal model. They pictured a decision maker facing a choice between two lotteries (sound familiar?) where he or she is to pick either Lottery A or Lottery B and receive a payoff depending on the draw of a numbered ticket from a hat:

|  | Ticket drawn | |
| --- | --- | --- |
|  | *1–30* | *31–100* |
| Lottery A | $30 | $0 |
| Lottery B | $0 | $10 |

That is, if you had picked Lottery A and a ticket between 1 and 30 came up, you would get $30; if you had picked Lottery B, you would get nothing. If 31–100 came up you would collect $10 if you had picked B, nothing if you had picked A. (Quick check: Which would you pick?)

Suppose you picked Lottery B and ticket 27 came up: you get $0. This is a poor outcome, obviously, but the economists argued that two emotions make it even worse. You compare your outcome to the $30 you would have if you had picked A, and you feel "regret." You also compare your outcome to the $10 you would have if you had been luckier, and you feel "disappointment." This formulation makes the comparisons very specific. "Regret" comes from comparing *across* alternatives, "disappointment" comes from comparing *within* alternatives. (We use quotes here to remind ourselves that these were just labels stuck on by the theorists. They never checked to see if the participants actually felt these emotions). This formed the basis of some very neat mathematical modeling of choice and some very nice laboratory data that apparently confirmed the models. Unfortunately, it turned out that the results were caused by a simple lab artifact (Starmer & Sugden, 1993) and work in this line came to an abrupt end. Not all psychologists have heard about the abrupt end, however, and many textbooks still contain the "regret is between, disappointment is within" formulation. Beware of economists bearing psychological gifts!

## Sunk Costs

Bad news about your elderly car: The garage just called to tell you that it needs a $200 brake job if you want to drive it again. And this is on top of the $600 you spent last month to have the transmission fixed. As you try to decide whether to spend the $200 or get rid of this car and buy another one, it's hard to get last month's $600 out of your mind. If you do not fix the brakes, that $600 is going to be wasted, which feels awful. Reluctantly, you conclude that it makes sense to spend the extra $200, and you tell the garage to go ahead.

In all likelihood, your emotions have caused you to commit a classic decision error: You have fallen into the "sunk cost trap," the error of treating non-recoverable earlier expenditures as though they are part of a later decision. If you have ever taken an introductory college economics class you will have been warned about this error. Unfortunately, economists are not very good at teaching us how to spot the trap and how to avoid it, and most of us fall prey to it more often than we should. Test yourself on these little stories: Has the person in the story fallen into the sunk cost trap?

- The new pizza restaurant offers "All you can eat for $5." Alan tries it, finds that the pizza is terrible, but eats several slices so as not to waste his $5.
- Same story, except that Alan's explanation is that eating a large lunch will save his having to buy dinner.
- Months ago Bonnie bought an expensive ticket, no refunds or exchanges, for tonight's concert. Unfortunately, she is coming down with the flu and the concert just got a terrible review in the local paper. She doesn't really want to go, but she does anyway, so as not to waste the ticket.
- Chuck has been on hold at the computer tech support hotline for 25 minutes. He considers calling back later when they will be less busy but decides to hold on longer.
- Jean has been in an abusive relationship with her boyfriend, Jim, for two years. Her friends all urge her to break it off, but

she stays in the relationship, arguing that she has too much invested to quit.

It is trickier than it looks. In the first story, Alan is clearly trapped. Assuming no refunds, his $5 is gone, and his choices are either to eat a lot of bad pizza or not. It should be an easy choice. In the second story, Alan, though perhaps not very smart, is at least acting in light of future consequences (saving his dinner cost), so no sunk cost there. Bonnie is also clearly trapped. She would not go to the concert if the ticket were free, so why should she go, and have a miserable time, just because she bought it? Chuck's position is less clear. If he thinks he's getting closer to the front of the line, it might make sense to hold on. If he's just trying to justify the time he has wasted so far, he's trapped. And Jean sounds to be thoroughly and disastrously trapped. She should be asking herself about the future of her relationship; the past is only relevant in that it tells her what sort of man she is with.

The sunk costs trap distorts decisions outside our personal lives as well. Barry Staw, in a series of studies, has shown the same effect in important organizational choices, such as increasing investments in unsuccessful projects (Staw & Fox, 1977). Even at the level of national policy it is easy to find rhetoric that turns upon the sunk cost trap. For example, during the Vietnam War it was argued that the U.S. should escalate its commitment in order to justify the losses it had already incurred (Staw, 1976).

Hal Arkes, a psychologist who has studied sunk cost extensively (e.g., Arkes & Blumer, 1985), thinks that the key psychological issue is our desire to avoid waste—or, at least, to avoid acknowledging waste. Avoiding waste is, obviously, a sensible rule for life: Don't take more food than you want to eat. However, suppose you already have over-filled your plate and find yourself full with food still left. Clearly, you made a mistake in estimating how hungry you were. But do you now want to make a second mistake, treating yourself as a human garbage disposal, in order to make up for the first mistake? It makes more sense to confess your mistake and stop eating, but most of us were taught to "eat what's on your plate"—and most of us carry a few extra pounds into middle age as a result. Avoiding the regret we might feel over the first poor decision, we drive ourselves into a second one, with more regret to come.

In an interesting wrinkle on the sunk cost effect, Orit Tykocinski and her colleagues have recently studied situations in which an initial failure to take advantage of an advantageous offer inclines people to pass up a later opportunity that, though good, is not quite as good as the original. They call this effect "inaction inertia," suggesting that once we have set off on the downward path of inaction, it is hard to stop ourselves from continuing down it. In a typical demonstration of the effect (Tykocinski & Pittman, 1998), half of a group of participants was told a story in which they had failed to take advantage of a 50% discount on an item they particularly want. The other half was not told about the sale. Both halves were told that the item is now on sale at a 20% discount. Do they think they will buy the item? Compared to participants who were unaware of the earlier 50% discount, far fewer of those who knew about it were willing to buy at the 20% discount. Again, regret avoidance seems to be the crucial link. Buying in the second sale forces the participants who knew about the earlier, larger, discount to experience the painful regret associated with missing out on the original opportunity. At least for many of us, the cost of passing up the second sale is worth it if it allows us to avoid acknowledging that first error. As with many of the sunk cost examples, decision makers may make a second mistake rather than acknowledging an earlier one and experiencing the resulting regret.

The simplest practical device to avoid these tempting traps is to keep straight what options are available and what their consequences might be: in our first example, "Keep car, repair brakes" might be one option, "Get rid of car, buy another" might be the other. The consequences of the first option will include the new brake job and its $200 cost, and the fact that the car has a repaired transmission. They will not, however, include the $600 already spent on that transmission. It is gone. It is not part of the current decision.

### Endowment and the Status Quo

Imagine the following scenario: You are a student in a large section of an economics course. As class starts one day, the instructor walks around the room carrying a large box of coffee mugs, each embossed with the university's crest—the sort of mug you see in every college bookstore. The instructor gives one of these mugs to half the students in the room, alternating along the rows of seats. He invites everyone in the room to examine a mug carefully and then provides an opportunity for trading. Students who got a mug fill out a form saying, "I would be prepared to sell this mug for any amount over $___." Students who did not get a mug fill out a form saying, "I would buy a mug for any price less than $___." How much trading would you expect to see?

To an economist, this question has a clear answer: About 50% of the students should engage in trading. The logic runs like this: It seems reasonable to think that different students evaluate the mugs differently, so irrespective of whether they got a mug or not, let us assume that about half of the students think the mugs are beautiful, memorable, or useful, and the other half think the mugs are ugly, vulgar, and useless. Let's call the two groups "mug lovers" and "mug haters." Since the mugs were given out at random, about half of those who got mugs are mug haters, which would be 25% of the class, and half of those who did not get mugs are mug lovers, which would be another 25% of the class. These two quarters of the class should be happy to trade with one another, with the result that about half the students should be involved in a trade (25% + 25% = 50%) with the haters getting cash (which they prefer to mugs) and the lovers getting mugs (which they prefer to cash). It should be a neat little classroom demonstration of the "gains to trade" argument, with everyone better off from the trades. But maybe not . . .

In fact, when researchers ran the mug experiment, they observed very little trading (Kahneman, Knetsch, & Thaler, 1991) because most mug owners asked too high a price and most non-owners offered too little. The results of follow-up experiments implied that this mismatch between prices and offers reflected something familiar—people come to like things they have and to value them accordingly. That is, the students who were initially given the mugs appeared to became attached to them and therefore were reluctant to give them up unless the amount they received was high enough to overcome their attachment—hence the high asking prices. Those who did not possess mugs offered what may have been a reasonable price for them, but that price fell short of the inflated asking price. This was labeled "the endowment effect." Once people have something they are attached to, they are reluctant to part with it at the market price, or perhaps even a higher price. What is more, the effect seems to happen very quickly after the item is acquired (Strahilevitz & Loewenstein, 1998).

The endowment effect is closely linked to another phenomenon called the "status quo bias," which is people's observed reluctance to change the current state of affairs without good reason—a bit like their unwillingness to give up a mug they own unless they receive an inflated price.

Samuelson and Zeckhauser (1988) examined nonoptional and optional decisions and the tendency in the latter case to maintain the status quo. They presented participants with various versions of six decision problems, each of which had two, three, or four alternatives and was presented in either of two conditions. In one condition change was nonoptional—it was inevitable, and the question was which alternative future was the best. In the other condition change was optional—one of the alternatives was identified by the experimenters as the status quo and the others were alternatives to it, but people could elect to stay with the alternative that had been designated as the status quo. For this second condition, the question for the participants was whether to remain with the status quo or replace it with one of the alternatives; they overwhelmingly elected to stay with the status quo. Later studies have found much the same results: for example, Silver (1989) found that merely telling people that one of two alternatives was the status quo biased them toward selecting that alternative, even when the other alternative was more attractive.

Real-life examples of the status quo bias abound. In countries (like most of Europe) where citizens are assumed to be organ donors unless they indicate otherwise, organ donation rates are as high as 70% to 80%. In countries (like the U.S.) where citizens are not donors unless they indicate a willingness to be, donation rates are as low as 10% to 20% (Johnson & Goldstein, 2003). Being a potential donor is the status quo for most Europeans, and not being a donor is the status quo for most Americans. The result of the universal disinclination to move from the status quo is that Europeans who need organ transplants are much more likely to get them than are Americans who need them.

In another example, in the early 1990s two states, New Jersey and Pennsylvania, allowed motorists to choose between two insurance policies, one (less expensive) that restricted the right to sue, the other (more expensive) that did not. New Jersey offered the cheaper policy as the default, which became the status quo for most citizens. Pennsylvania offered the more expensive as the default, but you might think that because the other policy was cheaper, people would make the effort to choose it. In fact, most Pennsylvania drivers simply stayed with the default insurance, the status quo (Johnson, Hershey, Meszaros, &

Kunreuther, 1992). The apparently innocuous "status quo" effect thus has large and significant effects on important real-world decisions.

It is easy enough to think of possible explanations for these interesting effects. Perhaps once I have a coffee mug I start to think of all the neat things I can do with it (pencil jar? paperweight? flower vase?), and the item becomes more valuable to me. Perhaps knowing very little about organ transplants or car insurance, I assume that the government has looked into the matter and selected the default as the option that makes sense for most people. However, perhaps the simplest explanation is the loss aversion built into prospect theory. Once we have something, having it becomes our reference point, so that parting with it is seen as a loss while its replacement (money, cheaper insurance), although seen as a gain, has to be very valuable in order to cancel out the loss. Losses are relatively more painful than equivalent gains are pleasurable, so unless the change is made very attractive (e.g., a very high offer for our coffee mug), we stay put.

## Overconfidence

Consider another seemingly simple classroom demonstration: Your instructor gives you a short quiz that lists 10 states in the U.S. and, for each state, asks you two questions. What is the capital of the state (fill in the blank)? And how sure are you that your answer is correct (circle a number between 0, I'm sure it is wrong, and 10, I'm sure it is right)? The instructor collects all the quizzes and tabulates the results. What do you think the results will look like?

Usually, the number of correct answers varies a lot: A few students know all the state capitals, some know none of them, and most are somewhere in between. But the interesting result is not how much the students know, it is whether or not they *know* how much they know. Does their confidence match their accuracy? That is, when the instructor looks at the answers for which students circled "I'm sure it is right," how many of them actually got the answer right? Similarly, for each point on the confidence scale, how many students were right for each level of confidence?

When this classroom exercise actually is done, students turn out to be overconfident. That is, of all the answers rated "I'm sure it is right," typically only about 75% of the students actually know the correct answer. Of the answers rated 50/50, only about 25% are correct. (Most of the answers rated 0 really are wrong, though now and then a right answer pops up in this category—lucky guesses?) This is a very common finding, both in casual classroom demonstrations and in careful research studies (e.g., Fischhoff, Slovic, & Lichstein, 1977): People's confidence generally is greater than justified given the quality of their performance.

Overconfidence is of no great consequence in classroom quizzes, of course. However, outside the classroom it can be very serious. If your investment adviser assures you that she is "100% confident" that a particular stock will go up, you may live to regret having invested a chunk of your savings in it. Similarly, if your surgeon tells you that he is 99% sure the operation he is recommending will repair your knee, what do you think the real chances are that you will be back on the ski slopes by the end of the year? What if your contractor is 80% sure he can have your kitchen remodeled in a month? (If you have ever dealt with contractors, you know this is wild-eyed overconfidence!) There are many such examples of important personal decisions in which decision makers rely on experts who provide assurance through telling them how confident they are about future events. Even though experts may be very good at what they do, prudence dictates that their confidence statements be taken with a grain of salt.

Interestingly, there is one area of expert judgment where the experts' confidence matches their accuracy: professional meteorologists estimating the probability of rain. Across all the times these experts say, "The probability of rain tomorrow is 40%," it really does rain on about 40% of the following days. When they say the probability is 90%, it nearly always rains the next day. And when they say the probability is 0%, you can safely leave your umbrella at home (Murphy & Winkler, 1974). This property, called "good calibration," is so exceptional in the world of confidence estimates that weather forecasters have been extensively studied to see what gives them their special edge. One part, not surprisingly, is that they are paid to be accurate and are penalized for over- or underconfidence. More important, they have good feedback and ample learning opportunities: They make similar forecasts day after day; there's no ambiguity about what event they are predicting; and they get immediate, clear feedback when it either rains or does not. Few everyday situations provide opportunities for clear feedback.

The more usual pattern, overconfidence, is an important problem in organizational life. Employees routinely overstate the probability (confidence) that their pet project will succeed (often shading their private overconfident guesses still farther to help them win support). Many projects then go on to fail or incur costly overruns. The distortion may be in either the estimate of how long the project will take (over-optimism) or in the estimate of the likely range of time it will take (as in, "I'm sure it will only take two to four weeks"). In one study of software writers (Connolly & Deane, 1997), nearly half the projects ended up with completion times that the programmers had earlier thought would be either "astonishingly short" or "astonishingly long," indicating that they had been confident that the project times would be more tightly clustered than actually turned out to be the case. It is easy to imagine how disruptive these errors are when others are basing their plans on the programmers' completion of their software projects.

### Feelings of Risk

Decision researchers have always been interested in people's feelings about risk, starting with Pascal's (in the 1600s) and Bernoulli's (in the 1700s) instructions to young noblemen about how to gamble. Some of the most basic issues remain unclear, however. Exactly *why* do most people refuse to play a coin-toss game in which they can win $10 on a head but lose $10 on a tail, which has an expected value of $0, or even win $10/lose $2.50, which has an expected value of $2.50? Do they have some strange anomaly in their utility functions? Is it because, as in prospect theory, they start with a reference point of zero, and the loss of losing looms larger than the gain of winning? Or is it just that they dislike the worrying feeling they would experience while the coin is in the air? Even more important, does the attitude toward risk that guides their behavior in simple gambling games carry over to other areas such as their willingness to engage in sky diving, exotic travel, or unsafe sex? (The evidence strongly suggests that the answer to this last question is "No." Many people are bold risk takers in one domain while being prudent and cautious in others.) There is even the puzzling finding that many people buy both insurance and lottery tickets, one reducing the risk they face, the other increasing it (Lopes, 1987).

A recent contribution to this long-running story is the "risk as feeling" research by Paul Slovic and his colleagues (Slovic, Finucane, Peters, & MacGregor, 2002) and, somewhat independently, by George Loewenstein and his colleagues (Loewenstein, Weber, Hsee, &

Welch, 2001). The core idea in this research reflects the theme of this chapter—when people assess risk they are guided as much by what they *feel* about the risky object or activity as by what they *think* about it. If someone asks you how risky a nuclear power plant is, for example, you might have immediate negative feelings about it—images of mushroom clouds and radiation release, harm to your unborn children. Especially if you have no solid information to the contrary, such negative feelings might lead you to overestimate the risks, and underestimate the benefits, of nuclear power.

Several classic studies (e.g., Slovic, 1987) strongly suggest that something like this is going on. When normal, moderately well-informed adults were asked to rate the seriousness of a whole list of risks—mountain climbing, swimming, various diseases, power mowers, and yes, nuclear power—the results tracked rather poorly against the data-based assessments made by experts. People tend to rate some risks lower than objective data would indicate (e.g., floods) and others higher (e.g., tornadoes). The key seems to be the feeling of *dread* the risk evokes. Floods seem so ordinary, and the way they do damage is so well understood, that they do not seem very dreadful (though they do, in fact, kill a lot of people and do a lot of damage). Nuclear power, on the other hand, is not well understood by most of us, and the ways in which it might damage us seem mysterious, making it a source of dread. Combining this sense of dread with several other relevant factors, such as whether the person engages in the activity voluntarily (e.g., mountain climbing) and whether it seems like the person can control the risk (e.g., driving), people rate risks by the severity of their emotions about them. Hence the large risk perceived for nuclear power plants: The dangers seem dreadful, ordinary people cannot control them, and their exposure to them usually is not something they have much control over. Added to this, the nuclear power industry seems to have lost the public's feeling of trust, at least in the U.S. (Slovic, 1993). Though the industry may be able to solve its technical problems, it has a long way to go before it overcomes the public's negative feelings about the nature of the risks it poses and its trustworthiness in dealing with them. The rational, analytical problems it faces may end up looking trivial compared to the emotional, intuitive assessments of the lay public.

This ends our discussion of emotions in decision making. This not an exhaustive list of the emotions that have been investigated, but these are the ones that have received the most attention and for which there is a literature large enough to warrant some conclusions. In the next chapter, we will continue this exploration of research that has gone beyond the first generation of behavioral research and theory, beyond heuristics and biases and prospect theory, to formulate behavioral theories about decision making that do not include the gamble analogy.

### ❖ SUMMARY

In this chapter we have looked at several topics in the growing research literature on the role of emotions in decision making. Most of what we have reviewed has grown out of a realization on the part of researchers that decision making is far more complex than characterized by prescriptive theory and normative models—even more complex than represented in heuristics and biases research and by prospect theory. This realization spurred efforts to explore beyond the prescriptive/normative bounds, and one focus of that exploration has been on the role of emotions in decision making.

The chapter began with a discussion of the impact of mood on decisions, even when the mood is induced by something as trivial as a kind word and a gift of candy. We then examined how regret and disappointment shape decisions, and how important it is to decision makers to be able to justify to themselves the choices they make and the processes by which they make them.

Next we saw how people may be willing to invest in a losing course of action merely because they have sunk so much into it that they hate to give it up, and why this seemingly sensible decision actually is a trap. We also saw how merely owning an object can inflate its value to the owner—the endowment effect—and how people tend to be biased in favor of the status quo over other alternatives, even when those other alternatives are more attractive than the status quo. And, we saw that people tend to be more confident in their judgments than their accuracy warrants—with the exception of meteorologists, who appear to be well calibrated. Finally, we saw that people evaluate risk by taking dread and other variables into account, often to the disadvantage of alternatives that actually are less risky than they think.

# 8

# Interpersonal, Organizational, and Group Decisions

*R* alph relaxed in his office. His sister-in-law, Professor Karma Howell, had spent two hours telling him about the research on emotion in decision making. He had found this interesting, but he still felt uncomfortable. It seemed as though the focus of everything he had learned to this point was about a single individual decision maker working alone. But he seldom made decisions all alone, and even when he did he had to think about how everyone else would react. And all that stuff about hiring new salespeople had been a group effort; he and Betty and Hank working together and being cranky together. He reached for the phone to call Karma; he wanted to know how the presence of other people colored decisions.

Nearly every decision involves other people one way or another. We are social creatures, and even when we make decisions alone we take into account the views and potential reactions of other people. More to the point, most of us spend most of our time with other people: our spouses, children, friends, and our colleagues at work. It therefore is more realistic to think of decision making as a social activity than it is to think of it as a solitary individual's activity.

When decision making is approached in this way three things immediately become clear. First, you must consider the possible effects of your decisions on others, partly out of a sense of fairness and partly to anticipate how they might react so you can temper your decisions accordingly. Second, and this follows from the first, you must cooperate with others in order to reach your own ends—success often is contingent upon the actions of others, and it is only through cooperation that all parties can attain the outcomes they desire. And third, anything that is important in interpersonal decisions probably is even more important, and complicated, in the context of organizations and groups.

## ❖  INTERPERSONAL DECISIONS

Our discussion of interpersonal decisions will focus on behavioral research that examines the descriptive adequacy of normative game models (called game theory) and normative negotiation models.

### Behavioral Game Research

Recall our description of the Prisoner's Dilemma in Chapter 4. Two prisoners are kept in separate rooms. Each is offered light punishment if he or she confesses and implicates the other person or heavy punishment if he or she keeps quiet but the other person confesses and implicates him or her, as opposed to very heavy punishment if they both confess or very light punishment if neither confesses. Note that for this game to be interesting there must be a possibility that both players care about what happens to the other player and both players try to forecast what the other will decide to do. If neither of these conditions holds, each player's optimal course is to be ruthless and betray the other player by confessing.

There are many variations on the Prisoner's Dilemma game and similar games, all of which require the players to make decisions in light of their assumptions about what the other player(s) will decide. It is this, perhaps most of all, that distinguishes games from the sorts of individual decisions that we have discussed in previous chapters. Game theory specifically acknowledges that decision making takes place in a social environment, but in its most rigorous form it regards the players much as prescriptive theory does—as thoroughly rational, strictly self-interested beings whose behavior is determined solely by the payoffs, although tempered by judgments about what the other player(s) might do (Luce & Raiffa, 1957).

Given the prescriptive viewpoint, game theory attempts to identify the players' optimal strategies, called "solution concepts." Many solution concepts have been offered, the best known of which is the "equilibrium solution" (Nash, 1951) for games in which players are not allowed to negotiate with each other. The equilibrium solution is self-enforcing in that if all the players adhere to it, it behooves no player to change his or her strategy (hence it is an equilibrium). There may be multiple Nash equilibria, which has led to attempts to identify a subset of them as the appropriate solutions, attempts known as "refinements" of the Nash solution. For different kinds of games there are different solution concepts, depending upon the particulars of the game.

The "centipede" game is fairly typical of the kind of research game theorists do. The diagram in Figure 8.1 is presented to the participants. The letters along the line at the top (the As and Bs) designate the two players' turns. Player A starts. She can choose either to stop the game, giving herself 10 points and Player B 1 point, or she can simply pass the play to Player B. Similarly, Player B can stop the game, giving Player A 2 points and herself 20 points, or she can pass the play back to Player A. The game proceeds until one or the other player stops it or until they reach the right-hand end of the centipede, where Player B must stop

**Figure 8.1**    Structure of the Centipede Game

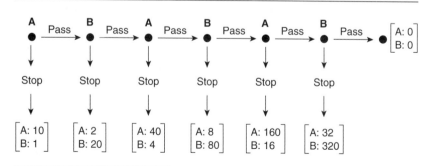

the game, giving Player A 32 points and herself 320 points. If she does not stop, both players receive 0 points and the game ends anyway.

Because the centipede diagram is sitting right in front of them, Player A can anticipate that Player B is bound to stop on the last leg of the centipede, so she is inclined to stop on the next-to-last leg rather than give the last leg to Player B. Similarly, Player B can anticipate Player A's anticipation of her strategy for the last leg and can presume that Player A will stop on the next-to-last leg, so she may decide to stop on the third-to-last leg. Of course, Player A can anticipate Player B's anticipation of her anticipation of her anticipation . . . well, you get the idea.

The upshot is that the solution concept is for Player A to stop on the first leg. However, participants generally do not stop early; they are more likely to play a turn or two, trusting their opponent to stay in the game (McKelvey & Palfrey, 1992). On the other hand, as the game progresses both players begin to worry and trust wears thin. The tricky part is to trust your opponent long enough to build up the payoffs, but not so long that she gets to stop first.

Insofar as it is possible to identify a solution concept for a game, or to delineate a set of appropriate solutions (strategies), game theory is a normative model in the sense discussed in previous chapters. And, as was stated above, just as behavioral decision research examines the degree to which normative models are adequate descriptions of relevant aspects of decision makers' actual behavior, behavioral game research examines the adequacy of normative game theory as a description of players' actual interpersonal game-playing behavior. Of particular interest are two non-economic factors (externalities) that research has repeatedly found to influence players' strategy selections: fairness and cooperation.

*Fairness*

Numerous studies show that players' decisions reflect a preference for fairness in the distribution of payoffs, which means that the game theory assumption of strict self-interest is incorrect. This does not necessarily mean that game theory is wholly wrong, because fairness can be interpreted as a determiner of utility by incorporating the player's concerns about the outcome to be received by the other player(s).

One paradigm for studies of fairness involves one player, A, choosing one of several possible distributions of money to be divided between herself and another player, B. For example, the experimenter might present A with the distributions 4, 10; 5, 5; or 12, 0, in which A would get the first amount and B would get the second. Player A chooses one of the distributions and negotiates with B, who must agree to using that distribution or neither player receives anything at all.

The theoretical solution is for A to choose the distribution that offers the largest total payoff and, in addition, demand a side payment from B that will end up giving A most of the payoff. With the distributions given above, A should choose 4, 10 and then demand a side payment of 8 or more to make the total at least 12, which is what A would get in the 12, 0 distribution if it had been chosen and agreed to by B. The idea is that B should agree to this deal because even a little something for agreeing to A's demands is better than nothing at all, which is what B would get for refusing A's demands. In theory, even if B stands to gain as little as one penny, he or she should agree to A's offer.

In fact, however, people who play A in these experiments seldom demand anything like the theoretically prescribed deal. Most often they split the payoffs equally between themselves and B, going for what they perceive to be the "fair distribution." On the other hand, the A players can be induced to offer deals that favor themselves if they are told that they had "earned the right" to play the role of A, or if they win that right in some preceding game of skill (Hoffman & Spitzer, 1985). As Camerer (1990) observes, unequal division can be acceptable if people think that the right to the larger share has somehow been earned. Apparently, earning the right allows unequal division of the payoffs to be regarded as fair, and fairness seems to be the dominant factor in the players' decisions.

Fairness also arises in what are called "ultimatum games." These are not unlike the game described above, but they lack the negotiation of a side-payment—A merely offers the division of payoffs to B, who must take it or leave it. Again, if B fails to take the offer, neither player gets anything. (The situation is analogous to buying something from a monopoly; you pay their price or go without.) As before, the theoretical prescription is for A to keep the largest share and offer B a pittance; B should accept any offer because it is better than nothing.

Again, fairness reigns. People who play the role of A seldom offer B less than 40% of the total payoff—not exactly a .50 –.50 split, but not .99 –.01 either. Moreover, people who play the role of B often refuse offers that give them less than about 20% of the payoff, contrary to the theoretical prescription that they should be grateful for any amount greater than zero. In short, people who play A tend to give fairer offers than they have to, and people who play B would rather receive nothing than accept an offer they see as grossly unfair.

Just as earning the right to an unequal distribution of payoffs seems to qualify the distribution as fair, demonstration of a true need for a disproportionate share of the payoff, as opposed to merely wanting it, also seems to qualify as fair. Of course, both earning and true need are externalities—not strictly part of the normative game theory model.

### Cooperation

The question of cooperation most often arises in the context of what is called "social dilemmas" and the issue of "free riding." The classical example of a social dilemma is the "dilemma of the commons" (Hardin, 1968). Imagine a village that has a common pasture on which each of the $n$ households can place one cow. The pasture can support only $n$ cows: any more leads to a reduction in food for the herd and a consequent reduction in the health of all of the cows. Thus it is in the best interest of the village as a whole to limit the number of cows to $n$, but it is in the best interest of each individual household to place a second cow on the pasture. The $n+1$ cow would slightly decrease the health of all the cows, including the extra one, but the "free riding" household would still be ahead by having two slightly unhealthy cows rather than just one very healthy cow. The hitch is, of course, that if every household behaves this way, the ever-growing herd will become increasingly unhealthy and everyone will be ruined. It is only by each player forgoing the opportunity to increase his or her advantage that the group as a whole can prosper.

A similar dilemma arises in the case of what are called "collective goods," for example, a public park or a public sports facility. Someone must fund the collective good in order for it to be provided. From a strictly self-interested viewpoint, an individual ought to elect to be a free rider—to use the park or sports facility but to resist contributing to its provision.

There have been numerous studies of social dilemmas and of contributions to the collective good. The major finding is that people tend to be cooperative even when they could do better by not being so. That is, they contribute more to the collective than they would if they were being guided strictly by self-interest. Indeed, people who value the collective good highly, or who have more resources, contribute even more (Rapoport, 1988). Moreover, if the players can discuss the game, or if the experimenter "preaches" about cooperation, contributions increase, especially if the contribution benefits the player's own colleagues (Camerer, 1990). In short, people tend to avoid taking the self-interested position of becoming a free rider.

The foregoing is merely the tip of the iceberg for behavioral game research. There are games of such wonderful complexity that one doubts that the players can comprehend them (indeed, players often simplify complex games by ignoring parts of them and making them into more tractable games). It is beyond the scope of our presentation to discuss them, but the results presented above give you the theme: By and large, unbridled self-interest is uncommon; people are sensitive to the economic factors embodied in the games, but they impose their own standards of fairness and cooperation. The resulting picture is of decision makers who are less ruthless and less selfish than game theory assumes.

## Behavioral Negotiation Research

Negotiation is a process in which two or more players decide what each will give and each will take in an exchange between them (Rubin & Brown, 1975). Negotiations are games, in the sense discussed above, but the rules of play are slightly different. As with games, the players presume that they have conflicting interests, but (1) communication is possible, (2) compromise is possible, (3) players may make provisional offers and counteroffers, but (4) offers and counteroffers do not result in outcomes until accepted by the players (Thompson, 1990). As with games, the normative model for negotiation derives from economics and prescriptive decision theory (Raiffa, 1982; Rapoport, 1966). The basic idea is that the players (and, for simplicity, we will assume that there are only two players—although they may represent constituencies) arrive on the scene with "reservation prices," which are the least they will settle for without walking away from the negotiation, and "targets," which is what they really want. The difference between the two players' reservation prices is called the "zone of agreement," the range of outcomes within which negotiation can take place.

Negotiations can be about dividing some fixed amount of a resource (distributive bargaining) or about adding to the resource (integrative bargaining). Negotiations in which the players do not have compatible interests involve distributive bargaining, and the normative prescription is to maximize one's gains at the expense of the other player. When there is at least some compatibility of interests, the negotiation calls for integrative bargaining, and the normative prescription is to seek the agreement that maximizes the players' joint profit. Integrative agreements allow both parties to do better than they would if they merely negotiated about the distribution of a fixed amount of a resource, because the essence of integrative agreement is that it expands the resource so each player gets more than he or she otherwise would receive. An integrative agreement is said to be "Pareto optimal" if no other agreement would improve the utility of one or both players while not hurting either player (Nash, 1950).

But do negotiators seek integrative solutions? Neale and Northcraft (1986) had both novices (students) and professional negotiators participate in a negotiation simulation. Actually, the experiment was done separately on the novices and the professionals. Half of each group was assigned the role of being a buyer (retail stores) and the other half assigned the role as seller (manufacturers of refrigerators). They were told that the issues for negotiation involved delivery terms, discount terms, and financial terms. Then they were given information about profits as a function of different levels and combinations of these three issues and asked to negotiate as many deals as they could in 25 minutes. The profits were set up so that integrative solutions were optimal, and the question was whether participants therefore would seek such solutions. The answer was that they did; they were not perfect at it, but they got better at it the more deals they made. Moreover, while the expert negotiators moved more quickly to integrative solutions and always did a better job, the novices improved with time and ended up performing nearly as well as the experts.

Just to help you think about integrative solutions, Follett (1940) provided the most frequently cited example: two people negotiating over the distribution of a basket of oranges discover that one wants the juice and the other wants the peels. Because of the discovery, conflict over distribution ceases and an integrative agreement leads to one player taking all of the juice and the other taking all of the peels. This agreement provides both players with more than they would have obtained had they merely divided the oranges, no matter what distribution they agreed upon. In general, differences between the players in terms of how they value the various characteristics of the resource of interest provide opportunities for integrative agreements.

### Fairness and Cooperation

Distributive and integrative agreements almost automatically evoke the two concepts we discussed when examining behavioral game research: fairness and cooperation. Fairness is of particular concern when the negotiation involves division of some fixed set of resources, and it clearly influences how players feel about the offers they make and receive and how they feel about the final agreement they reach. Cooperation is necessary if a resource is to be expanded—if a suitable integrative agreement is to be reached. When players ignore fairness or cooperation and only look out for their own interests, negotiations often reach an impasse and nobody profits. Players seem particularly sensitive to exploitative behavior on the part of opponents, particularly opponents who misrepresent their reservation price (Gruder, 1971). Similarly, when players try to control rather than cooperate, they are less likely to reach an integrative agreement (Tjosvold, 1978).

The desire for fairness and cooperation is influenced by the conditions under which negotiation takes place. In the first place, players' views about what is fair often are self-serving. Messick and Sentis (1979) asked players to specify a fair rate of pay for themselves when they had worked 10 hours and another person had been paid $25 for working 7, and a fair rate for the other person when they had been paid $25 for working 7 hours and the other person had worked 10 hours. In the first case they awarded themselves an average of $35.24 for the 10 hours they worked, and in the second case they awarded the other person only $30.29 for the 10 hours they worked. That hardly seems like perfect fairness.

On the good side, however, players tend to behave more generously when negotiation takes place face to face instead of through the mail or over the phone, and they are more generous when they expect to have to negotiate with the opponent in the future (Ben-Yoav & Pruitt, 1984a, 1984b). Understandably, they are less generous when the constituencies they represent pressure them to "win" (Neale, 1984; Tjosvold, 1977).

### ❖ ORGANIZATIONAL DECISIONS

To understand organizational decisions, we must recall that the members of organizations work together, however haphazardly, to construct socially shared frames for events. This relies upon the shared culture, the common core of understanding that exists throughout the organization, or at least in parts of the organization. It is this common culture, and the frames it provides, that allows people to work together and to communicate about the events that occur and the goals that they share. Without this shared understanding there would not be an organization in any real sense.

Shared understanding is never perfect. It frequently is the case that nobody knows all that is to be known about an issue and different people often know different things about it. This means that to one degree or another they all conceive of the problem differently. That is, they tend to frame things differently, meaning that they are all starting from different assumptions and are trying to tackle different problems—often the differences are small, but sometimes they are large.

The upshot is that, in the aggregate, most organizational decision problems are very ill defined and the decision options are not at all clear. Indeed, decision making is a decidedly disorderly process in which the search for a good definition of the problem engenders ideas about possible solutions that in turn influence the problem definition and further thinking about options. It clearly is a very complicated, convoluted, involved process that, to the outside observer, often looks like total chaos.

On top of all of this add coalitions and the differential power of the various participants, and things really get complex. Seldom are major decisions made by everyone who has a stake in what is decided, especially in large organizations. More often, decisions are made by representatives of the various units in the organization, each of which has its own interests, or representatives of various powerful coalitions in the organization, each of which has its own turf to guard and power to protect. The result is a form of negotiation, sometimes covert, sometimes overt, in which various representatives attempt to advance the interests of their sponsors by influencing the problem definition and option formulation as well as by having an impact on the final decision. Of course, if your power allows you to define the problem and delineate the options, you can constrain things so much that the decision is a foregone conclusion.

## Organizational Models

One way of attempting to impose order on the apparent chaos is to classify the various models of organizational decision making that guide both research and applied prescriptions, and to see what each contributes to a larger picture. Work on this was begun by Koopman and Pool (1991), and it is their general outline that we will follow here.

### The Rational Model

Most of the early descriptions of decision making in organizations were guided by the prescriptive/normative viewpoint described in previous chapters of this book. The model usually presumes that there is only one paramount goal and that the members of the organization, individually and collectively, strive to achieve that goal. It presumes that the decision makers have unlimited information and possess the cognitive ability to use it efficiently; they know all of the opportunities open to them and all of the consequences of pursuing one or another of those opportunities. Finally, it presumes that the optimal course of action can be revealed by applying the appropriate normative analysis and that choice of that course of action will, if only in the long run, prove to be more profitable than choice of any other course of action. The key concepts are rationality, analysis, orderliness, and maximization, which, as we have seen, people do not do very well.

### The Information Model

Doubts about the practicality of the rational model led to revisions, primarily in regard to assumptions about the cognitive abilities of decision makers. Simon (1945) and March and Simon (1958) pointed out that decision makers use only part of the information that potentially is available, both because they are cognitively limited and can handle only so much information at a time, and because there are resource constraints on acquiring complete information even if it is available. Decisions often are made when a sufficient option is encountered (called "satisficing") rather than after a prolonged search for the best option. Moreover, even when search is undertaken, it usually is limited—starting with options that have worked in the past and moving to new options only when old ones are demonstrably unsuitable. Indeed, only about 20% of the time are new options sought or considered.

*The Structural Model*

March and Simon (1958) suggest that the limited information processing and analysis capacities of individuals can be compensated for by properly structuring the organization—breaking it into appropriate units and apportioning various parts of the process to the units that have the corresponding capability. Although this may be a wise strategy, there still are problems with agreement about the organization's goals and adequate communication of those goals to the units. Even more telling is the lack of concentrated control over implementation of an option or part of an option—so if things do not go as planned, changes cannot quickly be made. The result is that decisions progress step by step rather than being made and committed to. This step-by-step process, called "incrementalism" (Lindblom, 1959) allows the decision maker or decision making unit to proceed cautiously in a general direction, changing things in light of feedback about the success of what is being done. In the course of this, wholly new options may evolve, options that were not obvious at the time the original decision was being considered. This process has been criticized as unduly conservative (Etzioni, 1967), but it has its defenders (Quinn, 1980).

Structural differentiation often proves to be inadequate because it promotes a limited view of the overall decision problem in favor of emphasis on the part for which a unit is responsible. Conflict often arises from a diversity of interests, from settling for local benefits at the expense of benefits for the organization as a whole, from an unwillingness of units to take risks for fear of losing out to other units and a resulting tendency to pass off hard problems to weaker units that are the least able to deal with them adequately. It is in this context that issues of power arise, how units (and individuals) derive power from their ability to control parts of the organization's environment, how difficult it is to replace them, how central they are to the organization's key activities, and so on (Hickson, Hinnings, Lee, Schneck, & Pennings, 1971). Certainly, exertion of power, struggles for power, and internal politics all heavily influence how decisions are made and how successfully they are implemented.

Often, structural differentiation is coupled with top-down managerial control, sometimes called bureaucratic organizational structure. Decision making can proceed rather efficiently in such organizations if top management lays out the guidelines for how decisions are to be handled by the units, and how those different decisions are to be brought together to form a plan of action for the organization as a whole. Mintzberg, Raisinghani, and Theoret (1976) referred to this form of decision control as "meta–decision making"—decisions about how decisions will be made. Combined with structural differentiation, meta–decision making can be a powerful way of confronting the limitations highlighted by the information model, discussed above, and is fundamental to the notion of strategic management.

## The Garbage Can Model

Consideration of the apparent chaos in organizations led Cohen, March, and Olsen (1972) to propose the garbage can model of managerial decision making, an evocative name that has afforded the model more attention than it perhaps deserves. Here organizations are seen as "organized anarchies," with unclear or inconsistent goals, using technologies that are not well understood by the organization's members, and relying upon decisions in which the members are inconsistent participants.

The basic premise is that organizations are collections of problems, solutions, participants, and choice opportunities in which participants must link problems and solutions (i.e., make decisions). These elements are randomly mixed together in a garbage can, which means that solutions can precede problems, or that both solutions and problems may await a choice opportunity, or that they all may come together when a particular set of participants convenes. In short, combinations of elements are intrinsically unpredictable—which is the attempt to mimic the apparent chaos in organizations. The model is an assault on the rationalistic description of decision making as identification of a problem, identification of options, evaluation of options, selection of an optimal option, and solution of the problem. It more closely resembles the idea of "a solution in search of a problem," and similar clichés characterizing decision making as it often is observed in organizations.

The garbage can model does not necessarily imply that organizations are wholly irrational. It merely suggests that the attention of participants is divided and that decisions do not derive from the unidirectional, linear processes prescribed by a more rationalistic approach. Indeed, the garbage can model says almost nothing about decision processes per se. Its description is similar to what might be given by the legendary Man from Mars who happens to land on a university campus. He hears the many different opinions, watches the different governance bodies, notes that nobody attends every meeting or understands every nuance of the problems under discussion, and observes that from this chaos some kind of direction emerges, even though no single person may be able to articulate it clearly. In spite of everything, the university appears to soldier on, to meet its obligations, to survive. Convinced that some sort of miracle has taken place, our Martian e-mails a description of what he has observed to the folks back home. The description might look a lot like the garbage can model.

## The Participation Model

Both the structural model and the garbage can model emphasize the roles of groups of participants in decision making. The participation model carries this farther by examining the advantages and disadvantages of member participation as well as the conditions under which participation is warranted.

It is argued that involvement of an organization's members in group decision making contributes to better decisions and greater satisfaction with, and greater confidence in, the decisions on the part of the participants. The advantage of better decisions seems obvious, although it really is not clear whether it means decisions that are made better, in the sense of more thoroughness, or whether it means that the decisions produce better results—decision researchers favor the first definition and decision makers prefer the second. The advantage of increased satisfaction with whatever is decided supposedly lies in a greater commitment on the part of the participants to implementation of the decision.

Because groups are composed of people who do not all have the same viewpoints and the same prior experience, it can be argued that the pool of resources is greater for groups than for individuals trying to make the same decisions. However, studies show that group discussion tends to focus on what is known by everyone, and relevant information possessed by individual members either goes unmentioned or tends to be ignored when it is brought up (Sniezek, Paese, & Furiya, 1990; Stasser & Titus, 1985).

An experiment by Heath and Gonzalez (1995) demonstrates how studies are done in this area, and provides interesting results. The experimenters were testing the hypothesis that an advantage of group interaction is that participants share information and therefore make better decisions. Pairs of participants were specially selected for their knowledge about football. Each week, each participant predicted the outcome of 14 football games by choosing the winner of each game and stating the probability that that team would win. Then they each met with a partner to "share information and opinions," after which they individually made new predictions. It was found that choices were not more accurate after the opportunity to exchange information about the teams, but that participants were significantly more confident in their post-discussion choices than in their earlier choices. The experimenters suggest that interaction in groups acts primarily to increase the members' confidence in whatever they subsequently decide as individuals rather than improving the quality of their decisions. Of course, the danger is that interaction will lead to confidence in what will in fact prove to be a poor decision (Janis, 1972, 1982; Sniezek, 1992).

Other research suggests that participation often decreases productivity (e.g., Locke & Schweiger, 1979; Wagner & Gooding, 1987). After all, group meetings and group discussions take up a lot of time that might otherwise be spent working, and the quality of the group decisions is not always very high. Detailed examination shows that participation is most useful if it can take advantage of expertise or if the reason for using it is to promote acceptance on the part of participants (Heller, Drenth, Koopman, & Rus, 1988; Koopman, 1980). Much the same conclusions are reached in studies of teamwork and team building (Katzenbach & Smith, 1993).

❖ GROUP DECISIONS

The participation model has had immense influence on small group research. The scope of this research extends well beyond our immediate interests, but there are three areas that are of particular pertinence to decision research: the conditions that call for group participation in decision making, the conditions that promote group generation of an increased range of decision options, and the conditions that lead to group consensus about one of those options and confidence in the correctness of that option.

### Participation

One of the focal points for thinking about participation has been the Vroom and Yetton (1973) model of managerial decision making.

Building on a store of earlier work on participation, the model holds that an organization's members can participate to different degrees in managerial decision making and that the leader's task is to select the right level of member involvement in light of the characteristics of the decision problem. The lowest level (A1) excludes them altogether; the leader makes the decision. The second level (A2) merely invites them to contribute information; the leader makes the decision, which may or may not reflect the input. The third level (C1) provides them with information about the problem and solicits each individual's ideas and suggestions; the leader makes the decision, which may or may not reflect the input. The fourth level (C2) provides them with information and solicits their collective ideas and recommendations; the leader makes the decision, which may or may not reflect the input. The fifth level (G) provides them with information about the problem and convenes them as a group to arrive at a consensus that becomes the organization's final decision.

The problem characteristics that determine which of these five levels of participation is appropriate are (1) the extent to which the quality of the decision is important, (2) the extent to which the leader possesses the expertise and information necessary to make the decision alone, (3) the extent to which the problem is clearly structured, (4) the extent to which member acceptance and commitment is critical to successful implementation of the decision, (5) the extent to which an autocratic decision by the leader will be accepted by members, (6) the extent to which members are motivated by the organization's goals rather than their own agendas, and (7) the extent to which members are likely to be able to reach consensus. The idea is that a leader can use these characteristics to make a meta-decision about which level to use for making a specific decision.

There have been numerous attempts to "test" the Vroom and Yetton model. Many of them have found that self-reports by managers about the level of participation used for various successful and unsuccessful decisions indicate greater success when the level conformed to the prescriptions of the model (Thomas, 1990; Vroom & Jago, 1978; Zimmer, 1978).

On the other hand, persistent criticisms of the model prompted Vroom and Jago (1988) to add five more situational characteristics to the seven listed above. These are (8) the extent to which members have sufficient information to make a quality decision, (9) the extent to which time constraints preclude involvement of members in the decision, (10) the extent to which it is prohibitive to bring together geographically dispersed members for group participation, (11) the extent to which the decision must be made quickly, and (12) the extent to which it is important to foster member development through participation.

Brown and Finstuen (1993) used the self-report method used in earlier research to examine the new version of the model. The results did not support the contention that the highest scoring level of participation was necessarily the best, but the model was successful in identifying the relative effectiveness of the five levels. Although the researchers interpret their results as providing strong support for the revised version of the model, they point out that the computational complexity of the structural equations raises questions about their practical usefulness for managers. On the other hand, the model provides a major service for managers and researchers alike by identifying the situational factors that influence the effectiveness of member participation in managerial decision making.

## Option Generation

Since 1957, when A. F. Osborn, an advertising executive, published his book about "brainstorming," there has been ongoing controversy about the value of group participation in option generation for decision making. Brainstorming is aimed at enhancing the group's creativity by encouraging free discussion and free exchange of ideas. It claims to work by separating idea generation from idea evaluation, on the premise that premature evaluation causes participants to become more cautious and less imaginative. Premature evaluation results in fewer new and potentially valuable ideas being available to the group during their deliberations—leading to conservative, familiar solutions to problems being chosen when the problems might profit from more adventurous approaches. The four rules of brainstorming are (1) criticism must be withheld during the generation stage so participants are not discouraged from contributing novel ideas; (2) odd, even crazy, ideas are encouraged so that unique, unapparent options can be discovered; (3) the more ideas, the better because quantity increases the chances that a good option will appear; and (4) using others' suggestions as a source of ideas about options is acceptable—sometimes called "piggybacking."

The usual measure of the effectiveness of brainstorming is the number and creativity of the ideas that are generated by a group as compared to the number and creativity of the ideas generated by a equal number of people working independently. Unfortunately, an extensive body of research shows that for both quality and creativity, brainstorming groups are seldom more effective, and certainly less efficient, than individuals—even when redundant ideas by individuals are not counted (Davis, 1992; Diehl & Stroebe, 1987; McGrath, 1984). Indeed, some research finds that, in direct contradiction of assumptions underlying brainstorming, evaluative groups are *more* productive than supportive groups (Connolly, Jessup, & Valacich, 1990).

### Consensus and Confidence

Beginning with the classic Asch (1956) experiments on conformity, small-group research has explored how the members of groups are influenced by group processes. Of this work, there are two areas of particular interest to us: the risky shift phenomenon and procedural effects.

In the 1960s it was reported that groups tend to be more extreme than individuals in their willingness or unwillingness to endorse risky decisions (Nordhoy, 1962; Stoner, 1961; Wallach, Kogan, & Bem, 1962). This difference can be viewed as a shift when one moves from individuals to groups, called the "risky shift" (or more appropriately, the "choice shift").

There has been an enormous amount of interest in the risky shift because it implies that group members end up agreeing to decisions that they would not make as individuals. One explanation is that group members can endorse a more risky alternative because responsibility is diffused across all of the members, but this fails to explain shifts in the conservative direction. Another explanation is that some decisions evoke members' social values for risk taking, and when, during the group discussion, they find that they are less extreme than some of the others in the group, they take an even more extreme position. Similarly, some problems evoke social values for conservatism, and the same mechanism comes into play during discussion of the problem, resulting in less extreme positions. However, shifts in both directions have been observed for problems that have no social content and thus could not evoke values favoring risk or conservatism.

The explanation that appears to have the most going for it is that shifts reflect the emergence of a dominant faction during discussions, and because participants assume that the majority has a right to have its decision be the group decision, opposition members subordinate their views (while not necessarily changing them) to the dominant view (Davis, 1992). This explanation is particularly plausible because the majority view usually becomes obvious, either in the course of the discussion or because procedures permit it to be emphasized. For example, it is common procedure for the group leader to summarize "the sense of the meeting," or for straw votes to be taken prior to a final vote. Straw votes, at least, have been shown to have a sizable impact on the opinions of members who hold other than the dominant view (Davis, Stasson, Ono, & Zimmerman, 1988).

Majority rule is but one convention that may influence the outcomes of group decision making. Others involve use of an explicit agenda for meetings, rules for speaking (recognition by the chair, turn-taking), voting procedures (secret ballot, show of hands), and criteria for arriving at a decision (majority, plurality, averaging). Each of these constrains how the discussion will proceed, how information is presented and persuasion is attempted, and how the final outcome will be determined. As an example of agenda effects, Davis, Tindale, Nagao, Hinsz, and Robertson (1984) showed that when charges against a defendant were considered in decreasing order of seriousness, juries were more inclined to convict on a serious charge than when the charges were considered in an ascending order. In another example, Plott and Levine (1976) influenced the decisions of a recreational organization by manipulating the agenda such that successive decisions narrowed down the options until only the one favored by the researchers remained.

Perhaps the most famous examination of group consensus in decision making was done by Irving Janis (1972), resulting in what he called "groupthink"—an overemphasis on consensus and a consequent failure to critically evaluate assumptions and options when the group is highly cohesive. Janis illustrated his ideas using six major decisions by groups acting for the American government. The theory involves three categories of necessary conditions: cohesiveness of the group, characteristics of the organization, and characteristics of the situation. When these conditions are right, groupthink occurs, resulting in defective decision making and inferior outcomes. Symptoms of groupthink are illusions of invulnerability, unanimity, and group morality; stereotyping of oppositions as "the enemy," weak, evil, or stupid; self-censorship in which members fail to bring up counterarguments or concerns;

censorship of others so that counterarguments do not reach influential members of the group; and direct pressure to keep errant members in line.

Like the garbage can model discussed above, the groupthink theory has an evocative label that perhaps gives the underlying ideas the appearance of more solidity than they deserve. In fact, the surprisingly sparse research literature on groupthink shows that support from experimental investigations is mixed at best; most of the support comes from case studies, in which both the selection of the particular case and the investigator's expectations can more easily influence the reported results (Park, 1990). Meta-analyses of experimental studies are not particularly encouraging either. For example, based on nine research reports (17 experimental conditions), Mullen, Anthony, Salas, and Driskell (1994) conclude that group cohesiveness, a major theoretical variable, does not itself impair decision quality; interpersonal attraction may have a deleterious effect, but apparently even it can be compensated for by commitment to the task. Until there is more, and better, research, the jury is out. Groupthink may well be a good theory, but as things stand, one simply does not know.

Consensus is one thing—a group member may vote with the majority for any number of reasons—but actually believing in the correctness of the decision is another thing. Belief, usually studied as confidence in the group's decision, is important because subsequent support of the decision implementation probably is dependent upon it. Actually, there are two ways of looking at confidence: the confidence of individual decision makers in their group's decision, and the confidence in that decision arrived at by the group as a whole. Comparison of the two shows that the group's confidence tends to be higher than the individuals' (Sniezek & Henry, 1989, 1990). Sniezek (1992) suggests that the higher group confidence may be the result of explicit or implicit pressure to achieve consensus and that consensus is treated as a cue to accuracy, thereby justifying higher group confidence. Indeed, Boje and Murnighan (1982) found that members of groups that reached consensus were satisfied with and accepting of their decisions and wanted to continue working together even though the decisions often were not as good as those of groups with lower consensus. As Sniezek (1992) reminds us, high confidence is not a good thing if the decision is not a good decision.

In closing, it is interesting to note that one of the pervasive arguments for using groups in organizational decision making is that it permits pooling of information held by the group's members and thus contributes to more informed, and presumably better, decisions. This suggests that because they are better informed, groups are correct in being confident about their decisions. Unfortunately, examinations of information sharing in groups shows that members do far less of it than this argument assumes; group discussion tends to focus on what is known by everyone, and uniquely held information tends to be ignored (Sniezek et al., 1990; Stasser & Titus, 1985).

❖ SUMMARY

Previous chapters have viewed decision making as a rather solitary activity. This chapter departs from that view by recognizing the interpersonal, organizational, and group nature of most decision making. We began by examining interpersonal decisions as they are studied using normative models (game theory and the normative negotiation model) that derive from prescriptive decision theory. In both cases it is found that fairness and cooperation are important aspects of observed behavior, neither of which is represented in the normative models.

We then examined the major models that drive thinking about decision making in organizations and groups and again found that prescriptive logic fares as badly for organizations as it does for individuals, and while each of the alternative models has its strengths, they also have their weaknesses. The participation model has been the main focus for much of the behavioral research on organizational decision making. The Vroom and Yetton (1973) and Vroom and Jago (1978) examinations of conditions that call for member participation in managerial decisions have had a major impact on academic research and exerted some influence on managerial practice, if only as a conceptual framework within which to consider participation.

Group consensus is consistently interesting to researchers and practitioners alike. The so-called risky shift phenomenon and groupthink are included in virtually every management textbook and are broadly accepted as persistent dangers when groups make decisions.

Researchers appear to be making progress on understanding choice shifts, but the jury is still out on groupthink.

Studies suggest that group interaction and group consensus may lead to overconfidence in group decisions, but the implications of this are dependent upon how that confidence influences commitment and investment in implementation of those decisions. This is an area of research that shows a great deal of promise from both a theoretical and a practical standpoint.

# 9

# Alternatives to Gambling

*R*alph had spent Saturday afternoon talking with his sister-in-law, *Professor Karma Howell. She had taken him through the research on emotions in decision making, and he could identify with everything she said. It seemed to him that psychologists were beginning to get a handle on emotion, but they clearly still had a way to go.*

*Afterwards, when they were having coffee at Starbucks, Ralph recalled something that had bothered him for weeks. It seemed to him that so much of the thinking about decision making involved gambles and all the concepts related to gambles. But when he thought about the decisions he made as part of his daily routine, he couldn't recall ever thinking that he was gambling. In fact, once he made a decision, he worked as hard as he could to make sure it turned out okay. He certainly was not passive like he was in Las Vegas, waiting for the roulette wheel to decide his fate. This "decisions = gambles" notion had never seemed right to him, so he asked Karma if there were any ways of characterizing decision making that might fit better with what he thought he did when he made decisions.*

The study of emotions in decision making (Chapter 7) and much of the work on organizational and group decisions are both departures from first generation decision research and theory. The third departure involves efforts to construct behavioral decision theories that do not incorporate the gamble analogy that is so central to prescriptive theory and first generation behavioral work. Together, the research on emotions, organizations, and groups and efforts to construct alternative decision theories constitutes a second generation of behavioral research and theory.

The effort to build gamble-less decision theories is motivated by the work of organizational researchers, systems designers, public policy and business researchers, and others who have found prescriptive theory and the first generation work inadequate for their practical needs, as well as by the doubt of some mainstream decision researchers about the viability, or necessity, of the gamble analogy and related concepts. Thus far the yield has been a series of small descriptive theories and astute observations (which will be described in this chapter) that have given guidance to the construction of a more comprehensive descriptive theory. The theories we will examine represent the newest (and if not always the newest, at least the most persistent) ideas about how decision making takes place naturally—without reference to gambling or the other features of prescriptive theory. None of them actually constitutes a full-blown theory, but each highlights one or more issues that a more comprehensive theory must address.

Our discussion of these theories will flow more easily if we impose some order. Let us divide them into four categories: recognition theories, narrative theories, incremental theories, and moral/ethical theories.

### Recognition Theories

*Policy.* The role of recognition in decision making has two facets. First, no matter how it is conceived of, decision making requires that the context be taken into account, and this means that the decision maker must be able to interpret ongoing events in terms of his or her past experience and existing store of knowledge. That is, much of the information that informs decision making derives from the decision maker's understanding about how the current situation came to be, how it relates to other situations that are occurring elsewhere at the same time, and how it relates to situations that will occur in the future. A decision maker armed with all the decision technology in the world would be completely stalled if he or she could not call on past experience and knowledge about ongoing events. In this sense, recognition is implicit in any theory of decision making.

The second facet of recognition is, however, the one that has received the most attention from decision researchers. In the context of organizations, Simon (1979) has described the role of standard operating procedures and programmed responses to specified situations as a form of decision making. Standard operating procedures usually are very specific: "When situation X arises, do Y." This requires the decision maker to recognize situations that fit the description of situation X. To the degree that situation X is specified in detail, recognition is merely a process of matching features of the present situation to the prototype, situation X. Of course, real situations seldom are an exact fit to the prototype, so some discretion is required, and it is this that qualifies the matching process as a decision: How close is close enough, and what do the points of mismatch mean?

When only general guidelines are given about situation X, the prescription for responding usually is called a "policy." That is, when situation X is a broad class of situations that cannot be defined in sufficient detail to permit feature-by-feature matching, the policy gives the decision maker only a general idea about the appropriate response. In this case, decision making is not so much "preprogrammed" as it is "constrained," where the constraints are imposed by the policy. Of course, here too recognition of the situation as an example of situation X involves decision making—so there are two decisions: "Is this a situation to which the policy is applicable, and, within the constraints of the policy, what should be done?"

From an organization's viewpoint, standard operating procedures and policies have the advantage that an important decision can be made once and then used on subsequent occasions for the same or similar situations. This is very efficient, but it also tends to be rather inflexible. It makes the behavior of members of the organization fairly predictable, but it also encourages stereotyped responses to situations that might profit from more creative and individualized decisions.

*RPD Theory.* The most extensive examination of recognition-based decision making has been undertaken by Klein (1993, 1996) and his associates. This resulted in a detailed theory called the recognition-primed decision (RPD) theory.

Klein (1989) stresses that situational conditions often diminish the applicability of problem analyses of the sorts prescribed by normative expected value theory. In such conditions the decision maker must rely on previously tried decision solutions, tempering them in light of the unique features of the present situation. Thus time pressure, prior experience, rapidly changing conditions, and the like recommend use of previously tried solutions, while conflict, the requirement to justify and optimize, and the like recommend use of more analytic, perhaps normative, approaches to making the decision.

For example, in the line of duty, firefighters and military officers often are under pressure to make rapid decisions based on their previous training. Examination of these decisions shows that they tend to be nonanalytical and heavily based on recognizing the situation as one for which this or that aspect of training provides a solution.

Klein's RPD theory begins with a decision about the familiarity of the situation. If it is not familiar, more information must be obtained. If it is familiar, thinking turns to goals and expectations about what ought to be happening if the situation is correctly recognized. If these expectations are satisfied, that is, the situation is correctly recognized, the question becomes one of what to do. Potential actions are not usually reflexive (although this can happen under extreme time pressure). Rather, the decision maker performs a mental simulation that permits him or her to imagine what might happen if the actions are performed. If the simulation suggests that the actions will successfully deal with the situation, they are implemented. If the simulation reveals potential problems, the actions are modified and the simulation is run again. This is repeated until a set of actions is derived that produces a successful mental simulation. Of course, if the situation is changing over time, this process must be constantly repeated in order to keep the actions attuned to the changing conditions. Thus the RPD theory has four main components: recognition of the situation, understanding of the situation (as revealed by whether it meets expectations as it unfolds and by recollection of typical actions from past experience), serial evaluation of the potential of various sets of actions for solving the problem, and mental simulation of the possible results of using an action in order to evaluate its potential.

RPD research is unlike any research we have described thus far. It is called the Critical Decision Method, in which non-routine events requiring decisions are obtained from interviews of real-life decision makers such as firefighters, military commanders, police officers, and design engineers. The purpose is to identify what options existed, which of these options were actively considered, important information, what the goal of the decision was, and how the goal shifted in the course of the decision, and the strategy used to make the decision. Interviews are recorded and raters identify the critical decision points and how the participant went about making the required decision. Results reported by Klein (1989) show that depending on the expertise of the decision maker and on the degree of latitude he or she has in approaching the decision, 40% to 80% of the decisions involve recognition in at least the initial stages. The more experience the decision maker has in the area in which the decision arises, the greater the role of recognition.

Recognition-based theories of decision making have the advantage that most of us can see ourselves doing what they describe. Moreover, they can draw on a considerable amount of research on memory and learning to provide both examples and mechanisms for their theoretical enrichment. Their disadvantage, however, is that they really never have progressed beyond the level of general description. Even though they inherently are psychological theories, there has been no effort to clearly delineate the psychological mechanisms by which they operate. Recognition is a very complicated process and a great deal of research has been done on it, yet it is taken as a given by these theories. Granted, for some applications the lack of specificity of the theories is acceptable, but as full-fledged behavioral theories they leave much to be desired.

Whatever remains to be done to more fully develop the recognition-based decision theories, the fact remains that they highlight an important aspect of decision behavior. It clearly is the case that once they have been made, many decisions are used over and over in similar situations. It clearly is the case that standard operating procedures and policies are similar but not identical, the latter involving more decision latitude. It clearly is the case that once a situation is recognized, the decision maker usually rechecks to make sure the recognition was accurate and that he or she understands what is going on. It clearly is the case that decision makers conceive of solutions (sets of actions) to decision problems and think about them (mental simulations) before implementing them. In short, recognition-based decision theories provide a great deal for a comprehensive second generation theory of decision making to deal with.

## Narrative Theories

When we acknowledge the importance of "thinking about" solutions to decision problems we must consider the nature of such thinking. It is here that the narrative-based decision theories make their contribution. The three most noteworthy theories are Jungermann and Thüring's (1987) scenario theory, Pennington and Hastie's (1986, 1988) story theory, and Lipshitz's (1993) argument theory.

*Scenario Theory.* On the presumption that decision making requires forecasting of future events, the scenario theory describes how a plausible narrative can be constructed to generate forecasts. The theory has four steps. In the first step, the frame within which the decision maker is working and the goal that is of interest within that frame are used as probes for retrieving relevant knowledge from memory. "Relevant" means knowledge that permits inferences of cause-and-effect, if-then propositions.

In the second step, the if-then propositions are used to construct a (cognitive) causal model that consists of a network of causal propositions. Construction uses both the known causal relationships that have been retrieved from memory and inferred causal relationships. The latter derive from the four "cues to causality" identified by Einhorn and Hogarth (1986): covariation of events, their temporal order, their spatial and temporal contiguity, and their similarity—to which can be added a fifth, the decision maker's intention to cause events to occur.

In the third step, plausible values are assigned to the "if" part of each of the if-then propositions in the model (i.e., if $X$ were the case, then $Y$ would occur). Each unique set of values assigned to the various propositions constitutes a scenario. Not all possible sets are admissible because the causal relations impose severe constraints.

In the fourth step, the model is "run" by working through the logical implications of a particular scenario, that is, the logical implications of a set of values assigned to each of the propositions. This produces a forecast for the scenario, which is an answer to the question, "Assuming that my causal model is reasonable, what would happen if $X_1, X_2, \ldots X_n$ were the case?" The "what would happen" is the forecast. A different scenario (a different set of value assignments) would yield a different forecast. Different scenarios can be compared, and the sensitivity of the forecasts to differences among them can be assessed. If many different scenarios lead to roughly the same forecast, the decision maker need not be too discriminating about value assignments. If markedly different forecasts are obtained, the decision maker can attempt to discover the crucial if-then propositions in the causal model and focus attention on their careful specification. In short, the causal model permits the decision maker to create multiple scenarios and multiple forecasts. He or she can then select the scenario that most closely represents reality, as it already is or as the decision maker plans to make it, and use that scenario's forecast as a basis for making decisions.

Lest causal models seem so abstract as to be implausible for day-to-day decision making, consider the following rather Machiavellian example. Suppose that I think that the manager of the office where I work has such a poisonous relationship with the district sales manager that either of them will do pretty much the opposite of anything the other suggests. Moreover, suppose I think that the district sales manager has a great deal of influence with the agency head in Phoenix, and that the agency head is in the position to recommend a friend of mine for a job in our Denver office. Therefore, I can imagine a scenario in which my office manager tells the sales manager that my friend should not be hired and, out of spite, the sales manager tells the Phoenix agency head to recommend my friend to the Denver office. If this chain of events seems plausible, my decision turns on selecting a way of getting my office manager to say bad things about my friend to the sales manager. I now can turn to imagining different ways of inducing the office manager to say bad things about my friend, and how different actions on my part might influence this chain of events. I also can imagine what might happen if other events changed the if-then relationships in my causal model—perhaps the Phoenix agency manager actually knows my friend and does not think much of him and therefore is resistant to pressure from the district sales manager. By mentally playing with different starting events (ways of getting my office manager to say bad things) and different states of if-then relationships in my model, I can generate an array of different scenarios. The one that seems the most plausible, or perhaps the least dangerous to my own job, can be used to guide my decisions and my actions.

Most causal models exist only in the heads of their authors, and as a result they tend to be rather simple. Perhaps too simple in many cases. It is, of course, possible to construct such models on a computer or using pencil and paper, and to have multiple contributors who share their knowledge and inferences. There are formal procedures for doing the latter, which goes beyond the scope of our discussion, but the reader should be aware that they exist. Formal models have the advantage of permitting more complex models than individuals can do in their heads, and they allow for a degree of objectivity and the use of multiple contributors' knowledge. On the other hand, they are complicated, expensive, and somehow coldly analytic. As a result, they often lose the intuitive compellingness that decision makers need to make confident decisions. In short, there is a trade-off between simplistic, cheap, but intuitively compelling mental models and more realistic, expensive, but rather coldly formal models.

*Story Theory.* Causal models of the kind we have been discussing focus on the future. Often, however, decisions flow as a logical consequence of one's interpretation of past events. For example, jury decisions about whether a defendant is or is not responsible for an unlawful event are dependent upon knowing about the circumstances leading up to the event. Pennington and Hastie (1986, 1988, 1992) examined the way in which jurors use evidence that is presented to them in the course of a trial. The research used volunteers from the jury pool for the Massachusetts Superior Court who had served on an average of three juries prior to the study. They were shown a videotape of a trial and were told that their task was to act as a jury member. The tape contained the usual information that is forthcoming in a trial. Afterwards each individual participant talked to the experimenter about the case and his or her decision while reaching an individual pre-deliberation verdict. This was tape-recorded for later analysis. Results showed that the "jurors" economically organized the information from the tape into a story that was inferred from the testimony in combination with their general knowledge about the world. Moreover, the stories were to the point; irrelevant information was not included. When information was lacking, the jurors made inferences based upon the parts of the story they had already constructed.

When completed, the story was used to make a decision about the appropriate verdict; the verdict that most closely "fit" the story was the one decided upon. But even though all of the stories shared a general structure, different jurors chose different verdicts depending upon the particular version of the story they had constructed. This is because the story often was based upon what the juror imagined he or she would do in the specific circumstances or what other people might be likely to do. That is, the story was heavily dependent upon the juror's implicit theory of human behavior—and not everybody had the same implicit theory.

Pennington and Hastie showed that construction of stories as a method of organizing knowledge, and the use of stories for decision making, is compatible with other linguistic comprehension models in modern cognitive theory—thereby tying decision making to a larger body of theory and research. They also point out that in contrast to the normative view of decision making, which tends to minimize interpretation and evaluation of information and to focus on direct relations among information and computations of the worth of options on a single dimension (utility), their research results show that the focus ought, in fact, to be on interpretation and evaluation.

It is interesting to compare the scenario theory and the story theory. They are similar in that they both involve construction of a mental model—a scenario or a story. They appear to be different because scenarios are used to forecast the future and stories are used to understand the past. However, scenarios also can be used to explain the past (Beach, Jungermann, & DeBruyn, 1996). This is done by assigning values to the causal model that describe how things were at some point in the past. Then the decision maker uses the scenario to make a "forecast" about the present. By changing the assigned values or by changing the structure of the causal model itself, the decision maker can generate a series of forecasts. If one of these forecasts resembles the present, the decision maker can assume that the scenario that generated it plausibly describes the chain of events that led to the present state of affairs. In short, the scenario can be regarded as an explanation of how things came to be the way they are. In this sense, the scenario that explains the past is comparable to a story that organizes knowledge about past events. In both cases, knowledge about the past constrains decisions and thus influences what the decision maker will do in the future.

*Argument Theory.* Theories that see arguments about the pros and cons of an option as central to decision making also assume that scenarios and stories are part of the decision process. However, they go beyond this to consider how a particular option is thought about, both before it is adopted as the chosen option and afterward when it must be defended to other people.

Lipshitz (1993) has suggested that the metaphor for decision making ought not to be gambling, or even choice. Instead it ought to be argument, in which a potential course of action is evaluated in terms of arguments for and against it. This permits one to consider potential outcomes and uncertainty about the eventuation of those outcomes (the components of expected value computations) as arguments, but it does not restrict consideration solely to these elements as prescriptive or first generation theory does.

Lipshitz's ideas, called the Argument-Driven Action (ADA) theory, are in the process of being crystallized, so it is difficult to characterize them clearly. The general idea is that the decision maker assesses the decision situation and, drawing upon past experience and existing knowledge, formulates a course of action that *matches* the demands of the situation—"What should be done in this situation?" This is akin to Klein's idea of recognition, but it involves more than mere recall of past actions in similar situations. At any rate, this first-cut at formulating an action is then *reassessed*, tempered and reshaped in light of arguments for and against it. This certainly is similar to the scenario-running form of mental simulation considered above, except that the emphasis is on using arguments to reshape the action to increase its match to the demands of the situation. Imagination is a primary tool in reassessment—just as it is in scenario construction. Arguments are phrased in the form "Do A because R," where A is an action and R is a reason. For example, "Do A because there are no objections to doing it or because all objections can be rebutted."

Research on the ADA theory, of which there is little thus far, resembles Klein's research on the RPD theory. Professional decision makers, often military officers, are asked to describe an important decision and what they thought about when they were making it. Analysis consists of looking at the chain of arguments that result in selecting this or that action as the incident unfolds. Thus, for example, Lipshitz (Beach & Lipshitz, 1993) examined the arguments given by Israeli Air Force General "Motti" Hod for the decisions that led Israeli fighter jets to force a Libyan airliner to crash-land in the Sinai, killing all but one person aboard, in 1973. The results are not the usual statistical tests to which most of us are accustomed. Rather, they are in the form of a coherent story in which successive decisions are related to one another through supportive arguments, information, and assumptions.

The ADA theory has a unique view of how uncertainty influences decision making. Normative theory ties uncertainty to whether or not outcomes will occur if the decision maker selects an action and generally views it in terms of probabilities of future events. The ADA theory views uncertainty as the source of motivation for decision making. That is, when there is uncertainty in the assessment of the situation, or in whether the formulated action will remedy the situation, the decision maker is motivated to modify the action so that uncertainty is reduced. It is this that moves the decision maker from merely using previously successful actions for this kind of situation to thinking about the action and revising it so it better matches the situational demands. In short, decision problems arise when there are objections to using a previously successful action; motivation to find a better action is provided by the uncertainty resulting from those objections; and reassessment (and revision) of the previous action is argument-driven, with the goal being to craft an action that better matches the situation, thereby reducing uncertainty.

This view of decision making has much in common with the theories we have discussed earlier in this chapter and almost nothing to do with the view advanced by prescriptive or first generation theory. It moves us from the idea of decisions as gambles because it conceives of uncertainty in an entirely new way, and it places the emphasis on a richer characterization of the cognitive processes underlying decision making. However, there is still more to be considered.

Svenson (1992) and Montgomery (1993) both have examined how decision makers think about a potential action both before and after it is decided upon. In many ways, these authors' views are like Lipshitz's except that they are a bit broader. The general idea is that the situation "nominates" a course of action, much as Lipshitz describes it. An action may be nominated by some salient characteristic, among which may be that it has worked in the past. The decision maker first *edits* the nominated action to clarify it and make it easier to think about. Then he or she subjects it to *differentiation* to make it sufficiently different from any alternative course of action. Differentiation means to stress its emotional, procedural, or structural attributes in a way that enhances the nominated action's apparent superiority to the alternatives. Moreover, differentiation takes into account future needs to defend the nominated action once it is the chosen action, thus insulating both the choice and the decision maker from future criticism. Differentiation continues after the action has been chosen, except that it now is called *consolidation*. Consolidation saves the decision maker from the agonies of post-decision cognitive dissonance (Festinger, 1964) or regret by affirming the superiority of the chosen action.

## Incremental Theories

The notion of incrementalism in decision making is not new. In fact, the first theory we will examine was proposed by Lindblom in 1959, and developed further by Braybrooke and Lindblom in 1963. Close reading of this work reveals that like most decision theories, the focus largely is on thought rather than action. Analysis of incremental action came later with the work of Connolly (1988; Connolly & Wagner, 1988). We will begin with the Lindblom theory and then move on to the Connolly theory. Both theories are instructive for any comprehensive second generation theory of decision making.

*Incremental Evaluation.* Lindblom's work is based on observation of public policy decisions, focusing on the difference between what is observed and what is required by the prescriptive theory of decision making, particularly in how options are evaluated prior to decision making.

Consider the conditions surrounding public policy decisions. First, the multiplicity of goals and values that are brought to bear on such a decision by the many different stakeholders makes it impossible to derive a single utility function upon which to base expected utility computations. Second, the ramifications of almost any public policy decision are so extensive (analogous to the widening circle of ripples when one drops a stone into a pool of water) that it is impossible to enumerate them, let alone evaluate them. Third, public policy decisions frequently are made in the face of absent or inadequate information and daunting ignorance about even their immediate consequences, and their remote consequences often are completely unknown. Even if the immediate and remote consequences of a decision could be identified, the costs of obtaining precise evaluations are enormous, if only because there are so many of them and because their utilities will differ for different stakeholders. Finally, for any but trivial decisions it is unlikely that all of the possible (or merely plausible) options will be known to the decision maker(s). Even if they were known, the cost in terms of time, effort, and money of analyzing all of them would be prohibitive. The upshot is that the rational evaluation prescribed by normative theory is impossible. On the other hand, policy makers cannot simply give up; they must adopt a strategy that both is realistic and gets the job done.

Here we come to one of the hidden gems in the Lindblom analysis, something that is seldom noted but that makes all the difference. It is that despite the rhetoric of politicians, public policy is shaped less by what policy makers want to move toward than by what they want to move away from. That is, change occurs only infrequently as a result of sweeping reform. Most often it occurs by "nibbling" away at problems, observing the results of small changes, making adjustments in the policy, and so on. Formally, the emphasis is on the undesirable parts of the status quo, and options are both generated and evaluated in terms of how those undesirable parts can be remedied. Because pre-decisional evaluation centers on the flaws in the status quo, it is not surprising that most remedies do not differ greatly from the status quo, differing only in the area of the flaws.

The observation that options are only marginally different from the status quo, and therefore from each other, dictates a change in how we view decision making. We must move away from the normatively prescribed overall analysis of options toward a tighter focus on decisions involving possible solutions to specific problems, from major public policy shifts driven by a universally accepted vision of the future to incremental changes aimed at solving problems without arousing the opposition of some or all stakeholders. These small remedies are provisional, in that they can be adjusted in light of feedback about their success in addressing one or another flaw in the status quo or in response to concerted pressure by opposing stakeholders. In some sense, incremental evaluation allows for the planning of small experiments in which success and failure will guide further action as decision making "feels its way along."

The salient features of incremental public policy evaluation are

1. Only those options are considered whose known or expected consequent states differ incrementally from the status quo and from each other.

2. Examination of options involves comparative analysis of no more than the marginal (incremental) differences in consequent states, rather than a more comprehensive comparison of the options and the states they offer.

3. Choice among options is dictated only by the attractiveness of the increments they offer.

4. The attractiveness of increments is influenced both by the remedies they offer and by what would be required to effect them.

5. The act of exploring increments often leads to greater understanding of the problems being addressed, leading to redefinition of those problems and to previously unsuspected options for solving them.

6. Because solutions to problems will be adjusted in light of feedback, decision making must be characterized as a series of small decisions rather than as a single definitive decision.

To summarize,

Since [public] policy analysis is incremental, exploratory, serial, and marked by adjustment of ends to means, it is to be expected that stable long-run aspirations will not appear as dominant critical values in the eyes of the analyst. The characteristics of the strategy support and encourage the analyst to identify situations or ills from which to move *away* rather than goals *toward* which to move. Even short-term goals are defined largely in terms of reducing some observed ill rather than in terms of a known objective of another sort. . . . Policy aims at suppressing vice even though virtue cannot be defined, let alone concretized as a goal; at attending to mental illness even though we are not sure what attitudes and behavior are most healthy; . . . at eliminating inequities in the tax structure even though we do not agree on equity; at destroying slums even though we are uncertain about the kinds of homes and neighborhoods in which their occupants should live. (Braybrooke & Lindblom, 1963, pp. 102–103)

Incremental evaluation pretty much leaves the policy maker buried in thought. It presumes that the decision maker(s) implements the option with the most attractive marginal increments, obtains feedback, and either proceeds or alters the policy in light of the feedback, but it does not provide much detail about how this happens. In this theory, options are merely policies, not specific courses of action—although Lindblom does not clearly differentiate between the two.

It is one thing to decide to do something and another thing to actually do it. Implementation has to deal with details and circumstances that are not specifically addressed by the policy, because policy cannot anticipate everything that might be encountered in the course of trying to accomplish it. The analogy is that a policy is like a road map and implementation is like actually driving your car down the bumpy road, detouring around repair crews, and keeping an eye out for landmarks that might signal progress toward the destination. Just as mapmaking and driving are different, formulating an attractive, plausible policy is different from executing the series of actions required to produce an acceptable approximation to that policy. What is needed is an incremental implementation theory to complement the incremental evaluation theory. Just such an implementation theory has been provided by Connolly (1988; Connolly & Wagner, 1988), called the "decision cycles" theory.

*Incremental Implementation.* Connolly (1988) begins his analysis much as Lindblom began his, with an argument against the universal applicability of normative decision theory.

> The central image [of normative theory] is that of a single decisive act by which the decision-maker hopes to move from a well-specified initial state (the unsolved problem) to a well-specified final state (the solved problem). The problem of felling a single tree highlights these characteristics, and we shall refer to analyses of this sort as 'tree-felling' theories. (p. 37)

In contrast, he proposes that many decision problems are less like "tree-felling" than like "hedge-clipping." "An unruly hedge and an undesired tree present the householder with rather different types of problems, and different strategies are called for in solving them" (Connolly, 1988, p. 37). The characteristics of problems that call for hedge-clipping, that is, for incremental implementation, are

1. The elements of the problem are interdependent. Felling a single tree does not affect the position of nearby trees, but clipping a limb of a hedge may have a large effect on the limbs around it.

2. Iterative solutions are possible. Felling a tree is pretty much all-or-none, but clipping a hedge can be done incrementally, in little

bits that nibble away here and there, each bringing the hedge closer to some desired state.

3. Corrections are possible and there is a range of acceptable solutions. Felling the wrong tree or felling it improperly usually cannot be corrected—the tree cannot be restored, and mistakes may result in a tree in your living room. Mistakes on hedges, on the other hand, seldom are serious because incremental clipping means that they are small. Moreover, recovery from errors generally is easy because the end-state of hedge-clipping is loosely defined; one can compensate for what might otherwise be an error by making the whole hedge lower or thinner than originally planned and still end up with an acceptable result.

4. The sequence of solution steps is flexible and robust in the face of interruptions. There is little latitude in how one goes about felling a tree, and once begun it is dangerous to leave the job until it is done. In contrast, one can approach hedge-clipping in a variety of ways, working first here and then there, leaving from time to time to do other things, all without impeding progress or compromising the final result.

To address decisions that have these four characteristics, Connolly extends a perceptual model first proposed by Neisser (1976). The latter posits a "perceptual cycle" that constantly updates a perceiver's knowledge (schema) of his or her environment through new information generated by active exploration guided by the existing schema. The new information results in modification of the guiding schema, which in turn guides new exploration, which generates even newer information, and so on. The strength of the model is the role of active exploration, rather than passive reception of information, in the construction and modification of subjective knowledge about the environment.

Connolly's adaptation of Neisser's model posits a "decision cycle" that functions in conjunction with Neisser's perceptual cycle. The decision maker's values, purposes, and goals constitute a cognitive-emotive schema that works in tandem with his or her perceptual schema to dictate goal-directed action. When this action is played out in the physical or social environment, it generates new information in the form of consequences. This new information modifies the decision maker's perceptual schema—his or her current knowledge about the environment. The modified schema, together with the decision maker's cognitive-emotive schema (values, purposes, and goals) prescribes changes in further goal-directed action, which generates new information, and so on. This interrelating of perceptual cycles and decision cycles has the effect of shifting the locus of decision making from the isolation of the decision maker's mind to the interaction of information-producing action in a progressively better understood environment. This shift to "decision-makers-in-context" (Connolly & Wagner, 1988, p. 190) produces the desired bridge between incremental evaluation, as described by Lindblom (1959; Braybrooke & Lindblom, 1963), and incremental implementation.

Incremental implementation often results in revisions of *both* perceptual and cognitive-emotive schemata. That is, feedback from incremental implementation not only provides information that prompts revision of one's knowledge of the environment, it also may prompt revision of one's values, one's intents and one's goals. Tree-felling decisions can produce similar results, but usually in the form of regret or guilt because by the time feedback is received it is too late to do anything—the tree is felled. Incrementalism, on the other hand, allows the opportunity to examine where things seem to be going and what is emerging as important. Sometimes the final state is the one that was sought. Often it is something else; as the process moves along, new opportunities arise and conditions change that evoke new values and change both tastes and goals. The result is a progressive modification of both the perceptual and the cognitive-emotive schemata that reflects learning from experience and a maturation and refining of both knowledge and desire.

Incremental implementation also influences commitment to decisions. Tree-felling requires monumental commitment, or at least the semblance of such; there is no turning back once action has begun. In contrast, incremental implementation almost demands low commitment to each small step because each step is merely an experiment, as it were. The results of the experiment inform subsequent action by prompting revisions of the perceptual and cognitive-emotive schemata. Because increment implementation is fluid, no step is itself particularly crucial, and commitment lies in loyalty to pragmatics and following the most reasonable (changing) path into the future—even the goals are changing, so it is not clear that commitment to any specific goal is appropriate. Indeed, trial periods, simulations, and actions that do not foreclose on future directions are precisely what is called for. All of these can be perverted into decision avoidance, but properly used they preserve the flexibility that is the genius of incremental implementation while avoiding the dangers of overcommitment inherent in the normative tree-felling prescriptions.

## Moral/Ethical Theories

The social sciences tend to underrate the importance of morals and ethics in human affairs. Perhaps because what is deemed moral in one culture or by one person is deemed immoral or amoral by others, we often regard morals and ethics as mere social conventions. This is a mistake. Behavior is very strongly influenced by individuals' bedrock beliefs about what is moral and ethical and therefore proscribed or prescribed. Obligation and commitment are major themes in virtually everyone's life, taking precedence over our preferences and self-interests. Only sociopaths and psychopaths fail to heed these constraints on behavior, and that is why their behavior is regarded as abnormal and potentially dangerous.

In addition to morals and ethics, we must include ideologies and beliefs and values in general. If one is fervently religious, one is obliged to behave in ways that are discernibly different from the behavior of people who are less religious. So too, if one believes that stealing is immoral, one's behavior will be far different from the behavior of those who do not see theft as a moral issue. Similarly, if one values government as a legitimate force in civic affairs, one pays taxes more willingly (and perhaps more honestly) than if one believes the opposite. In general, morals, ethics, ideologies, beliefs, and values all influence the decision process, both by prescription and proscription of particular courses of action and by making some decision outcomes more or less attractive than others.

*Deontology.* In ethics, "deontology" refers to the influence of moral obligation and commitment on human behavior. Normative decision theory fails to account for such influences, primarily by ignoring that they exist. However, as we have seen, even casual observation and a little introspection indicates that decisions are greatly shaped by these influences, and that it often is the major decisions that are most affected.

As discussed in previous chapters, prescriptive decision theory relies on the assumption that all value, whatever its source, can be measured on one scale, called utility. Further, it is assumed that the utility of an anticipated outcome of a decision is some combination (usually the sum) of the utilities of each of the outcome's component parts. These are very convenient assumptions, because both theory and applications would become quite complicated if different classes of outcomes and components of outcomes were to have different kinds of utility, especially if those different kinds of utility did not combine in a simple manner. Of course, different kinds of utility are precisely what is implied by Thaler's (1985) work on "mental accounting," but the differences that Thaler has identified are perhaps less disruptive to first generation theory than those implied by a deontological analysis.

The primary proponent of a deontological imperative in decision making is Amitai Etzioni (1988, 1993). His analyses suggest that decisions are not influenced solely by the pleasure or gain offered by the various options. He begins with the observation that most humans are solidly anchored in a social context. Thus the prescriptive theory view of a rational decision maker operating alone is seldom appropriate. Even when it is, the decision maker must take others' views into account, if only to avoid their approbation when the decision becomes known. For this reason, Etzioni proposes three sources of influence on decision making, which for convenience we will call utilitarian, social, and deontological. The utilitarian influence corresponds to utility in prescriptive theory. The social influence corresponds to both the codes of behavior for the individual's reference group and the cultural values of the larger community. The deontological influence reflects the moral and ethical considerations that guide the decision maker's behavior. In general, economics and normative decision theory study utilitarian influences, sociology and anthropology study social influences, and ethics studies deontological influences.

The difference between social and deontological influences on decisions are subtle but important. At the risk of oversimplifying, social norms exercise their influence by threatening approbation and ostracism if they are violated. In contrast, morals and ethics, although they derive from the community, are internal to the decision maker, exercising their influence by a sense of obligation, commitment, and duty, with conscience (and perhaps avoidance of guilt) rather than fear providing the motivation.

Etzioni (1988) begins his exploration of deontological influences on decision making with three questions. The first is about what the decision maker is trying to do. The utilitarian answer is that he or she is trying to maximize pleasure or self-interest. The social answer is that he or she is conforming to social norms and cultural demands in order to avoid punishment. The deontological view is that, indeed, decision makers evaluate their options in light of utilitarian and social considerations, but both of these are subsidiary to moral and ethical considerations. That is, utility, social norms, *and* morals must be taken into account if we are to understand human decision making.

The second question is about how decision makers choose the means for doing what they are trying to do. The utilitarian view is that they weigh the costs and benefits and select the course of action that promises the greatest net utility. The social view is that they select the course of action that conforms to the expectations of their reference group or the larger community. The deontological view is that they use their emotions and value judgments to reject courses of action that violate their moral or ethical codes or to select courses of action that are compatible with or prescribed by those codes.

The third question is about who makes decisions. The utilitarian answer is that individual decision makers do so on their own. The social answer is that, in effect, the decision is made by the reference group or community because it sets down the rules about how to behave, and the decision maker merely conforms to those rules. The deontological answer is that individuals make decisions in the context of groups and communities, guided by their own moral and ethical principles, which derive in large part from those groups and communities. Etzioni (1998) concludes,

At issue is human nature: How wise are we and what is the role of morality, emotions, and social bonds in our personal and collective behavior? Also at issue is the extent to which free-standing individuals are the foundation of our society; or does the foundation consist of persons integrated into small groups and communities? (p. xii)

## ❖ SUMMARY

We have examined four classes of ideas and theories that challenge the prescriptive, normative, first generation view of decision making and that require attention from any comprehensive second generation theory. First are the roles of situation recognition and policy in guiding behavior. Second are the roles of scenarios, stories, and arguments in understanding the past and present, in forecasting the future, and in justifying decision making. Third are the roles of incremental evaluation, with its emphasis on remedying what is wrong with the present situation, and incremental implementation, with its emphasis on decision cycles driven by feedback about progress. Fourth are the roles of morals and ethics in both proscribing unacceptable courses of action and in prescribing actions that the decision maker is obliged or committed to undertake.

This is an impressive list of ideas, especially when taken together with the issues raised earlier about emotions and about interpersonal, organizational, and group decisions. In the following chapter, we will examine a theory that attempts to accommodate some of these ideas and issues, at least insofar as it is possible to do so in one framework. This theory, called image theory, grew out of the ideas described above and, thus far, is the most fully developed second generation theory.

# 10

# Image Theory

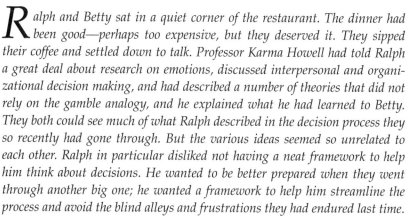

$R$ alph and Betty sat in a quiet corner of the restaurant. The dinner had been good—perhaps too expensive, but they deserved it. They sipped their coffee and settled down to talk. Professor Karma Howell had told Ralph a great deal about research on emotions, discussed interpersonal and organizational decision making, and had described a number of theories that did not rely on the gamble analogy, and he explained what he had learned to Betty. They both could see much of what Ralph described in the decision process they so recently had gone through. But the various ideas seemed so unrelated to each other. Ralph in particular disliked not having a neat framework to help him think about decisions. He wanted to be better prepared when they went through another big one; he wanted a framework to help him streamline the process and avoid the blind alleys and frustrations they had endured last time.

As they talked, Betty took notes until she had covered a page with scribbles and boxes and arrows. She glanced over what she had written and was surprised to find that it was beginning to hang together. In fact it resembled something Karma Howell had given her to read, something about images that she had not understood at the time but that somehow seemed to fit with what she and Ralph had been talking about and with the notes she had taken. Suddenly she remembered and she turned to tell Ralph about it.

In this chapter we will examine a second generation theory that addresses some of the issues raised in previous chapters. The goal of the theory, called image theory, is to describe decision making as it occurs rather than to prescribe how it ought to be done.

There are two versions of image theory, one for individual decision making (Beach, 1990) and one for decision making in organizations (Beach & Mitchell, 1990; Weatherly & Beach, 1996). In fact, they are the same theory in that the underlying logic is the same, but the emphasis and some of the vocabulary are different in the two versions. We will begin with the version for individuals and then describe the version for organizations.

Heeding the lessons learned in previous chapters, image theory views decision making as a social act. That is, decisions seldom are made in isolation—the decision maker always must be mindful of the preferences and opinions of other people. However, in all cases he or she must make up his or her own mind and then differences with others must be resolved in some manner. Thus while groups and organizations are not themselves decision makers, they impose constraints on individuals' decisions. Moreover, they often are the context within which individuals' decisions become consolidated to form a group product.

## ❖ IMAGE THEORY FOR INDIVIDUALS

Briefly, decision makers use their store of knowledge (images) to set standards that guide decisions about what to do (goals) and about how to do it (plans). Potential goals and plans that are incompatible with the standards are quickly screened out, and the best of the survivors is then chosen. Subsequent implementation of the choice is monitored for progress toward goal achievement; lack of acceptable progress results in replacement or revision of the plan or adoption of a new goal.

### The Images

Each decision maker possesses a store of knowledge that is far vaster than what is needed for the decision at hand. That store can conveniently be partitioned into three categories, which are called images because they are the decision maker's vision of what constitutes a valuable and properly ordered course of events. The categories are labeled the value image, the trajectory image, and the strategic image, and they will be explained in a moment.

The constituents of the images can be further partitioned into those that are relevant to the decision at hand and those that are not. The relevant constituents define the decision's frame, which gives meaning to the context in which the decision is embedded and which provides standards that constrain how the decision will be characterized and how it will be interpreted.

*Value Image.* The first image consists of the decision maker's values, morals, and ethics (Etzioni, 1988), which set standards for how things *should* be and how he or she and others *ought* to behave. Collectively these are called *principles.* These are "self-evident truths" about what he or she, or the group or organization, stands for, about the goals that are therefore worthy of pursuit ("Success in my occupation will help my children get a good start in life"), and about what are and what are not acceptable ways of pursuing those goals ("But success must not come at the price of being away from my family too much"). Even if these principles are difficult for the decision maker to articulate, they are powerful influences on his or her decisions. Whatever they may be, they are the foundation of one's decisions; potential goals and actions must not contradict them, or those goals and actions will be judged unacceptable. Moreover, the utility of the outcomes of decisions derives from the degree to which they conform to and enhance the decision maker's principles. The decision maker's store of principles is called the value image because it represents his or her vision about the state of events that would conform most closely to his or her beliefs, values, and ethics (Figure 10.1).

*Trajectory Image.* In addition to principles, the decision maker has an agenda of goals to achieve. Some goals are dictated by his or her principles ("I must get promoted to Unit Manager this year in order to progress in my career") and some are dictated by problems encountered in the environment—although principles still influence how these problems are addressed ("Because my boss refuses to recommend me for promotion, I must find a new job—but I wouldn't feel right about leaving without giving proper notice"). The decision maker's goal agenda is called the trajectory image because it is his or

**Figure 10.1**    Image Theory

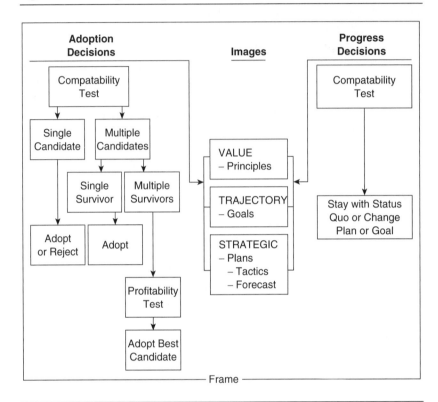

her vision about how the future should unfold and therefore sets standards for what is and is not appropriate behavior.

*Strategic Image.* Each goal on the trajectory image has an accompanying plan for its accomplishment. Plans have two aspects: the first is tactics, which is their concrete behavioral aspect. Because plans are inherently an anticipation of the future, their second aspect is forecasts. That is, plans require tactics to deal with local environmental conditions and constraints, and they provide a scenario for forecasting what might result if the tactics are successful (Jungermann & Thüring, 1987; Lipshitz, 1993; Pennington & Hastie, 1986, 1988, 1992). The various plans for the various goals must be coordinated so that they do not interfere with one another and so that the decision maker can maintain a reasonably orderly pursuit of his or her goals. The collection of plans is called the strategic image because it represents the decision maker's vision of what he or she is trying to do to achieve the goals on the trajectory image and sets standards for what is or is not appropriate behavior.

The principles, goals, and plans that constitute the three images are called the *constituents* of those images.

### Framing

As we saw in Chapter 2, a frame is that portion of his or her store of knowledge that the decision maker brings to bear on a particular situation in order to endow that situation with meaning. In image theory, the frame consists of the constituents of the three images that are deemed relevant to the decision at hand and that set the standards that influence that decision.

Framing occurs when the decision maker uses contextual information (cues) to probe his or her memory. If the probe locates a contextual memory that has features that are virtually the same as those of the current context, the current context is said to be *recognized* (Klein, 1989, 1996). Recognition serves two ends: first, it defines which image constituents are relevant to the context, and second, it provides information about goals that previously have been pursued in this kind of context and about the plans, both successes and failures, that have been used to pursue them. If a same or similar goal is being pursued this time, the plan that was used before may either be used again—called a *policy* (Simon, 1979)—or used as the foundation for a new plan.

### Decisions

There are two kinds of decisions: adoption decisions and progress decisions.

*Adoption Decisions.* Adoption decisions are about whether to add new goals to the trajectory image or new plans to the strategic image; sometimes new principles are added to the value image, but for adults this is infrequent and need not concern us here. The criterion for adding a new goal or plan is whether it meets the decision maker's standards, as defined by the image constituents that make up the decision frame. That is, is it incompatible with the decision maker's relevant principles or does it interfere with existing goals or ongoing plans? If the answer is "Yes," how incompatible is it? If it is not too incompatible, it might work out all right, but there is some point at which it simply is too incompatible and must be rejected rather than adopted.

Adoption decisions are accomplished first by *screening* options (possible goals and plans) in light of relevant principles, existing goals, and ongoing plans, and by *choice* of the best option from among the survivors of screening. If there is only one option and it passes screening, it is adopted without recourse to choice. Similarly, if there are two or more options and only one passes screening, it is adopted without a choice having to be made. But if there are two or more options and more than one passes screening, the best of the survivors must be chosen. The key point here is that choice, the subject of most of the literature on decision making, is rather less common than supposed. Screening is by far the more important decision mechanism, if only because most decisions involve only one option and the question is whether to pursue it, if it is a goal, or to implement it, if it is a plan (Lipshitz, 1993). Choice is, in fact, only a tie-breaker when screening fails to narrow the field down to a single acceptable option.

*Progress Decisions.* The second kind of decision is about whether a plan is making progress toward achievement of its goal (Connolly, 1988; Connolly & Wagner, 1988). These progress decisions rely on the forecast aspect of plans—the plan is used as a scenario to forecast the future, and if that future plausibly includes the goal, the plan is deemed to have met the standard and it is retained (Jungermann, 1985; Jungermann & Thüring, 1987). If the forecast does not include the goal, the standard has not been met and the plan must be rejected and a new or amended plan adopted in its place.

### Decision Mechanisms

There are two decision mechanisms in image theory: the compatibility test and the profitability test.

*Compatibility Test.* The compatibility test screens options for adoption on the basis of their *quality*. This is assayed in terms of the compatibility between the option and the standards defined by the three images. Actually, the focus is upon lack of quality, in that the option's incompatibility ($I$) decreases as a function of the weighted sum of the number of its violations of the standards, where the weights reflect the importance of the violation. (Note the similarity [but not the identity] between screening and Simon's [1955] concept of "satisficing.")

Violations are defined as negations, contradictions, contraventions, preventions, retardations, or any similar form of interference with the realization of one of the standards defined by the images' constituents. Each violation is all-or-none. The decision rule is that if the weighted sum of the violations exceeds some absolute *rejection threshold* the option is rejected, otherwise it is adopted. The rejection threshold is that weighted sum beyond which the decision maker regards the option as incompatible with his or her relevant principles, existing goals, and ongoing plans.

The (in)compatibility test can be formally stated as follows:

$$I = \sum_{t=1}^{n} \sum_{c=1}^{m} W_c V_{tc}; \; V_{tc} = -1 \text{ or } 0,$$

where incompatibility, $I$, is zero when a option has no violations and decreases (i.e., is more and more negative) as the number of violations increases; $t$ is a relevant attribute of the option; $c$ is a relevant standard; $V$ is a violation of standard $c$ by attribute $t$ of the option; and $W$ is the importance weight for each of the standards.

Thus while the violations are all-or-none ($-1$ or $0$), violations of some standards may count more than others ($W_c$) and compatibility is a continuous scale between $0$ and $-mn$, where $m$ is the number of standards and $n$ is the number of the option's relevant attributes (an attribute may violate more than one standard).

*Profitability Test.* When more than one adoption option survives screening, the decision maker must choose the best from among them. This is accomplished using the profitability test, which usually focuses on the *quantity* of the outcomes associated with the options rather than the quality of the options' fit with the decision maker's images. The profitability test is not, in fact, a single decision mechanism but a collective term for the individual's repertoire of strategies for making choices and the mechanism for selecting one of those strategies for use on a particular choice. Expected value maximization may be one of the strategies, as may any of a number of other strategies (Svenson, 1979); as we shall see, expected value maximization turns out to be the meta-strategy for the profitability test.

The underlying assumption is that each decision maker possesses a repertoire of choice strategies and that the strategy that he or she selects for the task at hand depends upon three categories of variables: characteristics of the choice, characteristics of the environment in which that choice is embedded, and characteristics of the decision maker (Beach & Mitchell, 1978; Christensen-Szalanski, 1978, 1980).

Characteristics of the choice include the unfamiliarity of the choice, ambiguity, complexity, and instability—where the latter means that the goal of the choice changes over time. Characteristics of the environment consist of irreversibility of the choice, whether the choice can be made iteratively (recall Braybrooke & Lindblom, 1963; Connolly, 1988; Connolly & Wagner, 1988; Lindblom, 1959), the significance of the choice, accountability for a choice that fails to yield acceptable outcomes, and the time and money constraints on the choice process. Characteristics of the decision maker consist of knowledge of different choice strategies (the breadth of his or her repertoire), ability to actually use the strategies, and motivation to expend the least possible time, effort, and money on the choice while still doing a good enough job.

The decision maker's repertoire is seen as containing strategies that range from the aided analytic (e.g., decision analysis), to unaided analytic (e.g., balancing pros and cons in one's head), to unanalytic strategies (e.g., coin tossing, asking others for advice).

As formulated by Christensen-Szalanski (1978, 1980), the meta-logic of the selection process is cost-benefit, where benefit is in terms of subjective expected utility. Where the utility of choosing a strategy that will produce what ultimately will prove to be a correct choice is designated $U_c$, the utility of a correct choice is $U_i$, the cost of using a given strategy is $U_e$, the subjective probability of a given strategy yielding a correct choice is $P_c$, and the subjective probability of that strategy yielding an incorrect choice is $1 - P_c$.

Assume that the decision maker believes that, in general, the more analytic a strategy, the higher the probability that it will yield a correct choice (an assumption for which there is evidence). Also assume that the decision maker believes that more analytic strategies cost more time, effort, and money to use. It follows, then, that the subjective expected utility for any strategy in the decision maker's repertoire is

$$SEU = P_c U_c + (1 - P_c) U_i$$
$$= P_c(U_c - U_i) + U_i$$

**Figure 10.2**    The Logic of Strategy Selection

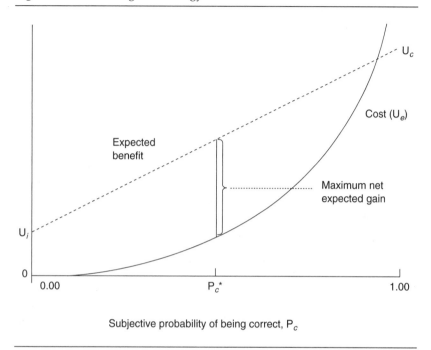

Subjective probability of being correct, $P_c$

SOURCE: Reproduced from Christensen-Szalanski (1978) by permission of the author and Academic Press, Inc.

which is the equation for the straight line in Figure 10.2. The abscissa is a probability scale and the ordinate is a utility scale. The straight line demarcates the range from the utility of an incorrect adoption choice, $U_i$, which is seen by the decision maker to be virtually assured at $P_c = 0$, to the utility of a correct choice, $U_c$, which is seen as virtually assured at $P_c = 1.00$. ($U_i$ is a positive number in the figure, but it could be negative if an incorrect choice would result in a loss.) The slope of the line is $U_c - U_i$, the difference between the utility of a correct choice and the utility of an incorrect choice.

The decision maker's repertoire of choice strategies can be arrayed along the abscissa of the figure according to the decision maker's subjective probabilities, $P_c$, that they will yield a correct adoption choice in the present situation. On the left will be the simple nonanalytic strategies, perceived to have low $P_c$, and on the right will be the aided analytic strategies, perceived to have high $P_c$. The unaided analytic strategies will be somewhere in the middle. Of course, which strategies are in the array and where they lie on the $P_c$ scale depends upon the individual decision maker's repertoire and his or her beliefs about the efficacy of each strategy.

Assuming that the strategies are arrayed from nonanalytic to aided analytic, and assuming that the perceived cost of using them varies from quite low for the nonanalytic strategies to quite high for aided analytic strategies, results in the increasing cost curve, $U_e$, in the figure. (The cost curve could be illustrated as a negative utility, but doing so complicates the rather simple picture that this method permits.)

The straight line in the figure represents the expected utility (benefit) of each strategy on the probability scale. The cost curve represents the cost of using each of those strategies. The difference between the expected benefit line and the cost curve represents the net expected gain of using each strategy. The optimal strategy for use on the adoption choice at hand is the one for which the net expected gain is maximal—which is the strategy that lies closest to the point at which the difference between the line and the curve is largest. This point, called $P_c^*$, is the optimal probability level for the choice strategy that is to be used. That is, using a strategy with a higher $P_c$ would increase the expected benefit, but it would increase the cost more, thereby reducing the expected benefit. Using a strategy with a lower $P_c$ would decrease the cost, but it would decrease the expected benefit more, thereby reducing the net expected benefit. Of course, the decision maker may not have a strategy in his or her repertoire with a $P_c$ that corresponds to $P_c^*$, in which case he or she should select the strategy whose $P_c$ most nearly corresponds to $P_c^*$.

At the moment the strategy is selected, the decision maker need not take into account anything about the individual adoption options that have survived screening by the compatibility test. The utilities of making a correct ($U_c$) or incorrect ($U_i$) choice derive from the various characteristics of the decision environment vis-à-vis the decision maker's principles (value image constituents), rather than from the features of the options themselves. Thus irreversibility, significance, accountability, and constraints on time and money induce a high utility for making a correct choice and a low (or negative) utility for making an incorrect choice. The decision maker's job is to balance these perceived utilities against the probabilities and costs associated with each of the choice strategies in his or her repertoire in order to select the strategy that offers the best hope of success at the lowest cost in resource expenditure.

## Research

There is a growing research literature on image theory. Rather than reviewing it all (see Beach 1990, 1993a, 1993b, 1996), let us examine a primary experiment, which is on screening, and then summarize the findings of the rest.

Beach and Strom (1989) asked undergraduate participants to assume the role of a newly graduated student who was looking for a job. The job seeker's preferences about 16 job characteristics were provided so that all participants were using the same standards. Then each participant was presented with an array of jobs. The 16 characteristics of each job were presented on 16 successive pages of a small booklet, one booklet for each job. Each characteristic violated or did not violate one of the job seeker's 16 standards. The characteristics violated different standards for different jobs and each job had a different number of violations. The participant read the information on the successive pages in a booklet until he or she decided to reject the job or to save it for his or her short list. By noting where the participant stopped looking through a particular booklet, the experimenters were able to calculate the numbers of violations and nonviolations that had been observed before the participant made the decision to reject the option or to place it in the choice set.

The results showed that rejection of options regularly occurred after observation of roughly four violations; this is the rejection threshold. There was no comparably constant number of nonviolations for deciding to place options on the short list. In fact, nonviolations played virtually no role at all in screening except to stop information search when no violations were observed (or else a perfect option never would be accepted because the search for violations would never stop).

The Beach and Strom (1989) study supports the image theory position that screening relies almost exclusively on violations of standards. It also demonstrates the existence of a rejection threshold, and suggests that for a specific decision task the rejection threshold may remain fairly constant. Subsequent research showed that screening not only turns on violations of decision standards, but decision makers regard screening as so different from choice that they often do not carry forward information used in screening when they evaluate surviving options before choosing the best (van Zee, Paluchowski, & Beach, 1992). They also may use the same information differently in screening and choice (Potter & Beach, 1994). In addition, screening out unsuitable options is the norm, although decision makers can be induced to focus on screening in the most acceptable options or to focus on regret for having eliminated attractive options, both of which result in more survivors in the choice set than normally would be the case (Ordóñez, Benson, & Beach, 1999). Moreover, the more violations an option is known to have, or the more important the standard is, the more likely decision makers are to regard even a small discrepancy from the standard as an additional violation (Benson, Beach, Mertens, & Payne, 2004). In short, screening is a different process from choice and requires a different way of thinking than is commonly used in thinking about choice.

Beach, Smith, Lundell, and Mitchell (1988) investigated compatibility in three business firms. The first firm, which manufactured athletic shoes, was in financial difficulty and was experiencing a large turnover among its executives. The second firm, a winery, was relatively new and was growing and changing in a rapid but planned manner. The third firm, which manufactured ski wear, was old, stable, and most of its employees had worked with it for a long time.

To begin, the executives of each firm were interviewed about the principles that were important to their firm, which turned out to be surprisingly different. Then, for each firm, various plans were drawn up for the introduction of a hypothetical new product. The plans were designed to violate more or fewer of the firm's principles. Then the plans were given to the executives, who rated each plan in terms of its compatibility with their firm's values. Results showed that the greater the number of violations the lower the compatibility rating, but of equal interest was the finding that the agreement among the executives differed from firm to firm. The agreement was less among the executives of the athletic shoe manufacturer than among the executives of the winery, which in turn was less than among the executives of the ski wear manufacturer. In fact, as you might expect, the less agreement among the executives about what their firm's principles were, the less agreement among them about whether a plan was compatible with those principles.

This experiment makes two contributions. First, it is a nonlaboratory study of compatibility, showing that compatibility is linked to violations of principles. Second, it shows that the more the members of an organization share a common view of what is important to that organization (culture), the more they agree about the appropriateness of a plan of action for that organization—which speaks to the organizational version of image theory that we will review in a few moments.

Research on strategy selection for the profitability test demonstrates that decision makers possess repertories of choice strategies, and that their selection of which strategy to use in a particular decision context is contingent upon the characteristics of the decision itself, of the decision environment, and of the decision maker. In a series of experiments, Christensen-Szalanski (1978, 1980) manipulated the payoffs for correct choices and the costs for executing various strategies and found that as the payoffs for correct choices increased, participants used more analytic strategies. In addition, he examined the effects of individual differences in decision makers' ability to execute strategies of differing degrees of analytic complexity and found profound effects on strategy selection and choice accuracy. That is, participants who admitted to avoiding mathematics and similar forms of disciplined analytic thought were less inclined to select analytic strategies than were Business School students (who had high mathematical scores on entry exams). Moreover, when participants became tired as a result of prolonged participation in experiments, they selected less analytic strategies, which Christensen-Szalanski interpreted as resulting from an increased cost to execute the more demanding strategies.

McAllister, Mitchell, and Beach (1979), using both practicing managers and business students as participants, found that increases in irreversibility, significance, and accountability resulted in increases in the use of more costly analytic strategies. Huffman (1978) showed that these same three variables and familiarity and complexity of the task influenced strategy selection. As environment and task demands increased, participants' willingness to expend resources on more analytic strategies increased.

Images also have been investigated, but not to the degree that is demanded by their central position in the theory. It is not clear exactly how images are best studied—by having participants describe the relevant constituents or by looking at the impact of images on decisions. Of course, both are plausible, but the first is difficult because participants often cannot put images into words very well. In one study (Bissell & Beach, 1996), workers in three firms were presented with a questionnaire that elicited their descriptions of "ideal" supervisory behavior and the behavior of their real supervisor. Presuming that the description of the ideal embodies their standards for supervision, the difference between it and the description of their own supervisor's behavior should indicate how compatible the two descriptions are. It was found that the rejection threshold was at about 10 to 12 violations of the ideal by the supervisor's actual behavior. Above this point workers were satisfied with supervision, with their jobs, and with the firm as a whole; below this point satisfaction with all three aspects of the workplace was low.

In contrast, Dunegan (1993, 1995, 2003; Dunegan, Duchon, & Ashmos, 1995; Pesta, Kass & Dunegan, in press) asks participants to "conjure up two images," one of the desired state of affairs and the other of the existing or expected state of affairs. Then they answer a series of questions about the compatibility of the two images. Dunegan and his colleagues find that image compatibility has a major impact on how information is used in decision making about such things as funding allocations, amounts of penalties to impose for deceptive business practices, and employee promotion decisions. This research also suggests that the positive and negative formulation effects so often observed in the research on prospect theory (Kahneman & Tversky, 1979) are mediated by images and image compatibility. For example, when participants are told that a group has failed in 20 of its last 50 projects, the image of how things can be expected to turn out is more negative than if they are told that the group has succeeded in 30 of its last 50 projects. Because of this, the image is less compatible with the ideal and participants tend to be less generous in allocating additional funds to continue work.

Clearly there is a great deal more to be done to explore the limits of image theory and to make the appropriate changes. It does, however, offer a vehicle for consolidating the ideas that are described in previous chapters, and it offers a research agenda that promises to be interesting. However, having said that, it is time to review, however briefly, the organizational version of image theory.


## ❖ IMAGE THEORY FOR ORGANIZATIONS

The reasoning underlying the organizational version of image theory is the same as for the individual version. That is, there are three images, adoption and progress decisions, and the compatibility and profitability tests for screening and choice. The difference lies in how the images are characterized and the implications of this characterization.

The image theory view is that organizations do not themselves make decisions (Davis, 1992). Rather, the individual members make decisions, either as agents of the organization or as a participant whose individual decision is in some way combined with the individual decisions of the other participants to arrive at a collective decision. The degree to which the decisions made by an agent of the organization make sense to other members, and the ease with which a collective decision can be reached, depends upon the degree to which the organization's members have similar underlying beliefs, values, goals, and plans. It is here that the images become crucial.

## Images

The organizational counterparts of the value, trajectory, and strategic images are called the organization's culture, its vision, and its strategy.

*Culture.* Like the value image, an organization's culture consists of beliefs and values. Here, however, they are the organizationally related beliefs and values that are shared, to one degree or another, by the members of the organization. The culture prescribes what is true, necessary, and desirable, and, therefore, the goals that the organization and its members ought to pursue and how they should be pursued. By the same token, it proscribes what is false, unnecessary, and undesirable, and, therefore, the goals and actions that the organization and its members ought not pursue and that they ought to resist when proposed by others. The culture provides answers to the question, "Who are we and what do we stand for?" (Weatherly & Beach, 1996).

Harrison (1972) lists the functions of organizational culture. It specifies what is important to the organization—the criteria for success and failure. It dictates how resources are to be used and to what ends. It defines where power lies and how it is to be used. It establishes what the organization and its members can expect from each other and how the members are to be rewarded and punished. And it instructs members about how they are to deal with each other and with the external environment. In short, the culture provides the guidelines for members' expectations and for their behavior.

*Vision.* Like the trajectory image, an organization's vision consists of its agenda of goals and their timelines for accomplishment. It may or may not be formally articulated by the organization's leaders—often it is simply understood throughout the organization. When it is formally stated it provides guidelines for planning activities. Vision provides answers to the question, "Where are we going and what are we trying to become?"

*Strategy.* Like the strategic image for individuals, an organization's strategy provides the general blueprint for accomplishing the goals encompassed in its vision (trajectory image). The strategy consists of numerous specific plans for accomplishment of specific goals—with different emphases for different parts of the organization but all contributing to the overall strategy and dedicated to realization of the vision. Strategy provides answers to the question, "How are we striving to achieve the goals that constitute our vision?"

### Research

Thus far, there has been little research on the organizational version of image theory. What there is has been motivated by the hypothesis that the greater the agreement among the members about the culture, the more agreement there will be among them about what constitutes appropriate goals and plans for the organization.

Using employees of an electric power company and of a commercial finance company as participants, Weatherly and Beach (1996) presented options that were and that were not compatible with the participants' company's culture and asked them which options should be chosen by their organization. The more compatible an option was with the participants' perceptions of their organization's culture, the more likely they were to endorse it as the appropriate choice, from a high of about 98% endorsement of compatible options to a low of about 20%, with a rejection threshold of about 5.5 violations.

In a second study, when options were presented to participants as having been chosen by management, the more compatible the option with the culture the greater the willingness of participants to endorse it, from a high of 98% for the most compatible options to a low of 59% for the less compatible options (suggesting a general tendency to go along with management decisions even when they are not truly acceptable). Both this result and the one described in the previous paragraph are congruent with Beach et al.'s (1988) results for the executives of the athletic shoe manufacturer, the winery, and the ski wear manufacturer discussed a few pages back.

In the third study, it was found that the less the compatibility between employees' descriptions of their organization's culture *as it should be* and their descriptions of the culture *as it is,* the less satisfied they reported themselves to be with their jobs, the less committed they reported themselves to be with the organization, and the more strongly they reported themselves to feel about leaving their jobs.

The results of the third study complement the findings of Shockley-Zalabak and Morley (1989), who examined the relationship between individuals' images of ideal organization and these same persons' images of the organization for which they worked. It was found that larger discrepancies between these two images led to lower satisfaction with the organization, lower evaluations of the organization's quality, and lower estimates of the chances that the organization would survive. In a similar vein, Bissell and Beach (1996) had employees of a controller's office in a state agency and of a pre-trial services office describe their images of ideal supervisory behavior and their images of their own supervisor's behavior. Results showed that employees' satisfaction with their jobs decreased as the discrepancy between ideal image and the actual image increased and that satisfaction with the organization decreased as job satisfaction decreased. Richmond, Bissell, and Beach (1998) obtained the same result with employees of a chain of fast food restaurants and Dunegan (2003) got it with members of the professional staff at a university.

These studies are merely a beginning. Clearly a great deal more needs to be done to investigate both the organizational and the individual versions of image theory. In addition, studies that integrate the two versions more tightly are called for. The goal, of course, is to produce a descriptive theory that covers both individual and organizational decisions with one small set of concepts and mechanisms, thus giving some degree of unity to what are now fairly different views of decision making.

### ❖ EXTENSIONS AND APPLICATIONS OF IMAGE THEORY

While there may be others that we do not know about, there are three main lines of research that have grown out of image theory. The first is application of image theory to examine employee decisions about quitting their jobs—called job turnover—done by Tom Lee and Terrance Mitchell at the University of Washington. The second is application of the theory to employee evaluations of fairness in the workplace—called organizational justice—done by Stephen Gilliland and his colleagues at the University of Arizona. The third is application of the theory to decisions about treatment programs for patients with mental health problems by Paul Falzer and his colleagues at Yale University. All three topic areas have a history of unsuccessful attempts to couch the decisions in terms of prescriptive theory or first generation behavioral theory. The researchers cited here each elected to recast the issues in terms of image theory and to create a research agenda to evaluate the value of doing so. We will end this chapter by briefly describing each of these endeavors.

## Job Turnover

Until the introduction of Lee and Mitchell's (1994) variant of image theory, called the Unfolding Model, research on job turnover was based on a common view: Employees became dissatisfied with their jobs for one reason or another, they searched for alternatives, and they then engaged in a mental expected value analysis to decide whether to stay where they were or go to the most attractive alternative job. Unfortunately, this reasonable-sounding process does not correspond well to observations of decision makers' descriptions of their deliberations about quitting.

The Unfolding Model has two central ideas. First, there are multiple paths by which people leave jobs. Second, these paths unfold over time, that is, they become apparent to the decision maker over time, and they unfold at different rates. The model describes four prototypical paths, of which Paths 2 through 4 utilize concepts from image theory.

Path 1 is followed when some significant event triggers a preexisting script that the decision maker follows. For example, when school starts in the autumn, many students quit their summer jobs to return to classes. Or, when the last child graduates from college, the child's mother may follow her plan to quit her job and take up gardening.

Path 2 is followed when something shocking occurs that causes the decision maker to reassess his or her commitment to his or her employer. For example, when passed over for promotion, a manager may consider what is important to her (value image), the career objectives that follow from her values (trajectory image), and where this job appears to be leading (strategic image). She then makes a progress decision by comparing the trajectory and strategic images; if the two are incompatible she quits her job. Note that no search for an alternative job is involved in Path 2.

Path 3 is followed when something shocking occurs and the decision maker follows Path 2 but follows it with a search for alternative jobs that are then screened for compatibility with the decision maker's standards, and the best of the survivors is chosen. For example, if an employee is accused by coworkers of making them look bad by working too hard, she may decide that this job does not further her desire to advance to a management job through demonstrated ability and hard work (Path 2). She may then begin to look for alternative jobs, rejecting those that do not have the potential for satisfying her desire for advancement and selecting the most promising from among those that are not rejected (Path 3).

Path 4 is followed when accumulated dissatisfactions, rather than a shocking event, initiates the process described for Path 3.

Initial research (Lee, Mitchell, Holtom, McDaniel, & Hill, 1999; Lee, Mitchell, Weiss, & Fireman, 1996; Mitchell & Lee, 2001), based on interviews and questionnaires, strongly suggests that the four paths describe the decision processes of most employees as they deliberate whether to voluntarily leave their jobs. The model is still being studied, one goal of which is to help employers understand how their actions trigger turnover decisions and how to use this understanding to reduce employee turnover.

## Organizational Justice

Gilliland and his colleagues have used image theory to investigate organizational justice—the mental processes underlying judgments about what constitutes fairness in the workplace, about whether one has been treated fairly, and how these judgments eventuate in decisions to leave the organization, to sue it, and so on. Previous research and theory in this area were based on classical expected value decision theory, on heuristics and biases, and on prospect theory, without particularly satisfactory results.

Gilliland and Paddock (in press) review the research and present their adaptation of image theory to organizational justice, calling it

Justice Integration Theory. Using image theory as the framework, the authors tie existing literature to the basic concepts and derive a list of propositions that can guide future research. It is indeed an impressive job and one that lays out a plan for a good deal of future research.

The research began before Justice Integration Theory was published, and so far it has been impressive. For example, Gilliland, Benson, and Schepers (1998), in the first empirical investigation of image theory and justice, presented student participants with scenarios and asked them to judge the fairness of an employer's actions and to decide what to do about it. The goal of this study was to compare the roles of violations and nonviolations in judgments of fairness and in subsequent decisions about what to do. Results showed that judgments about fairness were influenced by both violations and nonviolations, but decisions about what to do were influenced primarily by violations, with a rejection threshold of about three violations. The upshot of this research is that judgment and decision making are not the same thing, and that researchers would do well to mind the distinction.

In a second study, Paddock, Gilliland, and Goldman (2003) looked at fairness judgments and at decisions about what should happen as a result. This time the participants were people who actually had been laid off from their jobs. They were asked questions about the layoff procedure used by their former employers and then they were asked to decide whether that employer should be rewarded or punished. Interestingly, decisions about rewards were influenced primarily by violations, but decisions about punishments were influenced by both violations and nonviolations. That is, decisions to reward looked like regular decisions—the more violations there are, the less inclined one is to reward the employer. Decisions about punishment looked like judgments—punishment reflects violations but is tempered by nonviolations. This implies that for these decision makers, reward and punishment were not symmetrical; they are not two ends of the same stick. That is, the decision to reward or not is an all-or-none decision in the sense covered by image theory's compatibility test. The decision to punish or not is more like a judgment in the sense discovered by Gilliland et al. (1998)—a matter of degree.

Research on Justice Integration Theory continues, and it will be interesting to see what it produces. If the two existing studies are anything to go by, this appears to be a profitable line of work. It promises to illuminate both organizational justice and decision research, which makes it doubly valuable.

## Clinical Treatment Selection

Over the years, empirical research has identified effective practices for treating many mental health problems, called Evidence Based Practices (EBPs). EBPs seldom are one-size-fits-all; variations on an EBP allow treatment of variations on a particular category of problems. The task for the clinician is to decide which of the proven EPBs, and which variation of each, is appropriate for the client in question.

This may seem straightforward, but it turns out not to be. Researchers despair the fact that even when clinicians know about them, they frequently choose clinical lore and traditional treatment modalities over empirically tested EPBs. The question is why they make this choice. The answer begins with learning about how they make treatment decisions in general. Knowing this, it might be possible to present information in a way that would give EBPs a better chance of being chosen.

The clinical literature on EPB decision making customarily characterize clinicians as gamblers who bet on a particular treatment modality after having calculated the expected value of all available modalities. Time and again this characterization has proved to be both inaccurate and unhelpful. As a result, Paul Falzer (2003a, 2003b) and his colleagues at the Yale School of Medicine have cast the EPB decision in terms of image theory. Roughly, the idea is that clinicians value a certain level of functioning for their patients—the value image. This image will vary somewhat for different patients, depending on their diagnosis and the severity of their disorder; getting a severe schizophrenic to function adequately in a group home might be the best that can be hoped for, while it might be reasonable to expect to get someone with an obsessive disorder to the point of holding a job and having a social life.

The clinical diagnosis and supporting documents (interviews, tests, etc.) define the patient's present state, and the difference between the value image and the present state dictates the goals that make up the trajectory image. The idea is to move the patient from his or her present state to the state defined by the trajectory image.

The first decision is about adopting the treatment plan that will constitute the strategic image. This consists of the clinicians screening out unsuitable EBP, lore-based, or traditional modalities and selecting the best from among the survivors. The second decision is about progress as treatment is implemented. If treatment results in movement toward the goals on the trajectory image, the treatment is deemed successful and is continued. If progress is too slow or not at all, or even in some other direction, the treatment is abandoned and something new is tried (which actually may be the same treatment with a few alterations).

Falzer's use of image theory is more complex than this short description might imply, but this is the essence. Research is in its infancy but begins with a series of studies evaluating how well the image theory interpretation fits clinicians' observed decision processes. The strategy is to adapt techniques from earlier image theory studies for use with clinicians. Presuming that the fit is good, the next step will be to design interventions to help clinicians more easily evaluate EBPs in light of the goals on their trajectory images; EBPs are less familiar and less intuitively compelling than lore and tradition, and they therefore fail to evoke strong confidence in the resulting decision.

This ends our discussion of image theory; we will reserve a critique of the theory for the next, and final, chapter of the book.

## ❖ SUMMARY

Image theory is a second generation behavioral decision theory. Like first generation theory, it attempts to describe how decision makers actually make decisions rather than prescribing how they should make them, but image theory does not make use of the gamble analogy that underlies first generation work. Of course, image theory draws on the empirical research from first generation research, but its more immediate antecedents are outlined in the previous chapter—the small descriptive decision theories that eschew the gamble analogy. It certainly is not the end of the line as a second generation theory—it is but another step to future generations of behavioral research and theory.

Image theory assumes that decision makers come to the decision with a store of knowledge that can conveniently be divided into three categories, the three images. These are knowledge about what truly matters (beliefs and values), knowledge about what constitutes a desirable future (goals), and knowledge about how to go about securing that future (plans). The process by which relevant knowledge is brought to bear on a decision is called framing. Decisions consist of either augmenting one's knowledge (adoption decisions) or of assessing the effectiveness of one's actions (progress decisions). The most frequently used decision mechanism is the compatibility test (screening and progress decisions). When the compatibility test fails to provide an unequivocal decision, the decision maker turns to the profitability test, which in fact is a repertoire of strategies for making choices. The selection of a strategy from the repertoire is contingent upon the characteristics of the decision, the environment in which the decision is embedded, and of the decision maker.

The organizational version of image theory presumes that decisions are made by individuals in the organization and amalgamated to create an "organizational decision." The theory is the same as for individuals except that the relevant parts of the individual's knowledge base are specific to the organization. Thus knowledge about the organization's culture is part of the individual's value image, knowledge about the organization's vision is part of the individual's trajectory image, and knowledge about the organization's strategic plan is part of the individual's strategic image. When making decisions for and about the organization, the framing assures that these organizationally relevant parts of the individual's knowledge contribute to the decision process.

# 11

# The Future

*T*he light turned green and Ralph headed his car toward home. It had been a long couple of months, but he felt good about the outcome. The new salespeople were working out well. So that problem was solved, and he thought he somehow was better prepared for whatever came next.

He had learned a lot in this short time, especially about decision making. On the other hand, impressed as he was by all the theory and research that his sister-in-law had taught him, he was disappointed by how little help it was to folks like him. True, the multiple regression (cloning) stuff had worked well, but it left them with a large pool of qualified candidates, and the process of choosing from that pool had been brutal. Decision trees with all their fancy computations were too cold and cumbersome for him to even consider; he doubted he would feel comfortable with their prescriptions even if he used them. Neither generation of behavioral decision work was much better; it simply wasn't advanced enough to give him the kind of guidance he thought he needed. The heuristics and biases stuff just made him feel stupid, and image theory lacked the prescriptive structure he wanted for practical problems.

On the positive side, however, he now could think more objectively about how he approached decisions, and he could understand where some of his frustrations had come from. If nothing else, he had learned to make his goals and *decision criteria explicit so he could tell how and where he disagreed with other people and so he could detect contradictions in his own thinking. Next time, perhaps, he could make things go a little smoother.*

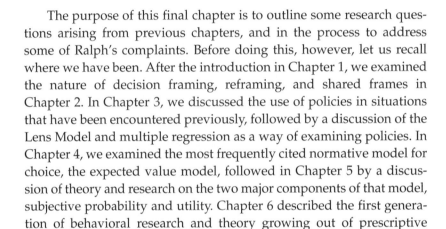

The purpose of this final chapter is to outline some research questions arising from previous chapters, and in the process to address some of Ralph's complaints. Before doing this, however, let us recall where we have been. After the introduction in Chapter 1, we examined the nature of decision framing, reframing, and shared frames in Chapter 2. In Chapter 3, we discussed the use of policies in situations that have been encountered previously, followed by a discussion of the Lens Model and multiple regression as a way of examining policies. In Chapter 4, we examined the most frequently cited normative model for choice, the expected value model, followed in Chapter 5 by a discussion of theory and research on the two major components of that model, subjective probability and utility. Chapter 6 described the first generation of behavioral research and theory growing out of prescriptive theory and its normative models. The first generation goal was to retain the general logic of prescriptive theory but to change its various aspects in a way that would produce behaviorally descriptive theory: heuristics and biases and prospect theory.

The success of first generation research and theory gave legitimacy to research that ranged beyond the confines of prescriptive theory and normative models. This is best represented by the work on the role of emotion in decision making that was described in Chapter 7. Then, to continue the broader view of decision making, in Chapter 8 we examined research on interpersonal, organizational, and group decision making, again seeing that theories deriving from prescriptive theory seldom were successfully descriptive. This led to Chapter 9 and the examination of a number of small theories that do not utilize prescriptive theory's gamble analogy. And, in Chapter 10, we finished our survey of the psychology of decision making with a description of the most thoroughly developed second generation theory advanced thus far, image theory. Which brings us to this, the final chapter, in which we will critique what has gone before and outline our guesses of how future behavioral research and theory will unfold.

## ❖ PRESCRIPTIVE THEORY

### Frames

If you read the latest journal articles you might think that framing pertains solely to prospect theory (Kahneman & Tversky, 1979) and to putting a positive or negative spin on identical payoffs for gambles (e.g., 60% successes vs. 40% failures). If, however, we view framing historically (Minsky, 1968), as the process of bringing relevant knowledge to bear on a situation, several research questions suggest themselves.

First, what are the general principles that govern how information influences framing? This includes current information about the situation as well as knowledge the decision maker has about what led up to the situation. Perhaps advertising provides a source for ideas about this; a great deal of effort has been put into ways to grab consumers' attention and influence how they perceive (frame) decisions about products. Are there principles from advertising and, say, the management of political campaigns, that generalize to the framing of everyday decisions? In short, perhaps there are natural laboratories that could provide useful suggestions for a theory of framing that can be tested in scientific laboratories. As part of this, studies of how experts frame decisions must be broadened to include areas other than just occupation-related decision making; we all are experts in our own lives, and experience clearly has an effect on how each of us frames everyday situations.

Research also is needed on how frames influence the construction and use of scenarios and mental models, how frames affect the stories we tell ourselves, and how they thereby affect subsequent decisions. Part of this involves how people communicate frames to influence another person's frame and to promote understanding of their own frames by other people. This in turn raises questions about how shared frames influence confidence in decisions; perhaps we are more confident if we know that other people see things the same way we do. It also raises questions about what happens when people who must work together have different frames for the same situation but do not realize it, and how resolution of the differences is handled.

Reframing also requires attention. If a problem is framed in a certain way and subsequent events prove that frame to have been inaccurate, how does reframing take place? Under what conditions do decision makers resist reframing—how wrong must the first frame be to prompt reframing?

Finally, framing need not always be intuitive and private. Sometimes frames are carefully and thoughtfully constructed, and often this is done in concert with other people. For example, when a committee or team is charged with examining a particular problem, much of their early effort may be invested in reaching a common understanding of what the problem is and what its possible ramifications may be. In some cases this exploration is done systematically (or at least in an orderly manner), and the question is whether there are ways of doing this that are efficient and that make subsequent decision making easier and insure more satisfying results.

### Policy

If we conceive of policies as preformulated action strategies for classes of similar situations, research must focus on how we recognize that a situation is a member of one or another class. This might draw upon what has been learned about stimulus and response generalization in learning theory, but the stimulus-response framework is perhaps archaic and too restrictive. Alternatively, cognitive research on memory certainly is relevant, and tying policy to this research would strengthen the rather tenuous links between cognitive science and decision research.

It also is important to learn more about the nature of behavioral policies, particularly their detail and breadth. One can imagine that for very repetitive, well-structured situations the policy might be highly detailed and prescriptive, while for more variable situations the policy might consist of guidelines that allow for changing conditions or for the uniqueness of a particular instance of the situation. Of course, organizational policies, as distinct from an individual's behavioral policies, also range from highly prescriptive to general guidelines, and therefore may provide ideas about how to think about individuals' policies that could result in useful theory and interesting research.

The Lens Model and multiple regression have been valuable in studying individuals' policies, and they probably will continue to be so, particularly for applied research aimed at a rough sketch of what is going on. However, for more detailed research they both may have outlived their usefulness. The Lens must be conceived of in more complexity if we are to better appreciate the nuances of decision makers' policies, and this will demand equally complex analytic techniques. Multiple regression provides a very simple picture of the structure of a decision maker's policy, but advances in structural modeling can provide richer pictures.

An interesting area of research about the nature of cues has been opened by Connolly (1977; Connolly & Srivastava, 1995). Sometimes cues are "clues," and sometimes they are "components" of the thing being evaluated, and the two interpretations have different implications. Clues are information about some unobservable state, and as such they help in diagnosing what that state might be. In our example in which Ralph and Betty tried to clone their good salespeople, the information on job applications was treated as clues about an unobservable sales ability.

Component information is quite different. Connolly's example involves two men who have purchased new cars, each of whom finds a defect in the ashtray of his car. One regards the defect as a clue about the quality of his car's construction; the defective ashtray suggesting lower-than-hoped-for quality. The other man regards the ashtray as a component of the car and the defect as a negligible decrease in his car's value.

Connolly (1977) showed that these different interpretations of cues require quite different policies: averaging of clue information and adding of component information. Connolly and Srivastava (1995) have demonstrated that decision makers, in fact, are sensitive to the distinction between clues and components, that they evidence the predicted difference in policies for the two kinds of information, and that subsequent behavior reflects the differences in policies. Moreover, whether decision makers interpret cues as clues or components depends upon how they frame the situation, and the researchers could manipulate the frame by the way in which they described the situation, which ties this research to our earlier discussion of research opportunities for framing. The compellingness of Connolly's differentiation and the empirical results of Connolly and Srivastava's research, both on policy and on framing, suggest that this is an important area of research.

## Choice

Prescriptive theory as the touchstone for behavioral research shows only minor signs of going away. It is seductive. It is reasonable to think that people behave in their own best interests. It is convenient to characterize these interests as the product sum of probability and utility, and to describe choice as simply the selection of the option with the largest product sum. Even when research shows that this is an inaccurate description, the model's predictions often are not too far off the mark (remember, accurate prediction is not necessarily accurate description). To tip the scales even farther, the decision aiding technology (decision trees, computer programs, and all the rest) that derives from prescriptive theory is highly developed and has a commercial market, and it is unlikely that its users will willingly abandon it.

On the other hand, the failures of normative theory are so well documented that virtually nobody who is familiar with the research believes it to be descriptively useful. First generation theory (i.e., prospect theory) keeps the general idea of subjective expected utility while making massive changes in the underlying components in order to make it descriptive. Prospect theory has generated a large amount of interesting laboratory research. However, as valuable as it has been, many researchers find it as constricting as the prescriptive theory it seeks to replace, if only because it too relies on the gamble metaphor and that metaphor appears to be only narrowly applicable outside the laboratory.

Another way of addressing the failure of prescriptive theory is to regard it as merely one out of many possible strategies for making choices, albeit the most thoroughly researched and logically well-developed. Then the question becomes one of who actually uses the strategy (or something like it), under what conditions they use it, and how closely their strategy follows the prescriptions of the normative model. Because the strategy is highly analytic, a good place to begin is to examine the conditions that generally promote analytic thought. Such work was begun in the 1980s (e.g., Barnes, 1984; Nisbett, Krantz, Jepson, & Kunda, 1983), but little seems to have been done since.

### Subjective Probability

Even if we demote prescriptive theory to merely being one of many strategies, subjective probability retains its importance. Be it a representation of uncertainty, risk, unpredictability, or whatever, it is clear that decisions are influenced by it. Early attempts to use probability theory as a normative model concluded that subjective probability does not behave as the theory demands. One result was that probabilities were replaced by decision weights in prospect theory.

There has been a great deal of research on risk, risk perception, and risk communication (e.g., Rück, 1993; Slovic, 1987), but it has not coalesced into a theory. If we think of decisions as involving both screening and choice, the role of risk in each must be considered (see Potter & Beach, 1994). If we acknowledge that decision makers have numerous strategies for making choices, the role of risk in each of them must be examined. If we recognize that a belief in luck influences many (most?) peoples' decisions, its links to perceived risk and to subjective probability deserve attention. However, before all of this is undertaken, researchers must become more sophisticated about what probability is (and is not) and how it relates to risk, lest they simply repeat the errors of the past. Hacking's (1975) book on the development of the concept of probability is a good place to start, and Gigerenzer's (1991) research is a good follow-up. Not every proportion is a probability and not every event has a clearly defined probability and not all uncertainty is perceived as riskiness. These concepts are substantially more elusive than generally imagined.

## Utility

From a behavioral viewpoint, utility is not so much a useful concept as it is a conversation stopper. There is not much to be said when the complex factors that drive decision making are presumed to result in a single point on a single scale. This impoverished description may be useful for economics, although Etzioni (1988) has argued persuasively to the contrary, but it is a liability for behavioral decision theory.

As stressed in second generation theories, the roles of the decision maker's principles (beliefs, values, morals, ethics, obligations, and duties) are so important that it is counterproductive to oversimplify them. Add to this the distinct need to account for the contributions of emotions and feelings to decisions, and the idea of reducing everything to a point on a single scale becomes somewhat absurd. If for no other reason, advances in the neurosciences (Damasio, 1994) demand that decision theorists and researchers (and economists) look beyond mere convenience to acknowledge that things are far richer, if less tractable, than has been admitted.

The upshot, perhaps, is that research on utility per se is not needed because the concept is no longer required. In contrast, research is sorely needed on all the things that the concept has obscured, and on how they contribute to decision makers' evaluations of subjective worth. In contrast to utility, subjective worth is bound to be multidimensional, and framing is likely to influence how it is evaluated and why it shifts as conditions change. Certainly, these issues merit research.

Finally, Thaler's (1985) work on "mental accounting" opens a potentially rich new research area. The observation that different categories of money are treated differently probably applies to the worth of things other than money; familiar possessions often are worth more than their market price, for example.

❖ FIRST GENERATION BEHAVIORAL
RESEARCH AND THEORY

Heuristics and biases and prospect theory, the first attempts to construct a behavioral theory of decision making, have been spectacularly successful, prompting a wide array of research and being adopted by other disciplines, such as economics. However, they both have problems: Heuristics and biases are theoretically shallow, and prospect theory retains the gamble analogy, which is increasingly seen as irrelevant to much of decision making. Therefore, it is likely that neither prospect theory nor heuristics and biases research will look much like their present forms 20 years from now. In every lively area of science, research programs and theoretical models evolve and change, and it would be very odd if these two survived. But something recognizably connected to them will surely remain. We need not be obsessed with human errors to recognize that people really do make mistakes—choices that in retrospect they wish they could make over. We hope researchers will stop explaining mistakes and biases by inventing more heuristics, but they surely will be asking: "Was that a sensible decision? Where did it go wrong? What can decision makers do to avoid falling into the same old traps?" We hope researchers will be more thoughtful about concluding what the "right answer" should be when reasonable people might disagree, but we also hope researchers do not lose their belief that some decisions really are better than others.

Prospect theory is, of course, a work in process, and its successes ensure that some version of it will be with us for a long time. After decades of battles along the intellectual border between economics and decision research, prospect theory has come to be seen as a bridge; it is common to read economics papers in which the psychology is drawn, not from some idealized rational chooser but from a recognizable, if simplified, prospector. Surely these intellectual gains should not be allowed to evaporate. The tension remains between keeping the theory reasonably compact and continuing to improve its descriptive realism. But Tversky and Kahneman's basic invention is brilliant: a theoretical form that is familiar to economists but that still accommodates many of the important psychological discoveries of decision psychology.

## ❖  EMOTIONS

Interest in the emotional aspects of decision making seems certain to continue. Here the linkage is between decision research and well-established bodies of work on emotions in the psychological mainstream. The traffic is two-way and has enriched both decision research and mainstream psychology. The work on mood, on regret and disappointment in shaping choice, the roles such emotions play in trapping decision makers in sunk costs or inaction inertia, and the speed with which their feelings of ownership develop in the endowment effect represent what must surely be just the tip of a large iceberg. Research on emotion in decision making has a lively future.

Just starting to emerge from the medical research laboratory to become part of decision research is the work on brain imaging. Here the research is developing at an astonishing rate, and it would clearly be foolish to make any predictions beyond the easy one: There is going to be more. Researchers are beginning to progress beyond their initial fascination with "put them in the magnet and see which bits of the brain light up" and are launching research programs with real decisional significance. Trying to guess where this brand-new field is likely to go is merely an opportunity to embarrass ourselves, so we will not even try. Our only prediction is that anyone launching a career in decision research would be well advised to take a few courses in the anatomy and physiology of the brain, and in advanced research techniques.

## ❖  INTERPERSONAL, ORGANIZATIONAL, AND GROUP DECISIONS

Decisions seldom are made in isolation, and they clearly reflect emotions, values, morals, and attitudes. Recognition of this raises interesting questions about the assumptions people make about other people's emotions, values, morals, and attitudes and, as a result, about how they will react to decisions that affect them. This in turn leads to questions about the origins of trust and the role of trust in interpersonal, organizational, and group decision making. Trust is discussed a good deal in management research, but it seldom is mentioned in decision research.

Trust also is linked to fairness and cooperation, which feature so prominently in the results of game theory and negotiation research, and in turn to research on equity and attribution. Of particular interest, because it has such broad implications for the rest of decision making, is the game theory finding that players can "earn" the right to disproportionate shares of resources. This, of course, is a common idea in everyday life, but the concept of rights has never played a role in decision theory or research. This has implications for the study of subjective evaluations of worth, discussed a moment ago, because it sets reference points for the "natural" distribution of resources. If, as is probable, the prospect theory notion that gains and losses are relative to a reference point is true, then the theory might profit from exploring the idea of "earned" rights being one kind of reference point. At any rate, trust, fairness, cooperation, and rights are such ubiquitous concepts in day-to-day interactions with other people that they deserve to be examined closely.

### Game Theory

Game theory holds considerable potential, but it has few ties to other areas that could make it richer. Social psychologists study many of the same problems as game researchers (e.g., the dilemma of the commons), but the two seem to have little communication. In part this is because social research is not as rigorous as game research, and game researchers appear to be put off by this. On the other hand, that rigor often makes game research very formal and abstract, which puts off social psychologists. The two groups really ought to talk to each other; little harm could result and there is a potential for something good evolving (Selten, 1990).

### Negotiation

Negotiation research also is frequently viewed as separate from mainline decision research. A potential point of intersection, however, is afforded by the role of negotiation in the consolidation of group members' individual decisions into a single decision. Whether it be by voting, consensus, by the leader recognizing the sense of the meeting, or by powerful members dominating the others, group members engage in complicated negotiations to combine their views and how to present the result to outsiders. There has been research on voting and on conditions that promote consensus, but they have not been brought together, and neither integrates well with negotiation research or decision research. In part this is because negotiation and voting research use different formal models and consensus research focuses on situation variables and process. Because there is neither common focus nor common language, the research does not fit together very well. Someone should put them together to create a theory of group decision negotiation.

## Levels of Discourse

Discussions of organizational decision making often suffer from a failure to clearly specify their level of analysis and then to stay on that level rather than moving back and forth. Work at the most molar level should consistently treat the organization as a single decision making unit, the decisions of which are implemented in an environment populated by other organizations. Work at the middle level should consistently treat the organization as a structured collection of members or employees, each of whom makes decisions that contribute to a collective decision that is then implemented according to the dynamics of the organization's structure and the situation. Work at the molecular level should consistently treat members of the organization as individuals working within the constraints and imperatives of the organization, with an emphasis on the cognitive and emotive processes that contribute to their decision making. The garbage can model (Cohen, March, & Olsen, 1972) is an example of what happens when the discussion switches among levels; it is neither molar, middle, nor molecular, but a mix of all three. As a result, in our opinion, it does not enlighten us about either the organization or the members, and it therefore is difficult to imagine how it could guide behavioral research.

If molar-level discussions have a common fault, it is that they tend to reify what is really only a useful fiction, that the organization itself makes decisions. If the middle-level discussions have a common fault, it is that they seem to revel in the disorder in organizational decision making, overlooking the role of theory in identifying order in apparent chaos. If molecular-level discussions have a common fault, it is that they ignore the fact that individuals are enmeshed in a social environment, and that the forces in that environment contribute hugely to decision making.

## Problems

Some might argue that the foundations for organizational decision theory exist, citing the garbage can model, participation research, groupthink, or the risky shift research. We already have commented on the garbage can model. And, contrary to how it is discussed in textbooks, the Vroom and Yetton (1973; Vroom, 1973) participation model is not really about group or organizational decision making. It is about the manager's decision whether to invite the participation of members in an organizationally relevant decision. As such, it is an interesting, and perhaps valuable, model but it does not contribute much to our understanding of what happens when decisions are made in groups or organizations.

Similarly, groupthink (Janis, 1972) might seem promising for studying individuals in a group decision setting, but it has not delivered on its promise. Thousands of students and businesspeople have been warned about the dangers of groupthink, but the relative paucity of research makes the warnings difficult to justify.

Things are better for risky shift. Even though the risky shift seems a bit elusive, and its causes are not altogether clear, research on it continues, as does other research on small groups. It is to be hoped that the results will eventually be of value to a broad theory of organizational decision behavior.

Paradoxically, the greatest promise for molar- and middle-level theories of group and organizational decision making may lie in advances in theory and research at the molecular level. That is, it may be impossible to understand what happens in groups and organizations until we better understand the individuals who belong to them. Until we have a better grasp of the role of morals, values, and emotions on individuals' decision making; until we see how people infer these same things for those around them; and until we see how the trust (or lack of it) engendered by these inferences influences individuals' decisions, we cannot understand the raw material that goes into group deliberations and the forces that influence its negotiated choices.

## ❖ ALTERNATIVES TO GAMBLING

Because of their need to address the question of how decisions should be made, many disciplines and occupations have devised theories about decision making, and few of these have incorporated prescriptive theory's gamble analogy. Our review of some of these theories raises questions that provide opportunities for research and for further theory construction.

### Policy

In addition to questions of situation recognition, policy research must address the fact that blind application of a previously successful response to a decision problem is unlikely to turn out well. Indeed, any policy must be modified to fit the unique demands of the situation at hand, and be it characterized as a scenario, a story, or a script, the mechanisms for appropriate modification are central to a useful theory of policy use. One approach to doing research on this might be to give participants descriptions of a policy for a familiar, real situation and observe how they revise it in light of changes in circumstances.

### Narratives

In addition to the role of narratives in policy, there is the larger question of their role in providing meaning to decision situations—in explaining the past and forecasting the future. Add to this the degree to which they are argument driven, which implies purposefulness in their construction, and the degree to which they are shaped by emotion, and the research agenda becomes very rich. In our view, narratives hold the key to progress in studying decision making. They encompass the past, the present, and the future. They provide a platform for expression of the decision maker's principles. They are colored by assumptions about social norms and interpersonal expectations. They may well be the primary vehicle for both understanding and decision making—where decisions grow "naturally" from the progressive development of the narrative. In short, the stories decision makers tell themselves may be central to how they pursue their futures, which, after all, is what decision making is all about.

## Incrementalism

The cognitive viewpoint holds that the gamble analogy of prescriptive theory has led to the mischaracterization of decisions. Seldom is the decision maker required to subscribe to a course of action and then wait passively for the results; most of us take pains to avoid such decisions. Most often we can experiment with what we do, advancing or retreating in light of how things are working. Indeed, the whole purpose of implementation is to influence events, to take command of the future, to work toward ends that fit with our vision of the future, no matter how ill-defined and fluid that vision may be. Passivity has no place in this. Commitment seldom is to the course of action per se; it is to the ends toward which one is striving. Consequently, only an extremely stupid or extremely desperate decision maker would irrevocably lock into a course of action, willingly forgoing the opportunity to revise both the ends and the means in light of information about progress and about the dynamic state of the environment. Most decisions "feel their way along," and in the course of doing so change the narrative that drives them. As things change, both as a result of what the decision maker does and for external reasons, strategies change and goals change. Often the decision maker ends up having done things and achieved ends that were totally unanticipated when the process began. Clearly this process requires our attention; research can be done if we do not try to force this dynamic process into a static model—if we begin to think of decision making as an ongoing story rather than as a single episode.

## Beliefs and Values

The powerful impact of decision makers' beliefs, values, morals, ethics, obligations, and duties demands further examination. This is not the same as research on moral behavior, which tends to focus on lapses, or studies of courage, which tend to focus on heroism—although lapses and heroism are important. More to the point is how principles are vested with emotion and feeling, and how this in turn influences such things as preemptive rejection (screening) of unacceptable options. Beyond this, however, is the contribution of principles to the perceived worth of potential consequences of decisions; utility theory has nothing to say about what makes things valuable. Similarly, principles influence the means selected to achieve worthwhile consequences; some acts are less worthy than others and some are simply unthinkable.

Related research questions involve how framing defines some principles and not others as relevant to the decision at hand, and what happens when the frame changes. Moreover, how are principles integrated into narratives in order to influence meaning and the direction of the narrative's development? And how do principles influence the interpretation of feedback about implementation as well as changes in the goal of implementation? These sorts of questions lead to research on individual differences, which, aside from risk aversion and mixed results on self-efficacy, has never been a particularly strong feature of decision work.

## ❖ IMAGE THEORY

Most of the research questions discussed above are at least obliquely relevant to image theory, but there also are questions that are specific to the theory.

### Images

Basic to the theory is the idea that knowledge is contained in mental representations called images. These are captured in part by concepts such as stories, scenarios, or scripts, but they are more than narratives. For many people, visual imagination is part of their mental images, as is emotion. Cognitive science and neuroscience are beginning to explore issues relevant to images and decision making, and behavioral decision research can contribute to this effort.

Attempts have been made to measure images, but they tend to boil down to lists of important factors, which rather misses the essence of things and probably obscures the emotional content of images. Techniques similar to those used for projective tests might be a better approach, although the results are less amenable to quantification than one might wish. Still, the goal is to understand images rather than find convenient ways of doing research, so a little creativity is to be encouraged.

### Adoption Decisions

Most image theory research has focused on screening of options and the compatibility test, and most of it has been done in the laboratory.

Results indicate that screening is perhaps the most important part of the decision process, if only because it dictates which options end up in the set from which a choice is made. The next step in this research should be to move from the laboratory to decision making in organizations. Because organizations require decision making to be semi-public, in that someone other than the decision maker must understand them, the process often is more open to examination than private decisions.

Choice has been studied in the context of the strategy selection model, which constitutes the profitability test portion of image theory. Unfortunately, the strategy selection model, while acceptable in principle, is flawed in detail—its driving mechanism is maximization of subjective expected utility, which is increasingly untenable. While it clearly is true that decision makers have numerous strategies for making choices, there must be an alternative to expected utility for describing the way in which they match a strategy to a choice situation.

### Progress Decisions

Image theory describes implementation monitoring in terms of ongoing decisions about whether acceptable progress is being made toward goals. The theory must be able to account for changes in goals and plans as implementation proceeds. This means that the role of information about progress is richer than mere feedback; it informs the images that define the goal and the plan and changes them in ways that are governed by the decision maker's principles. This takes place in an ongoing flow of interacting behavior and information, and image theory must be developed in order to deal with it.

### Organizations

Viewing the organization's culture, vision, and strategy as the counterpart of the individual's value image, trajectory image, and strategic image permits use of the same decision mechanisms for both versions of image theory. Research is needed to examine both the value and the descriptive adequacy of this parallel. The first step is to see whether the compatibility and profitability tests (i.e., screening and choice) work the same way for private and organizational decisions. For example, does the organization's culture exert the same kind of influence on its members' business decisions as their private principles exert on their private decisions? And what happens when the principles embodied in the organization's culture differ from the principles held by individual members; do people switch back and forth to fit the circumstances or does one set of principles override the other? This requires studies of cultural influences both on screening decisions and on choice, perhaps having participants make the same decision for themselves and for the organization when their private principles differ in some significant way from the organization's culture. The decisions should reflect the difference.

Research also should explore the parallels between an organization's vision and individuals' trajectory image. How do they guide both decision making and information seeking in support of both adoption and progress decisions? Similarly, what are the parallels between organizational strategy formulation and what individuals do when they set out to achieve goals? Individuals' strategies are unlikely to look like the formal strategic plans that some organizations generate each year, but they may resemble the plans that smaller businesses use—often encapsulated in the heads of a few top executives. In the latter case, both vision and plans are flexible and opportunistic, and in this sense they are very like their counterparts for individuals. Research should explore all of these parallels.

## ❖   SOME GUESSES ABOUT THE FUTURE

What would the table of contents of a book like this one look like if it were published 20 years from now? Of course, we can only guess, but we think that decision research, like psychology in general, will continue to have two dominant paradigms—analytic and descriptive. The analytic paradigm is represented in decision research by prescriptive theory and first generation behavioral research and theory; it reflects a taste for mathematics and a preference for the rigor and order of laboratory studies. The descriptive paradigm is represented in decision research by second generation research and theory. It reflects a taste for verbal models, with abundant boxes and arrows, and a tolerance (if not an actual appetite) for the ambiguity that comes from the use of real-world situations as vehicles for research. It would, perhaps, be a mistake to regard one paradigm as more scientific than the other; the difference is more in how they tell their stories than in substance.

Some speculation: We think that framing will become more important and that its link with policy will be a feature of future books on decision making. Work on policy will increase, but the Lens Model and multiple regression will be superseded by more flexible methods. Moreover, the definition of policy will broaden to permit ties to research on public policy and business policy. When this happens, the psychology of policy may become a special field of its own.

The expected value model will never go away completely, but its days are numbered. Whether it will rate more than passing mention in future texts depends on whether the author favors analysis or description. Similarly, subjective probability as a surrogate for subjectively experienced uncertainty or risk will be retained—the mathematics of probability theory is simply too seductive for some to give it up easily. Much the same will happen for utility, which is mathematically convenient but sterile; it will remain part of first generation accounts as they are increasingly adopted by economics.

Game theory and negotiation theory are presently at the crossroads. They both are born of the analytic paradigm and prescriptive decision theory, but empirical evidence is forcing them toward softer, less normative descriptions of the behaviors of interest. Few game theorists accept maximization as descriptive, but it is not clear what they will put in its place. Indeed, most of the research consists of demonstrating that people do not behave as game theory and negotiation theory prescribe (although, as Selten [1990] points out, "too many experimentalists are in search for a confirmation of orthodox theory and go to great lengths in explaining away deviations which cannot be overlooked" [p. 650]). Like the heuristics and biases studies, this research is in danger of producing nothing but examples of prescriptive decision theory's shortcomings, which soon loses its intellectual appeal. More to the point, if people do not behave like game theory or negotiation theory prescribe, what do they do? Is it orderly and coherent? Can it be theoretically described, with or without mathematics? In short, what happens in these research areas?

Organizational and group decision making is a treasure trove of unrealized research opportunities. Our impression is that current research merely describes the conditions under which various kinds of group decision outcomes are more or less likely to occur, but it seldom looks at decision making per se. This makes the existing research of little interest to decision researchers because it is seen as social psychology rather than decision psychology. One could argue, quite correctly, that you cannot have the latter without some appreciation of the former, but as things stand now it is not at all clear that the two literatures have much to say to each other. However, this is going to change as second generation research and theory develops, if only because it tends to be interested in real-life decision making, and real-life decisions mostly occur in groups and organizations. We predict that the textbook of the future will have a good deal of coverage of this topic, and that new researchers would be wise to get in on the ground floor; this is going to be big.

These research directions are only the high points, but they are what seem to us to be the most important directions. The history of the field shows a steady retreat from normative models imported from economics and statistics and a steady advance toward behavioral research and theories that may help us get a handle on what people are trying to do when they make decisions, thereby suggesting ways in which they can do it better (or at least less painfully). Much of this development derives from observations of real-life decision making, and from observed failures of the normative theories when confronted with day-to-day decision problems. It is our belief that first generation behavioral decision research and theory made enormous strides, and that the discipline is now in a second generation of advances as researchers become more comfortable with having departed from their prescriptive roots and allow themselves greater freedom to explore what happens when people make decisions. It is a good time to be working in this discipline, to be involved in creating the future generations of behavioral research and theory; the enterprise is exciting and fun, it is worthwhile, and the future looks bright.

# References

Anderson, J. R. (1981). *Cognitive skills and their acquisition*. Hillsdale, NJ: Lawrence Erlbaum.

Arkes, H., & Blumer, C. (1985). The psychology of sunk cost. *Organizational Behavior and Human Decision Processes, 35*, 124–140.

Asch, D. A., Baron, J., Hershey, J. C., Kunreuther, H., Meszaros, J., Ritov, I., et al. (1994). Omission bias and pertussis vaccination. *Medical Decision Making, 14*, 118–123.

Asch, S. E. (1956). Studies of independence and conformity: A minority of one against a unanimous majority. *Psychological Monographs, 70* (Whole No. 416).

Barclay, S., & Beach, L. R. (1972). Combinatorial properties of personal probabilities. *Organizational Behavior and Human Performance, 8*, 176–183.

Barnes, V. E. (1984). *The quality of human judgment: An alternative perspective.* Unpublished doctoral dissertation, University of Washington, Seattle.

Bayes, T. (1958). Essay towards solving a problem in the doctrine of chances. *Biometrika, 45*, 293–315. (Reprinted from *Philosophical Transactions of the Royal Society*, 1763, 53, 370–418.)

Beach, L. R. (1974). A note on the intrasubject similarity of subjective probabilities obtained by estimates and by bets. *Organizational Behavior and Human Performance, 11*, 250–252.

Beach, L. R. (1990). *Image theory: Decision making in personal and organizational contexts.* Chichester, UK: Wiley.

Beach, L. R. (1993a). Broadening the definition of decision making: The role of prechoice screening of options. *Psychological Science, 4*, 215–220.

Beach, L. R. (1993b). *Making the right decision: Organizational culture, vision and planning.* Englewood Cliffs, NJ: Prentice Hall.

Beach, L. R. (Ed.). (1996). *Decision making in the workplace: A unified perspective.* Mahwah, NJ: Lawrence Erlbaum.

Beach, L. R., Barnes, V. E., & Christensen-Szalanski, J. J. J. (1986). Beyond heuristics and biases: A contingency model of judgmental forecasting. *Journal of Forecasting, 5*, 143–157.

Beach, L. R., Christensen-Szalanski, J. J. J., & Barnes, V. E. (1987). Assessing human judgment: Has it been done, can it be done, should it be done? In

G. Wright & P. Ayton (Eds.), *Judgmental forecasting* (pp. 49–62). Chichester, UK: Wiley.

Beach, L. R., Jungermann, H., & De Bruyn, E. E. J. (1996). Imagination and planning. In L. R. Beach (Ed.), *Decision making in the workplace: A unified perspective* (pp. 143–154). Mahwah, NJ: Lawrence Erlbaum.

Beach, L. R., & Lipshitz R. (1993). Why classical decision theory is an inappropriate standard for evaluating and aiding most human decision making. In G. A. Klein, J. Orasanu, R. Calderwood, & C. E. Zsambok (Eds.), *Decision making in action: Models and methods.* Norwood, NJ: Ablex.

Beach, L. R., & Mitchell, T. R. (1978). A contingency model for the selection of decision strategies. *Academy of Management Review, 3,* 439–449.

Beach, L. R., & Mitchell, T. R. (1990). Image theory: A behavioral theory of decisions in organizations. In B. M. Staw & L. L. Cummings (Eds.), *Research in organizational behavior* (Vol. 12). Greenwich, CT: JAI.

Beach, L. R., & Phillips, L. D. (1967). Subjective probabilities inferred from estimates and bets. *Journal of Experimental Psychology, 75,* 354–359.

Beach, L. R., Smith, B., Lundell, J., & Mitchell, T. R. (1988). Image theory: Descriptive sufficiency of a simple rule for the compatibility test. *Journal of Behavioral Decision Making, 1,* 17–28.

Beach, L. R., & Strom, E. (1989). A toadstool among the mushrooms: Screening decisions and image theory's compatibility test. *Acta Psychologica, 72,* 1–12.

Beach, L. R., & Wise, J. A. (1969). Subjective probability estimates and confidence ratings. *Journal of Experimental Psychology, 79,* 438–444.

Behn, R. D., & Vaupel, J. W. (1982). *Quick analysis for busy decision makers.* New York: Basic Books.

Bell, D. E. (1982). Regret in decision making under uncertainty. *Operations Research, 30,* 961–981.

Benson, L. III, Beach, L. R., Mertens, D. P., & Payne, J. W. (2004). The violation threshold in pre-choice screening of decision options (Working paper). Tucson: University of Arizona, Department of Management and Policy.

Ben-Yoav, O., & Pruitt, D. G. (1984a). Accountability to constituents: A two-edged sword. *Organizational Behavior and Human Performance, 34,* 282–295.

Ben-Yoav, O., & Pruitt, D. G. (1984b). Resistance to yielding and the expectation of cooperative future interaction in negotiation. *Journal of Experimental Social Psychology, 20,* 323–353.

Bernoulli, D. (1738). Specimen theoriae novae de mensura sortis. *Comentarii Academiae Scieniarum Imperiales Petropolitanae, 5,* 175–192.

Bissell, B. L., & Beach, L. R. (1996). Supervision and job satisfaction. In L. R. Beach (Ed.), *Decision making in the workplace: A unified perspective* (pp. 63–72). Mahwah, NJ: Lawrence Erlbaum.

Boje, D. M., & Murnighan, J. K. (1982, October). Group confidence pressures in iterative decisions. *Management Science,* 1187–1196.

Braybrooke, D., & Lindblom, C. E. (1963). *A strategy of decision: Policy evaluation as a social process.* New York: Free Press.

Brehmer, B., & Joyce, C. R. B. (Eds.). (1988). *Human decision: The SJT view.* Amsterdam: North-Holland.

Brown, F. W., & Finstuen, K. (1993). The use of participation in decision making: A consideration of the Vroom-Yetton and Vroom-Jago normative models. *Journal of Behavioral Decision Making, 6,* 207–219.

Brunswik, E. (1947). *Systematic and representative design of psychological experiments, with results in physical and social perception.* Berkeley, CA: University of California Press.

Camerer, C. F. (1990). Behavioral game theory. In R. M. Hogarth (Ed.), *Insights in decision making: A tribute to Hillel J. Einhorn* (pp. 311–336). Chicago: University of Chicago Press.

Carnevale, P. J. D., & Isen, I. M. (1986). The influence of positive affect and visual access on the discovery of integrative solutions in bilateral negotiations. *Organizational Behavior and Human Decision Processes, 37,* 1–13.

Chase, W. G., & Simon, H. A. (1973). Perception in chess. *Cognitive Psychology, 4,* 55–81.

Christensen-Szalanski, J. J. J. (1978). Problem-solving strategies: A selection mechanism, some implications, and some data. *Organizational Behavior and Human Performance, 22,* 307–323.

Christensen-Szalanski, J. J. J. (1980). A further examination of the selection of problem-solving strategies: The effects of deadlines and analytic aptitudes. *Organizational Behavior and Human Performance, 25,* 107–122.

Christensen-Szalanski, J. J. J., & Beach, L. R. (1982). Experience and the base-rate fallacy. *Organizational Behavior and Human Performance, 29,* 270–278.

Cohen, M. S. (1993). The naturalistic basis of decision biases. In G. A. Klein, J. Orasanu, R. Calderwood, & C. Zambok (Eds.), *Decision making in action: Models and methods* (pp. 36–50). Norwood, NJ: Ablex.

Cohen, M. D., March, J. G., & Olsen, J. P. (1972). A garbage can model of organizational choice. *Administrative Science Quarterly, 17,* 1–25.

Connolly, T. (1977). Cues, components, and causal structure in laboratory judgment studies. *Educational and Psychological Measurement, 37,* 877–888.

Connolly, T. (1988). Hedge-clipping, tree-felling and the management of ambiguity: The need for new images of decision-making. In L. R. Pondy, R. J. Boland, Jr., & H. Thomas (Eds.), *Managing ambiguity and change* (pp. 37–50). New York: John Wiley.

Connolly, T., & Deane, D. (1997). Decomposed versus holistic estimates of effort required for software writing tasks. *Management Science, 43,* 1029–1045.

Connolly, T., Jessup, L. M., & Valacich, J. S. (1990). Effects of anonymity and evaluative tone on idea generation in computer-mediated groups. *Management Science, 36,* 698–703.

Connolly, T., & Reb, J. (2003). Omission bias in vaccination decisions: Where's the "omission"? Where's the "bias"? *Organizational Behavior and Human Decision Processes, 91,* 186–202.

Connolly, T., & Srivastava, J. (1995). Cues and components in multiattribute evaluation. *Organizational Behavior and Human Decision Processes, 64,* 219–228.

Connolly, T., & Wagner, W. G. (1988). Decision cycles. *Advances in Information Processing in Organizations, 3,* 183–205.

Connolly, T., & Zeelenberg, M. (2002). Regret in decision making. *Current Directions in Psychological Science, 11*, 212–216.

Damasio, A. R. (1994). *Descartes' error: Emotion, reason and the human brain.* New York: Grosset/Putnam.

Davis, J. H. (1992). Some compelling intuitions about group consensus decisions, theoretical and empirical research, and interpersonal aggregation phenomena: Selected examples, 1950–1990. *Organizational Behavior and Human Decision Processes, 52*, 3–38.

Davis, J. H., Stasson, M., Ono, K., & Zimmerman, S. (1988). Effects of straw pools on group decision making: Sequential voting pattern, timing, and local majorities. *Journal of Personality and Social Psychology, 55*, 918–926.

Davis, J. H., Tindale, R. S., Nagao, D. H., Hinsz, V. B., & Robertson, B. (1984). Order effects in multiple decisions by groups: A demonstration with mock juries and trial procedures. *Journal of Personality and Social Psychology, 47*, 1003–1012.

Dawes, R. M. (1971). A case study of graduate admissions: Application of three principles of human decision making. *American Psychologist, 26*, 180–188.

de Groot, A. D. (1965). *Thought and choice in chess.* The Hague: Mouton.

Diehl, M., & Stroebe, W. (1987). Productivity loss in brainstorming groups: Toward the solution of a riddle. *Journal of Personality and Social Psychology, 53*, 497–509.

Dinsmore, J. (1987). Mental spaces from a functional perspective. *Cognitive Science, 11*, 1–21.

Dougherty, T. W., Ebert, R. J., & Callender, J. C. (1986). Policy capturing in the employment interview. *Journal of Applied Psychology, 71*, 9–15.

Dunegan, K. J. (1993). Framing, cognitive modes and image theory: Toward an understanding of a glass half-full. *Journal of Applied Psychology, 78*, 491–503.

Dunegan, K. J. (1995). Image theory: Testing the role of image compatibility in progress decisions. *Organizational Behavior and Human Decision Processes, 62*, 79–86.

Dunegan, K. J. (2003). Leader-image compatibility: An image theory view of leadership. *Journal of Business and Management, 9 (Winter)*, 61–77.

Dunegan, K. J., Duchon, D., & Ashmos, D. (1995). Image compatibility and the use of problem space information in resource allocation decisions: Testing a moderating effects model. *Organizational Behavior and Human Decision Processes, 64*, 31–37.

Edwards, W. (1954). The theory of decision making. *Psychological Bulletin, 41*, 380–417.

Edwards, W. (1955). An attempt to predict gambling decisions. In J. W. Dunlap (Ed.), *Mathematical models of human behavior* (pp. 12–32). Stamford, CT: Dunlap and Associates.

Einhorn, H. J., & Hogarth, R. M. (1986). Judging probable cause. *Psychological Bulletin, 99*, 3–19.

Etzioni, A. (1967). Mixed-scanning: A "third" approach to decision-making. *Public Administration Review, 27*, 385–392.

Etzioni, A. (1988). *The moral dimension: Toward a new economics.* New York: Free Press.

Etzioni, A. (1993). *The spirit of community.* New York: Crown.

Falzer, P. R. (2003a). *Evidence and values in psychiatric decisions.* Paper presented at the Values in Psychiatric Diagnosis Research Working Group Conference, London, UK.

Falzer, P. R. (2003b). *Forging a new relationship between philosophy and science.* Paper presented at the Sixth International Conference on Philosophy, Psychiatry, and Psychology, Brasilia, Brazil.

Festinger, L. (1964). *Conflicts, decision and dissonance.* Stanford, CA: Stanford University Press.

Fischhoff, B., Lichtenstein, S., Slovic, P., Derby, S. L., & Keeney, R. L. (1981). *Acceptable risk.* New York: Cambridge University Press.

Fischhoff, B., Slovic, P., & Lichtenstein, S. (1977). Knowing with certainty: The appropriateness of extreme confidence. *Journal of Experimental Psychology, 3,* 552–564.

Fischhoff, B., Slovic, P., & Lichtenstein, S. (1980). Knowing what you want: Measuring labile values. In T. Wallsten (Ed.), *Cognitive processes in choice and decision behavior* (pp. 64–85). Hillsdale, NJ: Lawrence Erlbaum.

Follett, M. P. (1940). Constructive conflict. In H. C. Metcalf & L. Urwick (Eds.), *Dynamic administration: The collected papers of Mary Parker Follett* (pp. 36–47). New York: Harper.

Fryback, D. G., Goodman, B. C., & Edwards, W. (1973). Choices among bets by Las Vegas gamblers: Absolute and contextual effects. *Journal of Experimental Psychology, 98,* 271–278.

Galanter, E. (1962). The direct measurement of utility and subjective probability. *American Journal of Psychology, 75,* 208–220.

Gigerenzer, G. (1991). How to make cognitive illusions disappear: Beyond "heuristics and biases." In W. Stroebe & M. Hewstone (Eds.), *European review of social psychology* (Vol. 2). Chichester, UK: Wiley.

Gigerenzer, G., Hoffrage, U., & Kleinbolting, H. (1991). Probabilistic mental models: A Brunswikian theory of confidence. *Psychological Review, 98,* 506–528.

Gilliland, S. W., Benson, L. III, & Schepers, D. H. (1998). A rejection threshold in justive evaluations: Effects on judgment and decision making. *Organizational Behavior and Human Decision Processes, 76,* 113–131.

Gilliland, S., & Paddock, L. (in press). Images of justice: Development of justice integration theory. In S. W. Gilliland, D. D. Steiner, & D. P. Skarlicki (Eds.), *What motivates fairness in organizations? Vol. 4 in Research in Social Issues in Management.* Greenwich, CT: Information Age Publishing.

Gilovich, T., & Medvec, V. H. (1995). The experience of regret: What, when, and why. *Psychological Review, 102,* 379–395.

Gray, C. A. (1975). Factors in students' decisions to attempt academic tasks. *Organizational Behavior and Human Performance, 13,* 147–164.

Gruder, C. (1971). Relationships with opponent and partner in mixed-motive bargaining. *Journal of Conflict Resolution, 15,* 403–416.

Hacking, I. (1975). *The emergence of probability.* New York: Cambridge University Press.

Hammond, K. R. (1955). Probabilistic functioning and the clinical method. *Psychological Review, 62,* 255–262.

Hammond, K. R. (1971). Computer graphics as an aid to learning. *Science, 172,* 903–908.

Hammond, K. R., & Adelman, L. (1976). Science, values, and human decision. *Science, 194,* 389–396.

Hammond, K. R., Harvey, L. O., Jr., & Hastie, R. (1992). Making better use of scientific knowledge: Separating truth from justice. *Psychological Science, 3,* 80–87.

Hammond, K. R., Rohrbaugh, J., Mumpower, J., & Adelman, L. (1977). Social decision theory: Applications in policy formation. In M. Kaplan & S. Schwartz (Eds.), *Human decision and decision making in applied settings* (pp. 1–30). New York: Academic Press.

Hammond, K. R., Stewart, T. R., Brehmer, B., & Steinman, D. O. (1975). Social decision theory. In M. Kaplan & S. Schwartz (Eds.), *Human judgment and decision processes* (pp. 54–63). New York: Academic Press.

Hardin, G. R. (1968). The tragedy of the commons. *Science, 162,* 1243–1248.

Harrison, R. (1972, May/June). Understanding your organization's character. *Harvard Business Review,* pp. 119–128.

Hastie, R., & Pennington, N. (2000). Explanation-based decision making. In T. Connolly, H. Arkes, & K. Hammond (Eds.), *Judgment and choice: An interdisciplinary reader* (2nd ed., pp. 212–228). New York: Cambridge University Press.

Heath, C., & Gonzalez, R. (1995). Interaction with others increases decision confidence but not decision quality: Evidence against information collection views of interactive decision making. *Organizational Behavior and Human Decision Processes, 61,* 305–326.

Heller, F. A., Drenth, P. J. D., Koopman, P. L., & Rus, V. (1988). *Decisions in organizations: A three-country comparative study.* London: Sage.

Hickson, D. J., Hinnings, C. R., Lee, A. C., Schneck, R. E., & Pennings, J. M. (1971). A strategic contingency theory of intra-organizational power. *Administrative Science Quarterly, 16,* 216–229.

Hoffman, E., & Spitzer, M. (1985). Entitlements, rights, and fairness: An experimental examination of subjects' concepts of distributive justice. *Journal of Legal Studies, 14,* 259–297.

Huffman, M. D. (1978). *The effect of decision task characteristics on decision behavior* (Tech. Rep. No. 78–16). Seattle, WA: University of Washington, Department of Psychology.

Isen, A. M. (1993). Positive affect and decision making. In M. Lewis & J. M. Haviland (Eds.), *Handbook of emotions* (pp. 261–277). New York: Guilford.

Isen, A. M., Daubman, K. A., & Nowicki, G. P. (1987). Positive affect facilitates creative problem solving. *Journal of Personality and Social Psychology, 52,* 1122–1131.

Isen, A. M., & Means, B. (1983). The influence of positive affect on decision-making strategy. *Social Cognition, 2,* 18–31.

Isen, A. M., Nygren, T. E., & Ashby, G. F. (1988). The influence of positive affect on the subjective utility of gains and losses: It is just not worth the risk. *Journal of Personality and Social Psychology, 55,* 710–717.

Isen, A. M., & Patrick, R. (1983). The effect of positive feelings on risk-taking: When the chips are down. *Organizational Behavior and Human Performance, 31,* 194–202.

Isen, A. M., Rosenzweig, A. S., & Young, M. J. (1991). The influence of positive affect on clinical problem solving. *Medical Decision Making, 11*(3), 221–227.

Isenberg, D. J. (1984, November/December). How senior managers think. *Harvard Business Review,* pp. 81–90.

James, W. (1983). *The principles of psychology.* London: Macmillan. (Original work published 1890).

Janis, I. L. (1972). *Victims of groupthink.* Boston: Houghton Mifflin.

Janis, I. L. (1982). *Groupthink: Psychological studies of policy decisions and fiascoes.* Boston: Houghton Mifflin.

Johnson, E. J., & Goldstein, D. (2003). Do defaults save lives? *Science, 302,* 1338–1339.

Johnson, E. J., Hershey, J., Meszaros, J., & Kunreuther, H. (1992). Framing, probability distortions, and insurance decisions. *Journal of Risk and Uncertainty, 7,* 35–51.

Johnson-Laird, P. N. (1983). *Mental models.* Cambridge, MA: Harvard University Press.

Jungermann, H. (1983). The two camps on rationality. In R. W. Scholz (Ed.), *Decision making under uncertainty.* Amsterdam: North-Holland.

Jungermann, H. (1985). Inferential processes in the construction of scenarios. *Journal of Forecasting, 4,* 321–327.

Jungermann, H., & Thüring, J. (1987). The use of causal knowledge for inferential reasoning. In J. L. Mumpower, L. D. Phillips, O. Renn, & V. R. R. Uppuluria (Eds.), *Expert judgment and expert systems* (pp. 131–146). New York: Springer.

Kahneman, D., Knetsch, J., & Thaler, R. H. (1991). The endowment effect, loss aversion, and the status quo bias. *Journal of Economic Perspectives, 5,* 193–206.

Kahneman, D., & Tversky, A. (1973). On the psychology of prediction. *Psychological Review, 80,* 237–251.

Kahneman, D., & Tversky, A. (1979). Prospect theory: An analysis of decision under risk. *Econometrica, 47,* 263–291.

Kahneman, D., & Tversky, A. (1982). The psychology of preferences. *Scientific American, 246, 160–173.*

Kahneman, D., & Tversky, A. (1984). Choices, values, and frames. *American Psychologist, 39,* 341–350.

Katzenbach, J. R., & Smith, D. K. (1993). *The wisdom of teams.* New York: McKinsey.

Keren, G. B., & Wagenaar, W. A. (1985). On the psychology of playing blackjack: Normative and descriptive considerations with implications for decision theory. *Journal of Experimental Psychology: General, 114,* 133–158.

Klayman, J. (1988). On the how and why (not) of learning from outcomes. In B. Brehmer & C. R. B. Joyce (Eds.), *Human decision: The SJT view* (pp. 115–162). Amsterdam: North-Holland.

Klein, G. A. (1989). Recognition-primed decisions. *Advances in Man-Machine Systems Research, 5,* 47–92.

Klein, G. A. (1993). A recognition-primed decision (RPD) model of rapid decision making. In G. A. Klein, J. Orasanu, R. Calderwood, & C. E. Zsambok (Eds.), *Decision making in action: Models and methods* (pp. 138–147). Norwood, NJ: Ablex.

Klein, G. (1996). *Sources of power: The study of naturalistic decision making.* Mahwah, NJ: Lawrence Erlbaum.

Kolmogorov, A. N. (1950). *Foundations of the theory of probability.* New York: Chelsean. (Original work published 1933).

Koopman, P. L. (1980). *Besluitvorming in organisates.* Assen, the Netherlands: Van Gorcum.

Koopman, P., & Pool, J. (1991). Organizational decision making: Models, contingencies and strategies. In J. Rasmussen, B. Brehmer, & J. Leplat (Eds.), *Distributed decision making: Cognitive models for cooperative work* (pp. 19–46). Chichester, UK: Wiley.

Kort, F. (1968). A nonlinear model for the analysis of judicial decisions. *American Political Science Review, 62,* 546–555.

Lee, T. W., & Mitchell, T. R. (1994). An alternative approach: The unfolding model of voluntary employee turnover. *Academy of Management Review, 19,* 57–89.

Lee, T. W., Mitchell, T. R., Holtom, B. C., McDaniel, L., & Hill, J. W. (1999). A quantitative test of the unfolding model of voluntary turnover. *Academy of Management Journal, 42,* 450–462.

Lee, T. W., Mitchell, T. R., Weiss, L., & Fireman, S. (1996). An empirical examination of the unfolding model of voluntary employee turnover. *Academy of Management Journal, 39,* 5–36.

Lichtenstein, S., & Newman, J. R. (1967). Empirical scaling of common verbal phrases associated with numerical probabilities. *Psychonomic Science, 9,* 563–564.

Lindblom, C. E. (1959). The science of "muddling through." *Public Administration Review, 19,* 79–88.

Lipshitz, R. (1993). Decision making as argument-driven action. In G. A. Klein, J. Orasanu, R. Calderwood, & C. E. Zsambok (Eds.), *Decision making in action: Models and methods* (pp. 172–181). Norwood, NJ: Ablex.

Locke, E. A., & Schweiger, D. M. (1979). Participation in decision-making: One more look. In B. M. Shaw (Ed.), *Research in organizational behavior* (pp. 265–339). Greenwich, CT: JAI.

Loewenstein, G., Weber, E. U., Hsee, C. K., & Welch, E. S. (2001). Risk as feelings. *Psychological Bulletin, 126,* 910–924.

Loomes, G., & Sugden, R. (1982). Regret theory: An alternative theory of rational choice under uncertainty. *Economic Journal, 92,* 805–824.

Lopes, L. L. (1981). Decision making in the short run. *Journal of Experimental Psychology: Human Learning and Memory, 1,* 377–385.

Lopes, L. L. (1987). The psychology of risk. In L. Berkowitz (Ed.), *Advances in Experimental Social Psychology, 20,* 255–295.

Luce, R. D., & Raiffa, H. (1957). *Games and decisions: Introduction and critical survey.* New York: John Wiley.

March, J. G., & Shapira, Z. (1982). Behavioral decision theory and organizational decision theory. In G. R. Ungson & D. N. Braunstein (Eds.), *Decision making: An interdisciplinary inquiry* (pp. 52–68). Boston: Kant.

March, J. G., & Simon, H. A. (1958). *Organizations.* New York: John Wiley.

Markus, H., & Nurius, P. (1986). Possible selves. *American Psychologist, 41,* 954–969.

Markus, H., & Wurf, E. (1987). The dynamic self-concept: A social psychological perspective. *Annual Review of Psychology, 38,* 299–337.

McAllister, D., Mitchell, T. R., & Beach, L. R. (1979). The contingency model for selection of decision strategies: An empirical test of the effects of significance, accountability, and reversibility. *Organizational Behavior and Human Performance, 24,* 22

McCauley, C., Stitt, C. L., & Segal, M. (1980). Stereotyping: From prejudice to prediction. *Psychological Bulletin, 87,* 195–208.

McGlothlin, W. H. (1956). Stability of choices among uncertain alternatives. *American Journal of Psychology, 69,* 504–615.

McGrath, J. E. (1984). *Groups: Interaction and performance.* Englewood Cliffs, NJ: Prentice Hall.

McKelvey, R. D., & Palfrey, T. R. (1992). An experimental study of the centipede game. *Econometrica, 60,* 803–836.

McNeil, J. J., Pauker, S. G., Sox, H. C., & Tversky, A. (1982). On the elicitation of preferences for alternative therapies. *New England Journal of Medicine, 306,* 1259–1262.

Mednick, M. T., Mednick, S. A., & Mednick, E. V. (1964). Incubation of creative performance and specific associative priming. *Journal of Abnormal and Social Psychology, 69,* 84–88.

Messick, D., & Sentis, K. P. (1979). Fairness and preference. *Journal of Experimental Social Psychology, 15,* 418–434.

Minsky, M. (1968). *Semantic information processing.* Cambridge, MA: MIT Press.

Mintzberg, H., Raisinghani, D., & Theoret, A. (1976). The structure of "unstructured" decision processes. *Administrative Science Quarterly, 21,* 246–275.

Mitchell, T. R., & Lee, T. W. (2001). The unfolding model of voluntary turnover and embeddedness: Foundations for a comprehensive theory of attachment. *Research in Organizational Behavior, 23,* 189–246.

Montgomery, H. (1993). The search for a dominance structure in decision making: Examining the evidence. In G. A. Klein, J. Orasanu, R. Calderwood, & C. E. Zsambok (Eds.), *Decision making in action: Models and methods* (pp. 172–181). Norwood, NJ: Ablex.

Mullen, B., Anthony, T., Salas, E., & Driskell, J. E. (1994). Group cohesiveness and quality of decision making: An integration of tests of the groupthink hypothesis. *Small Group Research, 25,* 189–204.

Murphy, A. H., & Winkler, R. L. (1974). Probability forecasts: A survey of National Weather Service forecasters. *Bulletin of the American Meteorological Society, 55,* 1449–1453.

Nash, J. (1950). The bargaining problem. *Econometrica, 28,* 155–162.

Nash, J. (1951). Non-cooperative games. *Annals of Mathematics, 54,* 286–295.

Neale, M. A. (1984). The effect of negotiation and arbitration cost salience on bargainer behavior: The role of arbitrator and constituency in negotiator judgment. *Organizational Behavior and Human Performance, 34,* 97–111.

Neale, M. A., & Northcraft, G. B. (1986). Experts, amateurs, and refrigerators: Comparing expert and amateur negotiators in a novel task. *Organizational Behavior and Human Decision Processes, 38,* 305–317.

Neisser, U. (1976). *Cognition and reality.* San Francisco: Freeman.

Neisser, U. (1982). *Memory observed: Remembering in natural contexts.* San Francisco: Freeman.

Nisbett, R. E., Krantz, D., Jepson, C., & Kunda, Z. (1983). The use of statistical heuristics in everyday inductive reasoning. *Psychological Review, 90,* 339–363.

Nordhoy, F. (1962). *Group interaction in decision making under risk.* Unpublished master's thesis, Massachusetts Institute of Technology, Cambridge, MA.

Northcraft, G. B., & Neale, M. A. (1987). Experts, amateurs, and real estate: An anchoring-and-adjustment perspective on property pricing decisions. *Organizational Behavior and Human Decision Processes, 39,* 84–97.

Ordóñez, L. D., Benson, L., III, & Beach, L. R. (1999). Testing the compatibility test: How instructions, accountability, and anticipated regret affect pre-choice screening of options. *Organizational Behavior and Human Decision Processes, 78,* 63–80.

Paddock, L., Gilliland, S. W., & Goldman, B. M. (2003). *Positive and negative decisions in response to justice: More complex than the initial image theory account* (Research Report). Tucson: University of Arizona, Department of Management and Policy.

Park, W. W. (1990). A review of research on groupthink. *Journal of Behavioral Decision Making, 3,* 229–245.

Payne, J. W., Laughhunn, D. J., & Crum, R. (1980). Translation of gambles and aspiration level effects in risky choice behavior. *Management Science, 26,* 1039–1060.

Pennington, N., & Hastie, R. (1986). Evidence evaluation in complex decision making. *Journal of Personality and Social Psychology, 51,* 242–258.

Pennington, N., & Hastie, R. (1988). Explanation-based decision making: Effects of memory structure on judgment. *Journal of Experimental Psychology: Learning, Memory and Cognition, 14,* 521–533.

Pennington, N., & Hastie, R. (1992). Explaining the evidence: Tests of the story model for juror decision making. *Journal of Personality and Social Psychology, 2,* 189–206.

Pesta, B., Kass, D., & Dunegan, K. (in press). Image theory and the appraisal of employee performance: To screen or not to screen? *Journal of Business and Psychology.*

Peterson, C. R., & Beach, L. R. (1967). Man as an intuitive statistician. *Psychological Bulletin, 68,* 29–46.

Peterson, C. R., DuCharme, W. M., & Edwards, W. (1968). Sampling distributions and probability revisions. *Journal of Experimental Psychology, 76,* 236–243.

Peterson, C. R., Schneider, R. J., & Miller, A. J. (1965). Sample size and the revision of subjective probabilities. *Journal of Experimental Psychology, 69,* 522–527.

Peterson, C. R., Ulehla, Z. J., Miller, A. J., Bourne, L. E., & Stilson, D. W. (1965). Internal consistency of subjective probabilities. *Journal of Experimental Psychology, 70,* 526–533.

Phelps, R. H., & Shanteau, J. (1978). Livestock judges: How much information can an expert use? *Organizational Behavior and Human Performance, 21,* 209–219.

Phillips, L. D., & Edwards, W. (1966). Conservatism in a simple probability inference task. *Journal of Experimental Psychology, 72,* 346–354.

Plott, C. R., & Levine, M. E. (1976). A model of agenda influence on committee decisions. *American Economic Review, 68,* 146–160.

Potter, R. E., & Beach, L. R. (1994). Imperfect information in pre-choice screening of options. *Organizational Behavior and Human Decision Processes, 59,* 13–329.

Preston, M. G., & Baratta, P. (1948). An experimental study of the auction-value of an uncertain outcome. *American Journal of Psychology, 61,* 183–193.

Prinzmetal, W. (1995). Visual feature integration in a world of objects. *Current Directions in Psychological Science, 3,* 90–98.

Quinn, J. B. (1980). *Strategies for change: Logical incrementalism.* Homewood, IL: Irwin.

Raiffa, H. (1968). *Decision analysis.* Reading, MA: Addison-Wesley.

Raiffa, H. (1982). *The art and science of negotiation.* Cambridge, MA: Harvard University Press.

Rapoport, A. (1966). *Two-person game theory: The essential ideas.* Ann Arbor: University of Michigan Press.

Rapoport, A. (1988). Provision of step-level public goods: Effects of inequality in resources. *Journal of Personality and Social Psychology, 54,* 432–440.

Richmond, S. M., Bissell, B. L., & Beach, L. R. (1998). Image theory's compatibility and evaluations of the status quo. *Organizational Behavior and Human Decision Processes, 73,* 39–53.

Rohrbaugh, J. (1988). Cognitive conflict tasks and small group processes. In B. Brehmer & C. R. B. Joyce (Eds.), *Human decision: The SJT view* (pp. 199–226). Amsterdam: North-Holland.

Roose, J. E., & Doherty, M. E. (1976). Decision theory applied to the selection of life insurance salesmen. *Organizational Behavior and Human Performance, 16,* 231–249.

Rorer, L. G., Hoffman, P. J., Dickman, H. D., & Slovic, P. (1967). Configurational judgments revealed. *Proceedings of the 75th Annual Convention of the American Psychological Association, 2,* 195–196.

Rosch, E. (1976). Classification of real-world objects: Origins and representations in cognition. In S. Ehrlich & E. Tolving (Eds.), *La memorie semantique* (pp. 24–32). Paris: Bulletin de Psychologie.

Rubin, J. Z., & Brown, B. R. (1975). *The social psychology of bargaining and negotiation.* New York: Academic Press.

Rück, B. (Ed.). (1993). *Risk is a concept: Perceptions of risk perception*. Munich: Knesebeck.

Rummelhart, D. E. (1977). Understanding and summarizing brief stories. In D. LaBerge & S. J. Samuels (Eds.), *Basic processes in reading: Perception and comprehension* (pp. 62–93). Hillsdale, NJ: Lawrence Erlbaum.

Samuelson, P. A. (1963). Risk and uncertainty: A fallacy of large numbers. *Scientia, 9*, 108–113.

Samuelson, P. A., & Zeckhauser, R. (1988). Status quo bias in individual decision making. *Journal of Risk and Uncertainty, 1*, 7–59.

Schank, R. C., & Abelson, R. P. (1977). *Scripts, plans, goals and understanding*. Hillsdale, NJ: Lawrence Erlbaum.

Schoemaker, P. J. H. (1980). *Experiments on decision under risk: The expected utility hypothesis*. Boston: Nijhoff.

Selten, R. (1990). Bounded rationality. *Journal of Institutional and Theoretical Economics, 146*, 649–658.

Shanteau, J. (1992). The psychology of experts: An alternative view. In G. Wright & F. Bolger (Eds.), *Expertise and decision support* (pp. 11–24). New York: Plenum.

Shanteau, J., & Anderson, N. H. (1969). Test of a conflict model for preference judgment. *Journal of Experimental Psychology, 103*, 680–691.

Sheridan, J. E. (1992). Organizational culture and employee retention. *Academy of Management Journal, 35*, 1036–1056.

Shockley-Zalabak, P., & Morley, D. D. (1989). Adhering to organizational culture: What does it mean? Why does it matter? *Group and Organizational Studies, 14*, 483–500.

Silver, W. (1989). *Status quo effects on the framing effect*. Unpublished manuscript, University of Washington, School of Business, Seattle.

Simon, H. A. (1945). *Administrative behavior: A study of decision-making processes in administrative organization*. New York: Free Press.

Simon, H. A. (1955). A behavioral model of rational choice. *Quarterly Journal of Economics, 69*, 99–118.

Simon, H. A. (1979). Rational decision making in business organizations. *American Economic Review, 69*, 493–513.

Slovic, P. (1987). Perception of risk. *Science, 236*, 280–285.

Slovic, P. (1993). Perceived risk, trust, and democracy. *Risk Analysis, 13*, 675–682.

Slovic, P., Finucane, M. L., Peters, E., & MacGregor, D. G. (2002). The affect heuristic. In T. Gilovich, D. Griffin, & D. Kahneman (Eds.), *Heuristics and biases: The psychology of intuitive judgment* (pp. 397–420). New York: Cambridge University Press.

Slovic, P., & Lichtenstein, S. (1983). Preference reversals: A broader perspective. *American Economic Review, 73*, 596–605.

Slovic, P., Rorer, L. G., & Hoffman, P. J. (1971). Analyzing use of diagnostic signs. *Investigative Radiology, 6*, 18–26.

Sniezek, J. A. (1992). Groups under uncertainty: An examination of confidence in group decision making. *Organizational Behavior and Human Decision Processes, 52*, 124–155.

Sniezek, J. A., & Henry, R. A. (1989). Accuracy and confidence in group judgment. *Organizational Behavior and Human Decision Processes, 43,* 1–28.

Sniezek, J. A., & Henry, R. A. (1990). Revision, weighting, and commitment in consensus group judgment. *Organizational Behavior and Human Decision Processes, 45,* 66–84.

Sniezek, J. A., Paese, P. W., & Furiya, S. (1990). *Dynamics of group discussion to consensus judgment: Disagreement and overconfidence.* Unpublished manuscript, University of Illinois at Urbana-Champaign.

Spranca, M., Minsk, E., & Baron, J. (1991). Omission and commission in judgment and choice. *Journal of Experimental Social Psychology, 27,* 76–105.

Starmer, C., & Sugden, R. (1993). Testing for juxtaposition and event-splitting effects. *Journal of Risk and Uncertainty, 6,* 235–254.

Stasser, G., & Titus, W. (1985). Pooling of unshared information in group decision making: Biased information sampling during discussion. *Journal of Personality and Social Psychology, 48,* 1467–1478.

Staw, B. M. (1976). Knee-deep in the big muddy: A study of escalating commitment to a chosen course of action. *Organization Behavior and Human Performance, 16,* 27–44.

Staw, B. M., & Fox, F. (1977). Escalation: Some determinants of commitment to a previously chosen course of action. *Human Relations, 30,* 431–450.

Stoner, J. A. F. (1961). *A comparison of individuals and group decisions involving risk.* Unpublished master's thesis, Massachusetts Institute of Technology, Cambridge.

Strahilevitz, M. A., & Loewenstein, G. (1998). The effect of ownership history on the valuation of objects. *Journal of Consumer Research, 25,* 276–289.

Svenson, O. (1979). Process descriptions in decision making. *Organizational Behavior and Human Performance, 23,* 86–112.

Svenson, O. (1992). Differentiation and consolidation theory of human decision making: A frame of reference for the study of pre- and post-decision processes. *Acta Psychologica, 80,* 143–168.

Thaler, R. H. (1985). Mental accounting and consumer choice. *Marketing Science, 4,* 199–214.

Thaler, R. H. (1990). Saving, fungibility, and mental accounts. *Journal of Economic Perspectives, 4,* 193–205.

Thomas, J. C. (1990). Public involvement in public management: Adapting and testing a borrowed theory. *Administration Review, 50,* 435–445.

Thompson, L. (1990). Negotiation behavior and outcomes: Empirical evidence and theoretical issues. *Psychological Bulletin, 108,* 515–532.

Thüring, M., & Jungermann, H. (1986). Constructing and running mental models or inferences about the future. In B. Brehmer, H. Jungermann, P. Lourens, & G. S. Sevòn (Eds.), *New directions in research in decision making* (pp.163–174). Amsterdam: North-Holland.

Tjosvold, D. (1977). Commitment to justice in conflict between unequal status persons. *Journal of Applied Social Psychology, 7,* 149–162.

Tjosvold, D. (1978). Control strategies and own group evaluation in intergroup conflict. *Journal of Psychology, 100,* 305–314.

Trice, H. M., & Beyer, J. M. (1993). *The cultures of work organizations.* Englewood Cliffs, NJ: Prentice Hall.

Tversky, A. (1967). Additivity, utility, and subjective probability. *Journal of Mathematical Psychology, 4,* 175–202.

Tversky, A. (1969). The intransitivity of preferences. *Psychological Review, 76,* 31–48.

Tversky, A., & Kahneman, D. (1974). Judgment under uncertainty: Heuristics and biases. *Science, 185,* 1124–1131.

Tversky, A., & Kahneman, D. (1981). The framing of decisions and the psychology of choice. *Science, 221,* 1124–1131.

Tversky, A., & Kahneman, D. (1982). Causal schemas in judgments under uncertainty. In D. Kahneman, P. Slovic, & A. Tversky (Eds.), *Judgment under uncertainty: Heuristics and biases* (pp. 117–128). New York: Cambridge University Press.

Tversky, A., & Kahneman, D. (1983). Extensional versus intuitive reasoning: The conjunction fallacy in probability judgment. *Psychological Review, 90,* 293–315.

Tversky, A., & Kahneman, D. (1992). Advances in prospect theory: Cumulative representation of uncertainty. *Journal of Risk and Uncertainty, 5,* 297–323.

Tykocinski, O. E., & Pittman, T. S. (1998). The consequences of doing nothing: Inaction inertia as avoidance of anticipated counterfactual regret. *Journal of Personality and Social Psychology, 75,* 607–616.

van Zee, E. H., Paluchowski, T. F., & Beach, L. R. (1992). The effects of screening and task partitioning upon evaluations of decision options. *Journal of Behavioral Decision Making, 5,* 1–23.

von Mises, R. (1957). *Probability, statistics, and truth.* London: Allen & Unwin. (Original work published 1928).

von Neumann, J., & Morgenstern, O. (1947). *Theory of games and economic behavior.* Princeton, NJ: Princeton University Press.

von Winterfeldt, D., & Edwards, W. (1986). *Decision analysis and behavioral research.* Cambridge, UK: Cambridge University Press.

Vroom, V. H. (1973, Spring). A new look at managerial decision making. *Organizational dynamics,* pp. 66–80.

Vroom, V. H., & Jago, A. G. (1978). On the validity of the Vroom-Yetton model. *Journal of Applied Psychology, 63,* 151–162.

Vroom, V. H., & Jago, A. G. (1988). *The new leadership: Managing participation in organization.* Englewood Cliffs, NJ: Prentice Hall.

Vroom, V. H., & Yetton, P. W. (1973). *Leadership and decision-making.* Pittsburgh, PA: University of Pittsburgh Press.

Wagenaar, W. A. (1988). *Paradoxes of gambling behavior.* Hillsdale, NJ: Lawrence Erlbaum.

Wagenaar, W. A., & Keren, G. B. (1986). The seat belt paradox: Effect of adopted roles on information seeking. *Organizational Behavior and Human Decision Processes, 38,* 1–6.

Wagner, J. A., & Gooding, R. Z. (1987). Shared influence and organizational behavior: A meta-analysis of situational variables expected to moderate participation-outcome relationships. *Academy of Management Journal, 30,* 524–541.

Wallach, M. A., Kogan, N., & Bem, D. J. (1962). Group influence on individual risk taking. *Journal of Abnormal and Social Psychology, 65,* 77–86.

Weatherly, K. A., & Beach, L. R. (1996). Organizational culture and decision making. In L. R. Beach (Ed.), *Decision making in the workplace: A unified perspective* (pp. 117–132). Mahwah, NJ: Lawrence Erlbaum.

Wheeler, G., & Beach, L. R. (1968). Subjective sampling distributions and conservatism. *Organizational Behavior and Human Performance, 3,* 36–46.

Wise, J. A. (1970). Estimates and scaled judgments of subjective probabilities. *Organizational Behavior and Human Performance, 5,* 85–92.

Wright, G., & Bolger, F. (1992). *Expertise and decision support.* New York: Plenum.

Yantis, S. (1995). Perceived continuity of occluded visual objects. *Psychological Science, 6,* 182–186.

Yates, J. F. (1990). *Judgment and decision making.* Englewood Cliffs, NJ: Prentice Hall.

Zeelenberg, M., van den Bos, K, van Dijk, E., & Pieters, R. (2002). The inaction effect in the psychology of regret. *Journal of Personality and Social Psychology, 82,* 314–327.

Zimmer, R. J. (1978). *Validating the Vroom-Yetton normative model of leader behavior in field sales force management and measuring the training effects of TELOS on the leader behavior of district managers.* Unpublished doctoral dissertation, Virginia Polytechnic Institute, Blackburg.

# Index

# About the Authors

**Lee Roy Beach** is McClelland Professor Emeritus of Management and Policy in the Eller College of Management at the University of Arizona. He received his Ph.D. in experimental psychology from the University of Colorado and began his career as a human factors researcher for the U.S. Navy. After completing postdoctoral work in decision making at the University of Michigan, he taught cognition, perception, and decision making in the Department of Psychology at the University of Washington, where he moved from assistant to full professor and served as Chair. He has been a Visiting Scholar at Cambridge University (UK) and Leiden University (the Netherlands) and a Visiting Professor at the University of Chicago. He is the author of over 100 scholarly articles and has written or edited six books on organizational behavior and decision making, of which the latest is *Leadership and the Art of Change* (Sage, 2005). He has been the recipient of numerous awards for research and teaching, and prior to retiring he was a Fellow of the American Psychological Association and the American Psychological Society, and a member of the Society for Organizational Behavior and the Society for Judgment and Decision Making.

**Terry Connolly** is the FINOVA Professor and former Head of the Management and Policy Department in the Eller College of Management at the University of Arizona. He has held academic appointments at the University of Illinois, Georgia Institute of Technology, the University of Chicago, and Uppsala University (Sweden). He holds a B.S. in electrical engineering (Manchester University, UK), an M.A. in sociology, and a Ph.D. in organizational behavior and systems theory (Northwestern University). He has published more than 100 scholarly articles on a variety of topics related to judgment and decision making and has written or edited four books, most recently an anthology titled *Judgment and Decision Making: An Interdisciplinary Reader*, 2nd ed. (with Arkes and Hammond, 2000). He is past president of the Society for Judgment and Decision Making, and a Fellow and Charter Member of the American Psychological Association. His recent work has been concerned with the role of emotions, and especially of regret, in decision making.